The Internet
Illustrated

The Internet
Illustrated

Patrick Carey
Angela Ambrosia

Course Technology, Inc. One Main Street, Cambridge, MA 02142

An International Thomson Publishing Company

Albany • Bonn • Boston • Cincinnati • London • Madrid • Melbourne • Mexico City
New York • Paris • San Francisco • Singapore • Tokyo • Toronto • Washington

The Internet — Illustrated is published by Course Technology, Inc.

Managing Editor: Mac Mendelsohn
Series Product Manager: Nicole Jones Pinard
Product Manager: Kim T. M. Crowley
Production Editor: Christine Spillett
Text Designer: Leslie Hartwell
Cover Designer: John Gamache

©1995 Course Technology, Inc.
A Division of International Thomson Publishing, Inc.

For more information contact:
Course Technology, Inc.
One Main Street
Cambridge, MA 02142

International Thomson Publishing Europe
Berkshire House 168-173
High Holborn
London WCIV 7AA
England

International Thomson Publishing GmbH
Königswinterer Strasse 418
53227 Bonn
Germany

Thomas Nelson Australia
102 Dodds Street
South Melbourne, 3205
Victoria, Australia

International Thomson Publishing Asia
211 Henderson Road
#05-10 Henderson Building
Singapore 0315

Nelson Canada
1120 Birchmount Road
Scarborough, Ontario
Canada M1K 5G4

International Thomson Publishing Japan
Hirakawacho Kyowa Building, 3F
2-2-1 Hirakawacho
Chiyoda-ku, Tokyo 102
Japan

International Thomson Editores
Campos Eliseos 385, Piso 7
Col. Polanco
11560 Mexico D.F. Mexico

Trademarks

Course Technology and the open book logo are registered trademarks of Course Technology, Inc.

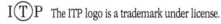 The ITP logo is a trademark under license.

Some of the product names in this book have been used for identification purposes only and may be trademarks or registered trademarks of their respective manufacturers and sellers.

Disclaimer

Course Technology, Inc. reserves the right to revise this publication and make changes from time to time in its content without notice.

ISBN 1-56527-528-4

Printed in the United States of America

10 9 8 7 6 5 4 3 2

From the Publisher

At Course Technology, Inc., we believe that technology will transform the way that people teach and learn. We are very excited about bringing you, instructors and students, the most practical and affordable technology-related products available.

The Course Technology Development Process

Our development process is unparalleled in the educational publishing industry. Every product we create goes through an exacting process of design, development, review, and testing.

Reviewers give us direction and insight that shape our manuscripts and bring them up to the latest standards. Every manuscript is quality tested. Students whose background matches the intended audience work through every keystroke, carefully checking for clarity and pointing out errors in logic and sequence. Together with our technical reviewers, these testers help us ensure that everything that carries our name is as error free and easy to use as possible.

Course Technology Products

We show both *how* and *why* technology is critical to solving problems in the classroom and in whatever field you choose to teach or pursue. Our time-tested, step-by-step instructions provide unparalleled clarity. Examples and applications are chosen and crafted to motivate students.

The Course Technology Team

This book will suit your needs because it was delivered quickly, efficiently, and affordably. In every aspect of business, we rely on a commitment to quality and the use of technology. Every employee contributes to this process. The names of all our employees are listed below: Diana Armington, Tim Ashe, Debora Barrow, Stephen M. Bayle, Ann Marie Buconjic, Jody Buttafoco, Kerry Cannell, Jei Lee Chong, Jim Chrysikos, Barbara Clemens, Susan Collins, John M. Connolly, Stephanie Crayton, Myrna D'Addario, Lisa D'Alessandro, Jodi Davis, Howard S. Diamond, Kathryn Dinovo, Jennifer Dolan, Joseph B. Dougherty, Patti Dowley, Laurie Duncan, Karen Dwyer, MaryJane Dwyer, Kristin Dyer, Chris Elkhill, Don Fabricant, Jane Fraser, Viktor Frengut, Jeff Goding, Laurie Gomes, Eileen Gorham, Catherine Griffin, Jamie Harper, Roslyn Hooley, Marjorie Hunt, Matt Kenslea, Marybeth LaFauci, Susannah Lean, Brian Leussler, Kim Mai, Margaret Makowski, Tammy Marciano, Elizabeth Martinez, Debbie Masi, Don Maynard, Kathleen McCann, Sarah McLean, Jay McNamara, Mac Mendelsohn, Karla Mitchell, Kim Munsell, Michael Ormsby, Debbie Parlee, Kristin Patrick, Charlie Patsios, Darren Perl, Kevin Phaneuf, George J. Pilla, Nicole Jones Pinard, Nancy Ray, Brian Romer, Laura Sacks, Carla Sharpe, Deborah Shute, Roger Skilling, Jennifer Slivinski, Christine Spillett, Audrey Tortolani, Michelle Tucker, David Upton, Jim Valente, Mark Valentine, Karen Wadsworth, Renee Walkup, Tracy Wells, Donna Whiting, Rob Williams, Janet Wilson, Lisa Yameen.

Preface

Course Technology, Inc. is proud to present this new book in its Illustrated Series. *The Internet — Illustrated* provides a highly visual, hands-on introduction to the Internet. The book is designed as a learning tool for Internet novices but will also be useful as a source for future reference.

Organization and Coverage

The Internet — Illustrated contains eight units that cover skills required to access and navigate the Internet. In these units students learn how to send and receive e-mail, join newsgroups, telnet, ftp, and use browsers.

Approach

The Internet — Illustrated distinguishes itself from other textbooks with its highly visual approach to computer instruction.

Lessons: Information Displays

The basic lesson format of this text is the "information display," a two-page lesson that is sharply focused on a specific task. This sharp focus and the precise beginning and end of a lesson make it easy for students to study specific material. Modular lessons are less overwhelming for students, and they provide instructors with more flexibility in planning classes and assigning specific work. The units are modular as well and can be presented in any order.

Each lesson, or "information display," contains the following elements:

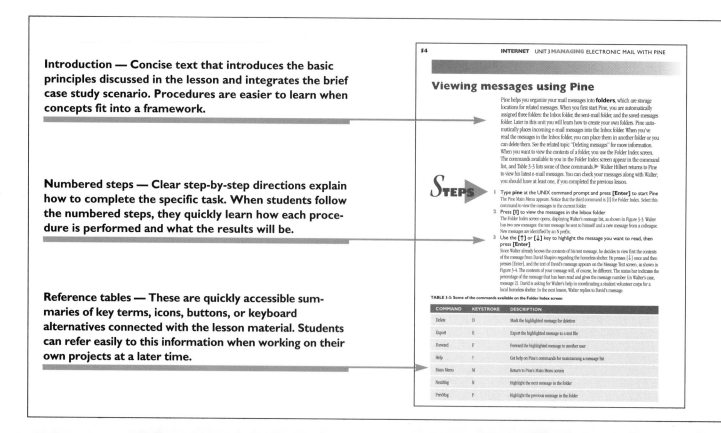

Introduction — Concise text that introduces the basic principles discussed in the lesson and integrates the brief case study scenario. Procedures are easier to learn when concepts fit into a framework.

Numbered steps — Clear step-by-step directions explain how to complete the specific task. When students follow the numbered steps, they quickly learn how each procedure is performed and what the results will be.

Reference tables — These are quickly accessible summaries of key terms, icons, buttons, or keyboard alternatives connected with the lesson material. Students can refer easily to this information when working on their own projects at a later time.

Features

The Internet — Illustrated is an exceptional textbook because it contains the following features:

- "Read This Before You Begin" page — This page, which appears before Unit 1, provides essential information that both students and instructors need to know before they begin working through the units.

- Real-World Case — The case study used throughout the textbook is designed to be "real-world" in nature and representative of the kinds of activities that students will encounter when working on the Internet. With a real-world case, the process of solving the problem will be more meaningful to students.

- End of Unit Material — Each unit concludes with a meaningful Concepts Review that tests students' understanding of what they learned in the unit. The Concepts Review is followed by an Applications Review, which provides students with additional hands-on practice of the skills they learned in the unit. The Applications Review is followed by Independent Challenges, which pose case problems for students to solve. The Independent Challenges allow students to learn by exploring, and develop critical thinking skills.

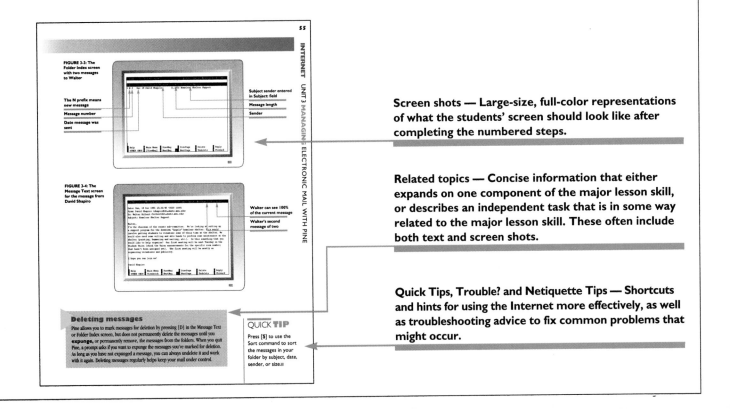

Screen shots — Large-size, full-color representations of what the students' screen should look like after completing the numbered steps.

Related topics — Concise information that either expands on one component of the major lesson skill, or describes an independent task that is in some way related to the major lesson skill. These often include both text and screen shots.

Quick Tips, Trouble? and Netiquette Tips — Shortcuts and hints for using the Internet more effectively, as well as troubleshooting advice to fix common problems that might occur.

The Supplements

Instructor's Manual — The Instructor's Manual is quality assurance tested. It includes:

- Solutions to all lessons, Concept Reviews, Application Reviews, and Independent Challenges
- Unit notes, which contain tips from the authors about the instructional progression of each lesson
- Extra problems
- Transparency masters of key concepts

Test Bank — The Test Bank contains approximately 50 questions per unit in true/false, multiple choice, and fill-in-the-blank formats, plus two essay questions. Each question has been quality assurance tested by students to achieve clarity and accuracy.

Electronic Test Bank — The Electronic Test Bank allows instructors to edit individual test questions, select questions individually or at random, and print out scrambled versions of the same test to any supported printer.

Acknowledgments

I want to especially thank and praise my Product Manager, Kim Crowley, who kept this project going forward with good humor and grace. Special thanks go to Angela Ambrosia, who, with her expertise as an Internet instructor, was a valuable member of the team. Christine Spillett, the Production Editor, has also earned accolades for managing a difficult and crazy schedule, not made any easier by the author's tardiness! Morten Eidal, Barbara Talmage, and Chris Greacen did a fabulous job of testing the examples used in the book and offering valuable advice, a task not made any easier by the ever-changing nature of the Internet. Finally, thanks to my Development Editor (and wife), Joan Carey, for transforming the text from a book about the Internet into a teaching tool.

Patrick Carey

Brief Contents

From the Publisher v

Preface vi

Read This Before You Begin 2

UNIT 1 Getting Started with the Internet 3

UNIT 2 Using Electronic Mail 27

UNIT 3 Managing Electronic Mail with PINE 49

UNIT 4 Joining Interest Groups with Usenet 71

UNIT 5 Connecting with Telnet and FTP 87

UNIT 6 Browsing with Gopher 107

UNIT 7 Finding Data on the Internet 127

UNIT 8 Introducing the World Wide Web 149

x

Contents

From the Publisher   v

Preface   vi

Read This Before You Begin   2

UNIT I   **Getting Started with the Internet**   3

Exploring the Internet   4
    History of the Internet   5
Understanding networks   6
Connecting to the Internet   8
Logging on   10
    Commercial service providers   11
Understanding UNIX   12
    Using operating systems other than UNIX 13
Viewing your directory   14
Creating a directory   16
    UNIX command switches   17
Discovering your Internet host's address   18
    Network protocols   19
Using domain names   20
    Domain name aliases   21
Logging out   22
    Who controls the Internet?   23
Concepts Review   24
Applications Review   25
Independent Challenges   26

UNIT 2   **Using Electronic Mail**   27

Understanding parts of an e-mail message   28
    E-mail addresses   29

Sending an e-mail   30
    E-mail command switches   31
Viewing and maintaining a message list   32
    Folders   33
Replying to a message   34
    Aliases   35
Understanding mailing lists   36
    Mailing lists and Bitnet   37
Understanding netiquette   38
    Smileys   39
Using Listserv   40
Subscribing to a mailing list   42
    Unsubscribing from a mailing list   43
Using mailing lists   44
    File archives   45
Concepts Review   46
Applications Review   47
Independent Challenges   48

UNIT 3 Managing Electronic Mail with Pine   49
Understanding Pine   50
    Other mailers and off-line mail readers   51
Composing a message using Pine   52
    Context sensitive key combinations   53
Viewing messages using Pine   54
    Deleting messages   55
Working with messages   56
Attaching files to messages   58
    Inserting a text file   59
Saving an attached file   60
    Exporting messages   61
Creating and using folders   62
Creating and using an address book   64
Creating a distribution list   66
    Modifying a distribution list   67

Concepts Review 68

Applications Review 69

Independent Challenges 70

UNIT 4 **Joining Interest Groups with Usenet** *71*

Understanding Usenet news 72

The history of Usenet 73

Finding newsgroups with trn 74

Unsubscribing from all newsgroups 75

Subscribing to a newsgroup 76

Working with the article selection list 78

Reading newsgroup articles 80

Posting articles to Usenet 82

Concepts Review 84

Applications Review 85

Independent Challenges 86

UNIT 5 **Connecting with Telnet and FTP** *87*

Telneting to other machines 88

Port numbers 89

Suspending Telnet 90

Terminal types 91

Obtaining files using FTP 92

File types 93

Navigating FTP directory trees 94

Readme files 95

Downloading a Text File 96

Local and remote directories 97

Downloading multiple files 98

Wildcards 99

Receiving a binary file 100

Compressed files 101

Suspending an FTP session 102

Uploading files with FTP 103

Concepts Review 104

Applications Review 105

Independent Challenges 106

UNIT 6 **Browsing with Gopher** *107*

Using a Gopher client 108

    Gopher client software 109

Viewing text files 110

Navigating Gopher 112

    The origins of Gopher 113

Connecting to other Gopher servers 114

Using Gopher to access anonymous FTP servers 116

Using Gopher to download a binary file 118

    Menu item types 119

Using Gopher to access Telnet sites 120

Creating bookmarks 122

    Suspending Gopher 123

Concepts Review 124

Applications Review 125

Independent Challenges 126

UNIT 7 **Finding Data on the Internet** *127*

Using Archie to find a file 128

Controlling output 130

    Types of searches 131

Establishing search criteria 132

Using an Archie client 134

Using Veronica 136

Conducting advanced Veronica searches 138

    Search parameters 139

Connecting to a WAIS client 140

    WAIS clients 141

Selecting a source 142

Conducting a search 144

Concepts Review	146
Applications Review	147
Independent Challenges	148

UNIT 8   Introducing the World Wide Web   *149*

Understanding the World Wide Web	150
Jump destinations	151
Usenet use groups related to the Web	151
Using browsers	152
Starting Mosaic	154
Navigating the Web	156
Understanding URLs and HTTP	157
Connecting to Gopher	158
Searching the Web	160
Using multimedia	162
Visiting interesting URLs	164
Concepts Review	166
Applications Review	167
Independent Challenges	168

TABLES

Table 1-1: Basic Internet tools — 4

Table 1-2: Popular Internet service providers — 11

Table 1-3: UNIX command parts — 15

Table 1-4: Some common UNIX commands — 18

Table 1-5: Some top-level domains — 20

Table 2-1: Common fields appearing in the header — 29

Table 2-2: Common UNIX mail commands — 32

Table 2-3: Sampling of Internet Acronyms — 39

Table 2-4: Common Smileys — 39

Table 2-5: Common Listserv commands — 45

Table 3-1: Parts of the Pine opening screen — 50

Table 3-2: Commands available on Compose Message screen — 53

Table 3-3: Some of the commands available on the Folder Index screen — 54

Table 3-4: Commands available on the Current Message screen — 57

Table 3-5: Folder List screen commands — 63

Table 3-6: Commands available on the Address Book screen — 65

Table 4-1: Common Usenet news categories — 74

Table 4-2: Common trn newsgroup selection level commands — 77

Table 4-3: Common trn article selection level commands — 79

Table 4-4: Common trn paging level commands — 82

Table 4-5: Common trn commands to send articles — 83

Table 5-1: A few popular Telnet sites — 89

Table 5-2: Telnet commands — 91

Table 5-3: Popular anonymous FTP sites — 93

Table 5-4: Basic FTP commands — 94

Table 5-5: FTP commands to transfer files — 96

Table 5-6: Compressed file formats — 101

Table 6-1: Public access Gopher servers via Telnet — 108

Table 6-2: Gopher text file commands — 110

Table 6-3: Commands used to navigate Gopher menus — 112

Table 6-4: Domain names of some popular Gopher servers — 115

Table 6-5: Common Gopher labels — 118

Table 6-6: Miscellaneous Gopher commands — 123

Table 7-1: Popular Archie servers — 129

Table 7-2: Commonly used Archie server commands 133

Table 7-3: Parameters used with the Archie client 135

Table 7-4: Veronica switch names to use in search parameters 138

Table 7-5: Public-access WAIS clients 140

Table 7-6: WAIS client software 141

Table 7-7: SWAIS commands 144

Table 8-1: World Wide Web browsers 153

Table 8-2: Elements of a Mosaic page 155

Table 8-3: Gopher menu icons 159

Table 8-4: Popular Web search engines 161

Table 8-5: Locations of viewers for Windows and Macintoshes 163

The Internet

UNIT 1   Getting Started with Internet

UNIT 2   Using Electronic Mail

UNIT 3   Managing Electronic Mail with Pine

UNIT 4   Joining Interest Groups with Internet

UNIT 5   Connecting with Telnet and FTP

UNIT 6   Browsing with Gopher

UNIT 7   Finding Data on the Internet

UNIT 8   Introducing the World Wide Web

Read This Before You Begin

To the Student

The step-by-step lessons in this book follow the day-to-day activities of students at a fictional school called MidWest University who use the Internet for their extra-curricular activities, their homework, on the job, and in other situations. As you work through the lessons, you will find that in many cases you are asked to pick a topic of your own and to consider the steps as examples. Because Internet access varies widely from site to site and because the Internet is constantly changing, your situation will almost always differ slightly (and sometimes not so slightly) from the examples shown in the lessons. Rather than trying to duplicate the output shown in the figures (in some cases this will be impossible), concentrate more on the general principles behind the examples. The best way to approach the Internet is with a sense of adventure and fun. Don't be afraid to explore on your own, and share what you find with your instructor, your classmates or even some of the people you encounter on the network.

To the Instructor

Teaching students how to efficiently access the Internet can be a daunting task. The Internet is in a constant state of flux, and since there is no central authority you won't always be notified of these changes. You may find out about a change only when a perplexed student approaches you, wondering why an example doesn't work anymore. This book presents many examples based on a fictional school called MidWest University. Although most of the examples involve real sites, real files, and real sessions, inevitably things will have changed since this book went to press. It is important that you personally verify the examples in this book before you use them to instruct your students. You can also help your students by suggesting alternative sites since the ones used in the examples might suffer from overload. Finally, try to anticipate how you can help make your students' tasks easier by, for example, sending them e-mail before you assign the e-mail unit. Some universities design Internet servers specifically for the purpose of instructing their students how to use the Internet because it gives them control over the files and utilities. You might want to consider such a strategy.

The examples in this book assume the UNIX operating system, except for Unit 8, which assumes that the students are using Windows. If you are using a different operating system, you might want to use this book as a starting point to discuss some of the basic concepts of the Internet. The following versions of various Internet tools appear in the figures:

Unit 3: Pine version 3.89
Unit 4: trn version 3.4.1
Unit 6: Gopher version 2.0.14
Unit 8: Mosaic for Windows version 2.0 alpha 7 (This unit will work with other browsers)

Depending on the version numbers of the applications you're running, your results and commands might be slightly different.

UNIT I

OBJECTIVES

▶ Explore the Internet

▶ Understand networks

▶ Connect to the Internet

▶ Log on

▶ Understand UNIX

▶ View your directory

▶ Create a directory

▶ Discover your Internet host's address

▶ Use domain names

▶ Log out

Getting Started
WITH THE INTERNET

*I*magine you are walking into a library for the first time. You see a bewildering array of books, magazines, videos, CDs, and other media, yet you have no idea how to find what you want. Your first encounter with the Internet may be a little like that, but once you become familiar with some basic Internet tools, you will find that you have a library as big as the world at your fingertips. This unit introduces you to the Internet and the machine you'll use to explore it—the computer. You will also start learning the fundamentals of UNIX, the most common language of the Internet world. ▶ MidWest University (MWU), a fictional school, has recently been linked to the Internet for the very first time. Olivia Sanchez, an MWU student, is eager to learn how to navigate the Internet, and she starts by learning about the computer system at her own site. ▶

Exploring the Internet

The **Internet** is a structure made up of millions of interconnected computers whose users can communicate with each other and share information; more than 3 million computers are hooked into the Internet. The physical structure of the Internet uses fiber-optic cables, satellites, phone lines, and other telecommunications media to send data back and forth, as shown in Figure 1-1. Any user whose computer can be linked to an Internet site can be a part of the worldwide Internet community. See the related material "History of the Internet" in this lesson for information on how the Internet got started. ▶ Now that MidWest University is connected to the Internet, its students are starting to learn the basic Internet tools shown in Table 1-1. Consider the advantages they gain by using the Internet:

■ **Communicate with users across the world**
With Internet access, MidWest University students and faculty can contact friends and colleagues electronically, at almost any Internet site on Earth.

■ **Form interest groups**
Those who use the Internet can join groups of other Internet users to share ideas and information or common interests and abilities.

■ **Retrieve data instantly**
With the Internet, students and faculty at MidWest University have access to data stored on computers across the world, which they can retrieve and store on their computers for their own research.

■ **Access software easily**
Software from commercial vendors and other sources can be easily obtained from the Internet.

TABLE 1-1: Basic Internet tools

TOOL	DESCRIPTION
Electronic mail (e-mail)	Most Internet users have an e-mail address. With e-mail, you can bypass the post office and send your messages quickly over the Internet to another user.
Telnet	Telnet connects your computer to other Internet computers. With Telnet you can work on a computer across the world as easily as you can work on a computer across the room.
FTP (File Transfer Protocol)	FTP is used for transferring files between computers on the Internet. Using FTP, you can receive documents or the latest software.
Usenet	Usenet newsgroups are a convienient way for Internet users to exchange messages on various topics with other users who share their interests.
Gopher and the World Wide Web	Gopher and the World Wide Web are Internet applications that attempt to organize in a user-friendly way the vast array of resources available on the Internet.
Archie, Veronica, and WAIS	These are Internet applications that help you search through the Internet for specific items. Archie searches FTP sites, Veronica searches Gopher menus, and WAIS searches file content.

FIGURE I-I: Structure of the Internet

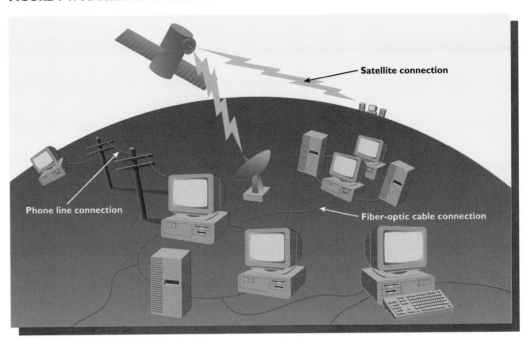

History of the Internet

Networks were first developed in the late 1960s by strategic thinkers who realized that if the communications network was controlled in one central location, it could be easily disabled in the event of a nuclear war. This would not be a problem if the network was decentralized so that no one component was necessary. The Department of Defense sponsored the Arpanet program to create such a high-speed computer network. Arpanet started with four computers in 1969, and this number grew steadily during the 1970s. Arpanet's decentralized structure made expansion easy and also allowed other networks to connect to it, creating a network of networks. In the late 1980s the National Science Foundation took over much of the functionality of the Arpanet through its own network, NSFnet, which connected universities and gave researchers access to supercomputers. Today most four-year colleges are connected to NSFnet, a part of the Internet. Of course, those students who have become accustomed to using networks and then graduate quickly petition their employers to get connected to the Internet.

Understanding networks

The Internet is often said to be a collection of networks. A **network**, which is created whenever two or more computers are connected, allows computers to share data or resources. Understanding network terminology will give you a clearer picture of how the Internet functions. As you read through this lesson, you might encounter a number of unfamiliar terms. Figure 1-2 should help you understand how networks are structured and how you fit into the larger picture as a network user. As you proceed through this book, you will regularly encounter these terms in the context of particular Internet tools. You have to be able to connect to your site's network before you can access the Internet, and having at least a basic understanding of network setup is important. ▶ The network at MidWest University has the following characteristics, which are common to all networks:

■ Each computer connected to a network is called a **host**. Hosts can be either single-user computers (like a PC) or computers that allow multiple users simultaneous access (like a mainframe).

■ Many users access the network by linking to a host from a **terminal**, a device that can be as simple as a keyboard, monitor, and cable or phone line connecting a user to the host computer. At MidWest University, students use hundreds of terminals to connect to just a few hosts. The host for MidWest University graduate students, for example, can accommodate many users simultaneously. It's important to understand the distinction between the host and the terminal. The host is the computer that is part of the network, and the terminal is the device that connects you to the host. Sometimes hosts can act as terminals if they are used to control the operations of another computer on the network.

■ One way resources are shared on a network is through the client/server relationship. The **server** is a computer that provides a resource to the network and the **client** is the computer that accesses that resource. For example, one of MidWest University's computer labs has a computer with a laser printer connected to it whose sole purpose is to print students' documents. When a student wants to print a document, the host that she is connected to acts as the client and sends the print job to the computer which acts as a print server.

■ A **file server** is a special kind of server that stores and manages files that it makes available to users on the network. For example, the computers at MidWest University all have word-processing programs installed on them, but the documents the students create with those programs are stored on the file server.

■ The resource provided by the server need not be an object such as a file or printer. It could also be an action performed by the server, like searching the network for specific pieces of information. A client on the network would formulate a query, send the query to a server, and the server would perform the search and report the results back to the client. In the upcoming units you'll learn about several important servers on the Internet, including the mail server that facilitates the transfer of electronic mail between users and the Archie server that searches the Internet for files matching user-specified criteria.

FIGURE 1-2: Parts of a network

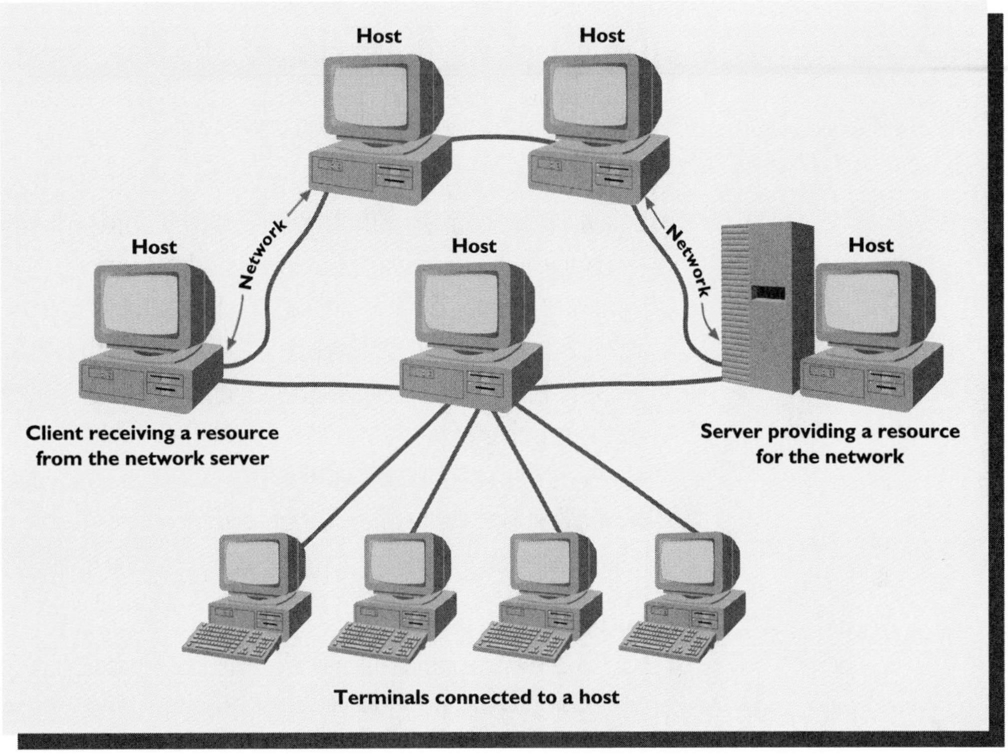

Host

Host

Host

Host

Host

Host

Network

Network

Client receiving a resource from the network server

Server providing a resource for the network

Terminals connected to a host

QUICK **TIP**

If your PC has communication software and a modem, it can connect to a network host over the phone line and pretend to be a terminal.

Connecting to the Internet

How you connect to the Internet depends on the location of your computer and its hardware configuration. Your computer must be a host on a network with Internet access or you must have access to a terminal connected to a host on a network with Internet access. A university computer on a campus network is probably already linked to the Internet, although it is possible some isolated computer labs are not yet connected. Check with your system administrator to determine whether the computer you are using is linked to the Internet. If necessary, you can purchase access from a commercial service and connect to that service using your computer's modem. Usually this involves paying a monthly service fee and a charge based on the number of hours you're connected to the host per month. Figure 1-3 shows how a modem connection works. Table 1-2 lists some popular service providers.

 MidWest University offers Internet access to every one of its students, but for those who aren't so lucky, here are some possible alternatives:

■ **Universities**

Many colleges now provide Internet access for their students and faculty. In some situations, members of the community can also access the university's computers.

■ **Private businesses**

More and more private businesses are using the Internet to advertise their services and keep in contact with important clients. Employees of these businesses can use many of the Internet tools discussed in this book.

■ **Online services**

On-line services, such as CompuServe and America Online, are now including partial or full Internet access as part of their service. Subscribers usually have to pay more for this service.

■ **Public libraries**

Publics libraries are placing card catalogs on-line and allowing users to access the catalogs of other libraries in the country through the Internet.

FIGURE 1-3:
Modem connection

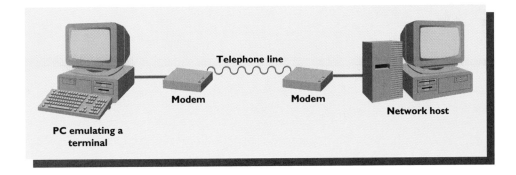

TABLE 1-2: Popular Internet service providers

SERVICE PROVIDER	AREA SERVED	FOR INFORMATION CALL
America Online	U.S. and Canada	1-800-827-6364
Committee on Institutional Cooperation Network	Midwestern states	1-313-998-6102
CompuServe	U.S. and international	1-800-848-8990
Delphi Internet Services Corp.	Massachusetts	1-800-695-4005
Express Access Online Communications Service	Virginia, Maryland, and D.C.	1-301-220-2020
MCI Mail	U.S. and international	1-800-444-6245
NetCom On-Line Communication Services, Inc.	California	1-408-554-8649
New England Academic and Research Network	New England states	1-617-873-8730
Northwestern States Network	Pacific Northwestern states	1-206-562-3000
Southeastern Universities Research Association	Southeast states	1-301-982-4600
Southwestern States Network	Southwest states	1-303-491-7260
SprintLink	U.S. and international	1-800-817-7755
The Whole Earth 'Lectronic Link (The WELL)	California	1-415-332-4335
The World	Massachusetts	1-617-739-0202

QUICK **TIP**

If you decide to use a commercial Internet service, make sure that it provides all the Internet tools you want (you'll learn about these tools in upcoming units).■

Logging on

While deciding how to connect to the Internet may take some time, once you have access, getting onboard is easy. In most cases, you use a terminal to **log on**; that is, connect to a host computer that has Internet access. Before you can log on, you must be registered to use the computer; that is, you must have an account on the host. Some universities automatically create accounts for students when they register for classes. There are three steps to logging on. First, you must connect to the host. Second, you enter your **user name**, a short name or nickname that identifies you. Your site may assign you a user name or you might be able to choose your own. Third, you enter a secret **password**, a string of characters that you select, which protects you from having others access your files and mail. The related material "Commercial service providers" in this lesson discusses a variation you might encounter as a new user when logging on. ▶ Olivia Sanchez, a student at MidWest University, logs on to her account. Try logging on with her to your site's network.

1 **Initiate the connection to the network host**
Initiating the connection may involve sitting down at a computer terminal (as is the case for Olivia) or dialing into the host from a PC in your home. In some cases, when you access the network host, the first thing you see is a prompt asking for your user name. A **prompt** is a phrase, word, or symbol on your computer's screen that asks for information. Your screen might say, for example, "User name:" or "login:" You might have to initiate the login procedure by pressing [Enter], choosing a command from a menu, or some other simple action. See your instructor for help if you aren't sure how to access the network host.

2 **Type your *user name* after the user name prompt, then press [Enter]**
Your user name is often your last name, although it may also be your first initial followed by your last name or some other combination of letters in your name. If you aren't sure what your user name is, check with your system administrator. Case is important, so make sure you are using the appropriate combination of upper and lowercase letters. Figure 1-4 shows Olivia's user name, "sanchez," which she types to connect to the host. Your entry will of course be different, as is the case for most of the figures in this book, which show fictional examples. When you compare your screen to Figure 1-4, your user name should appear after your computer's prompt (though, depending on your system,) your screen may not look anything like Figure 1-4. Moreover, notice that text entered by the user appears in blue, to help you distinguish what is typed from what appears on the screen. Once you enter your user name, the system prompts you for a password.

3 **Type your *password* after the password prompt, then press [Enter]**
For security reasons, your password may not appear on the screen, or it may appear as a series of asterisks. You are now logged on, and you can proceed to use the Internet.

FIGURE I-4: Login prompt

User name (you should enter your own)

Password may not appear as you type it

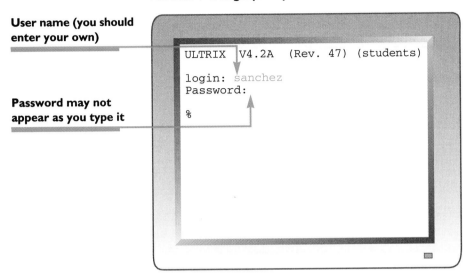

```
ULTRIX  V4.2A  (Rev. 47) (students)

login: sanchez
Password:

%
```

Commercial service providers

Some commerical service providers let you log on and register at the same time. If so, the first time you access the system the service prompts you to enter a user name that indicates you are a new user, such as "new," "newuser," or "guest." The service then prompts you for personal information such as your name, address, what password you want, and how you want to pay for the service.

Understanding UNIX

When working with a computer, you need to know something about the computer's operating system. An **operating system** is a program that manages your computer resources, such as memory, disk drives, or data files. You may be familiar with operating systems like DOS. The operating system you are most likely to encounter when you access the Internet is an operating system called **UNIX**. Because of its universality on the Internet, this book assumes that you are using UNIX. If you are using a different operating system the commands will be different, but the general features of each Internet tool will be the same. See the related topic "Using operating systems other than UNIX" in this lesson for more information. The appearance of the operating system and how you interact with it is called its **interface**. You communicate with the interface to invoke the operation you want to perform, like saving or printing a file. Operating systems can have several kinds of interfaces. In this book you encounter the following three kinds:

▪ A **menu-driven interface** presents you with lists of choices, or **menus**, from which you select the operation you want. Usually you select a menu option by typing a letter or number that corresponds to a menu choice or by highlighting the menu choice and pressing [Enter]. In a later unit, you'll be introduced to an Internet tool called Gopher, which uses a menu-driven interface.

▪ A **graphical user interface** (known as a **GUI**) uses a pointing device, such as a mouse, to click buttons, icons, or other graphical symbols to invoke specific operations. The Windows operating system is well known for its user-friendly GUI. As GUIs become more common, new Internet tools (such as Mosaic, which you'll learn about later in this book) are increasingly using this interface to a great advantage for the user.

▪ A **command-driven interface** requires you to type **commands**, or special words that are part of the operating system's language, to invoke specific operations. Users who work regularly with command-driven interfaces tend to memorize the most common commands, but if you are not used to working with this interface you may need to keep a list of commands handy. The UNIX operating system is a command-driven interface. The more UNIX commands you are aware of, the easier it will be for you to use the Internet. Figure 1-5 shows a very simple UNIX session; a user types the necessary commands to print a file named "history101.txt" (perhaps a paper for a History 101 class) and then logs out to end the session (you'll learn how to log out later in this unit). Don't try to enter these commands now; just use them as an example. Table 1-3 discusses the parts of this UNIX session.

FIGURE 1-5: Sample UNIX session

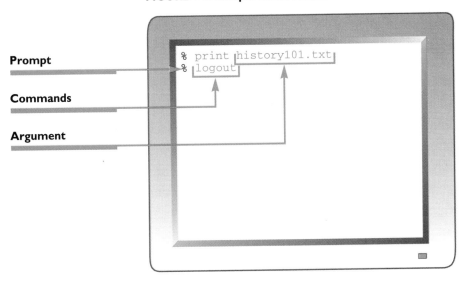

Prompt

Commands

Argument

Using operating systems other than UNIX

As the Internet increases in popularity, more users are accessing the network with a PC running Windows or OS/2 or with a Macintosh. Many UNIX computers offer a graphical user interface called **X-Windows** that reduces the need to learn the UNIX operating system. However, the most common way to use the Internet today is still with UNIX and UNIX commands.

TABLE 1-3: UNIX command parts

PART	DESCRIPTION	EXAMPLE AS SHOWN IN FIGURE 1-5
prompt	A phrase, word, or symbol on your computer screen that indicates that the computer is ready for you to enter information. You've already used the user name and password prompts to log on. A **command prompt** is a specific kind of prompt that indicates the computer is ready to receive commands that you type.	The UNIX prompt appears as the percent symbol (%). Other common command prompts are the $ and > symbols. Throughout this book you will see references to the % prompt, but be aware that yours may be different.
command	A word or string of characters from an operating system's command language that invokes a specific operation.	The UNIX print command tells the computer to print a file, while the logout command lets you exit your session.
argument	Additional information that you enter after a command that tells the operating system what the command should operate on. In this book, arguments are shown in italics; for example, "print *filename*."	The UNIX print command requires a file name, history101.txt, as an argument so that it knows which file to print. Notice that the logout command does not require an argument.

Viewing your directory

To get acquainted with UNIX, let's try a UNIX command that tells you what files you have in your account. If you are a new user at your site, you may not have any. As you proceed through this book, though, you will learn how to retrieve files, so it's best to get an early understanding of how to handle files in UNIX. The UNIX operating system groups files together in lists called **directories** in much the same way you might group documents in folders within a file cabinet. A directory contains not only files but may also contain other directories, called **subdirectories**. The organization of directories and directories-within-directories is called a **directory tree** because a diagram of the relationship between the directories resembles the branches of a tree. Figure 1-6 shows a sample directory tree at MidWest University. Directories are separated from subdirectories with a forward slash (/). You can organize the files in your account by creating a directory tree that best meets your needs. However, issues of file management and directory structure are beyond the scope of this book. Your instructor may have materials you can use to learn about organizing the files in your account. For now, check the status of your account by using the UNIX **ls** command, which lists the contents of your various directories. ▶ Olivia uses the ls command to examine the contents of her directory. Follow along with her.

1   Be sure you are logged on to your computer, as described earlier in this unit
The UNIX command prompt % should appear on your screen, ready to accept a command.

2   Type **ls** at the UNIX command prompt, then press **[Enter]**
The command "ls" is the UNIX word for the request, "May I please see the contents of my directory?". This command is the equivalent to the dir command in DOS. Olivia's computer responds by displaying a list of files in her directory, as in Figure 1-7. Your list of files will look different.

FIGURE 1-6: Sample directory tree structure at MidWest University

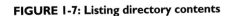

students directory

sanchez directory

/students

/students/hilton   /students/wu   /students/sanchez   /students/jones   Individual student accounts at MWU

/students/sanchez/personal   /students/sanchez/homework   sanchez subdirectories

Subdirectories for Olivia's classes → /students/sanchez/ homework/english   /students/sanchez/ homework/math   /students/sanchez/ homework/ot   /students/sanchez/ homework/chemistry

Files in Olivia's ot directory → signlanguage.txt   disabilities.txt

FIGURE 1-7: Listing directory contents

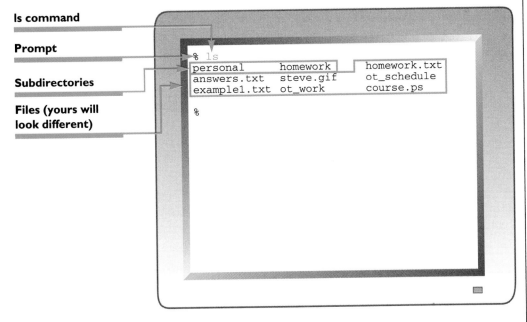

ls command

Prompt

Subdirectories

Files (yours will look different)

```
% ls
personal      homework       homework.txt
answers.txt   steve.gif      ot_schedule
example1.txt  ot_work        course.ps
%
```

Creating a directory

You could spend a whole semester learning the intricacies of UNIX. While UNIX commands can be confusing, experienced users are able to take advantage of UNIX's power to create sophisticated and useful programs. Table 1-4 displays some common UNIX commands that you might find useful for the purposes of this book. If you're going to be using UNIX extensively, however, you should consult a UNIX reference book or ask your instructor for more information. For now, take a look at a few UNIX commands that are used to manipulate file directories. The related topic "UNIX command switches" in this lesson gives you more options when issuing UNIX commands. Since you'll be getting files from the Internet in later units, it would be a good idea to create a special directory in which to place these files.
▶ Olivia decides to create a directory called "internet" into which she'll store her Internet-related files. Follow along with her.

I **Be sure you are logged on to your computer, as described earlier in this unit**
The UNIX command prompt % should appear on your screen, ready to accept a command. Now, Olivia uses the mkdir command (short for "make directory"), which takes as its argument the name of the directory she wants to create, to make a new directory.

2 **Type mkdir internet at the command prompt and press [Enter]**
Olivia has now created a subdirectory called internet using the UNIX mkdir command. Now she moves into that directory to view any files that exist there.

3 **Type cd internet and press [Enter]**
The cd command is short for "change directory;" it moves you to the internet directory you just created.

4 **Type ls to view the contents of the internet directory**
The contents of that directory are empty, as you can see from Figure 1-8, since Olivia has not had a chance to populate it with any files. Now she moves back to her home directory using the cd command.

5 **Type cd .. and press [Enter]**
The double dots (..) tell UNIX to move up in the directory tree, back where you started at the UNIX command prompt.

FIGURE 1-8: UNIX commands to create a subdirectory

No files appear after the "ls" command because you just created this directory

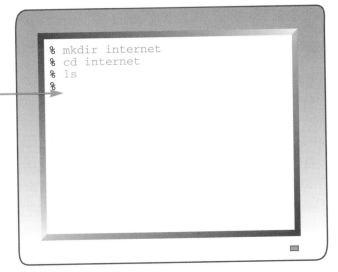

```
% mkdir internet
% cd internet
% ls
%
```

QUICK TIP

You can get information on UNIX commands, arguments, and switches by typing "man *command name*" at the command prompt (for example, to learn more about the ls command, type "man ls").■

UNIX command switches

You can modify the actions of many UNIX commands using switches. **Switches** are options that you add to the command to change its output or action. You identify a switch by typing a preceding hyphen (-). For example, typing "ls" at the command prompt lists the contents of the current directory, but typing "ls -l" lists not only the contents but also includes additional information, such as the size of each file or the time and date the file was last changed. Finally, typing "ls -F" lists the contents of the directory and identifies any subdirectories with a forward slash (/).

TROUBLE?

If you can't figure out the command you need to perform a task, use the apropos command. For example, typing "apropos *directory*" lists and briefly describes all the UNIX commands related to directories.■

TABLE 1-4: Some common UNIX commands

COMMAND	ACTION	COMMAND	ACTION
cd *directoryname*	Move to the directory titled *directoryname*	**more *filename***	Display the contents of *filename* one full screen at a time
cp *file1 file2*	Copy the contents of *file1* into *file2*	**mv *file1 file2***	Move (or change the name of) *file1* to *file2*
print *filename*	Print the file titled *filename*	**passwd**	Change your current password
ls	List the contents of the current directory	**pwd**	Display the name of the current directory
mkdir *directoryname*	Create a directory titled *directoryname*	**rm *name***	Remove the file or directory titled *name*

Discovering your Internet host's address

Each computer on a network has a unique name called a **host name**, usually displayed when you first log on, which identifies the computer to other computers on the network. Host names usually consist of one word (it can be playful, like "Snoopy," or serious, like "Accounts"). Recall, though, that because the Internet is a network of networks, a computer from another network needs a way to distinguish one computer from another. After all, there may be more than one computer on the Internet named "Gandalf." On the Internet, each host is assigned a unique address, called its **IP address** (Internet Protocol address). IP addresses consist of four numbers separated by periods (each lower than 256). Sample IP addresses include 137.18.128.6 or 192.74.137.5. As you can imagine, it would be difficult to remember these addresses, so **domain names**, names that identify computers to other hosts, are assigned for each IP address. The domain names for the two sample IP addresses are "house.gov" and "world.std.com." See the related topic "Network protocols" in this lesson for information on how computers on a network communicate. You can use the **nslookup** command to discover the IP address and domain name for your host. This command tells UNIX to get IP address and domain name information from a name server on the Internet (**name servers** are servers that provide a registry of Internet domain names and IP addresses).

▶ Olivia tries to find the IP address and domain name for her host. Follow along with her.

1 Be sure you are logged on to your computer, as described earlier in this unit
The UNIX command prompt % should appear on your screen, ready to accept a command.

2 Type **nslookup hostname** (where *hostname* is the name of the computer you're working on), then press **[Enter]**
Olivia types "nslookup students". As shown in Figure 1-9, the IP address for Olivia's host at MidWest University is 144.92.222.126 and the domain name is "students.mwu.edu." Remember this example is fictional. Your address and domain name will be different.

FIGURE 1-9: UNIX "nslookup" command

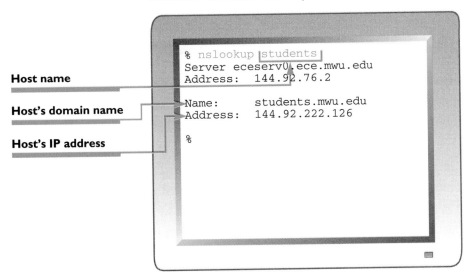

Host name

Host's domain name

Host's IP address

```
% nslookup students
Server eceserv0.ece.mwu.edu
Address:   144.92.76.2

Name:      students.mwu.edu
Address:   144.92.222.126

%
```

Network protocols

The rules that govern how different hosts on a network communicate and share resources is called a **protocol**. You can think of it this way—the Internet is related to the protocol in the same way that mail is related to the envelope. All post offices demand a common format for addressing envelopes, and similarly all Internet hosts use a common protocol or format called **TCP/IP** (Transmission Control Protocol / Internet Protocol). Any computer that communicates with other hosts on the Internet must support TCP/IP.

TROUBLE?

If your host computer doesn't recognize the nslookup command, it could mean that it determines Internet addresses by a different method than using a domain name server. Ask your instructor about your host name and address.■

QUICK TIP

If you don't know the host name of your computer and you're working on a UNIX computer, you can find the name by typing "hostname" at the command prompt and pressing [Enter].■

Using domain names

Even though domain names are easier to remember than IP addresses, they can still be intimidating. In the previous lesson, you saw a host at MidWest University with the domain name "students.mwu.edu." Domain names reflect a hierarchy of groups that are responsible for the computers or networks underneath them, as shown in Figure 1-10. As you read from left to right in the domain name you go up in the hierarchy. Some hosts have more than one domain name, as discussed in the related topic in this lesson, "Domain name aliases." As you work with other Internet hosts and domain names, you'll begin to recognize the types and locations of different computers from their Internet domain names. The final domain is known as a **top-level domain**. Table 1-5 shows some top-level domains. For the domain name "students.mwu.edu" you can derive the following information:

- **students** is the host name of the computer

- **mwu** is the educational institute, MidWest University

- **edu** is the group for all educational institutions in the United States

TABLE 1-5: Some top-level domains

DOMAIN	LOCATION	DOMAIN	LOCATION
au	Australia	gov	Government agencies
ca	Canada	int	International organizations
ch	Switzerland	jp	Japan
com	Commercial sites	mil	Military
de	Germany	net	Networking organizations
edu	Educational institutes	nz	New Zealand
es	Spain	org	Nonprofit organizations
fr	France	uk	United Kingdom

FIGURE 1-10: Domain name structure for "students.mwu.edu"

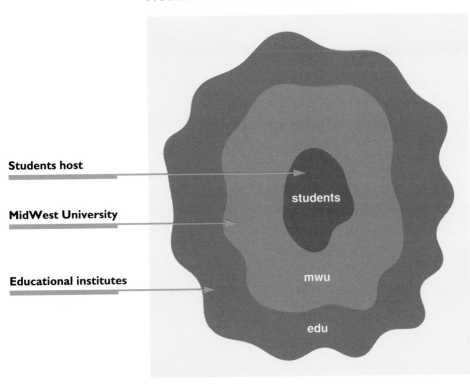

Students host

MidWest University

Educational institutes

Domain name aliases

A single host can have more than one name. For example, the host with the IP address 198.105.232.1 has two names: "ftp.microsoft.com" and an **alias**, or alternative name, "gowinnt.microsoft.com." The alias highlights a particular service the host provides to the network. The alias for this host indicates that it makes files publicly available to the Internet using the file transfer protocol (FTP)—a method of transferring files you'll learn about in a later unit.

Logging out

After you have finished your session, you should log out. Failure to log out might allow another person access to your account (if you are working from a public terminal). Some computers only allow a fixed number of users at the same time, so to be courteous you should log out to allow other users to get on. If you pay a fee-per-minute charge for Internet access, failure to log out promptly will cost you money. Finally, many systems have an automatic time-out mechanism that logs you out after a certain amount of time has passed with no activity (that is, if you haven't entered any commands). ▶ Olivia logs out now that she's had a chance to work on her site's network. After you've logged out, take a look at the related topic "Who controls the Internet?" in this lesson for some interesting information on the nature of the Internet, which you will get to know over the course of this book.

1 Be sure you are logged on at the UNIX command prompt, %

2 Type **logout** after the prompt, then press **[Enter]**
See Figure 1-11. Olivia is now disconnected from the Internet.

FIGURE 1-11: Logging out

Who controls the Internet?

The Internet is so big and sprawling you might wonder who controls it. The short answer is nobody. Remember the Internet was designed to be decentralized so that the failure of one part would not bring down the whole system. The long answer is more complicated. The closest thing to a governing body is the Internet Society (ISOC), a voluntary organization advocating the worldwide exchange of information through the use of Internet technology. The ISOC invites members to belong to a board called the Internet Architecture Board (IAB), which determines network standards and conventions that each host on the Internet must adhere to. Another volunteer organization, the Internet Engineering Task Force (IETF), works on the operational and technical problems of the Internet. Some Internet users have mixed feelings about the interest of the federal government in the "Information Superhighway." While there is a great desire to see Internet access promoted and expanded, some still feel that freedom from government regulations is the way to go.

CONCEPTSREVIEW

**Label each of the elements shown
in this short Internet session.**

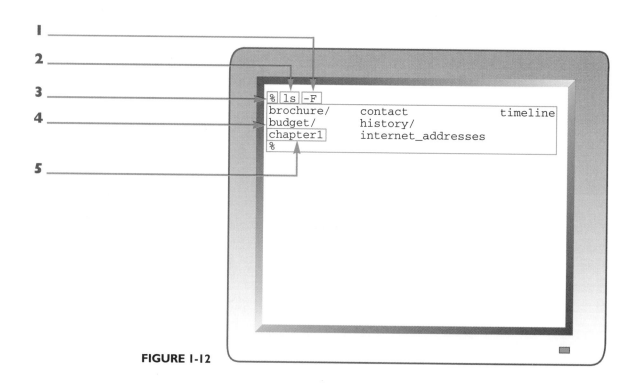

```
% ls -F
brochure/        contact                    timeline
budget/          history/
chapter1         internet_addresses
%
```

FIGURE I-12

**Match each of the descriptions with the term
it describes.**

6 List of files

7 Host providing a resource to
other computers on a network

8 An operating system commonly used by Internet users

9 Two or more connected computers allowing for the sharing of data and resources

10 Computer using a resource
provided by another host on a
network

a. network

b. client

c. server

d. directory

e. UNIX

Select the best answer from the list of choices.

11 The acronym GUI means:

  a. Group user information

  b. Graphical user interface

  c. Government user interconnections

  d. Get a UNIX interface

12 DOS and UNIX are all examples of:

  a. Internet servers

  b. network protocols

  c. operating systems

  d. Internet clients

13 A network protocol is:

  a. the rules of etiquette the network users should follow
in dealing with other users

  b. a set of rules for creating valid passwords

  c. the rules governing how hosts communicate and share
resources

  d. determined separately by each network host

14 If you start a word-processing program on your computer, but the files you're editing are provided by another host on the network, the host providing the files is an example of a:

a. server

b. client

c. service provider

d. host

15 A domain name ending with the letters "mil" tells you that the host:

a. is located in Milwaukee

b. is on a military network

c. transfers data at one million bytes per second

d. uses an arbitrary combination of letters, so it tells you nothing

16 UNIX commands:

a. are case sensitive

b. are case insensitive

c. are limited to eight characters

d. must end with a semicolon

17 Which of the following is a valid IP address?

a. 128.104.28.3

b. 128.63

c. 128.312.48.4

d. 128.33.4.62.29.35

18 To get help with the UNIX command "ls" type:

a. help ls

b. man ls

c. man LS

d. whatis ls

19 Which one of the following statements is true?

a. Every client on a network is a host.

b. Every host on a network is a client.

c. Terminals are always hosts.

d. Hosts cannot be terminals.

APPLICATIONS
REVIEW

1 Begin by accessing the Internet.

a. Sit down at your computer; if it is a terminal connected to the Internet, you can skip part b.

b. Dial in to an Internet site using your modem.

2 Log on.

a. Enter your user name and press [Enter].

b. Enter your password and press [Enter].

3 Use a few UNIX commands to get information about your status.

a. Type "ls" and press [Enter] to see the contents of your directory.

b. Type "hostname" and press [Enter] to find out the name of your host.

c. Type "apropos host" and press [Enter] to get information on different UNIX commands relating to hosts.

4 Log out.

a. Type "logout" and press [Enter].

INDEPENDENT
CHALLENGE I

In the first lesson of this unit, you saw a few examples of how people can use the Internet to communicate and share resources. You may be surprised as you become more familiar with the Internet by the wide variety of topics that it offers to users. You will find it easier to approach the Internet as a beginner if you have some specific questions to answer. Try formulating some ideas on areas that you'd like to explore on the Internet.

To complete this independent challenge:

I Write a list of topics (perhaps from your course work, hobbies, or job) that you think might be interesting to explore on the Internet over the course of your work with this book. Be creative! Current Internet reference bibliographies list topics as varied as White House press briefings, tattoos and body decoration, high-performance automobiles (hot rods), Hindustani classical music, bicycle-racing techniques, molecular biology databases, and so on; the Internet is an almost inexhaustible source of information!

2 Draft some specific questions that you can try to answer as you learn more about the Internet. Some examples are "What time is high tide in San Francisco next Friday?" or "If I want to attend an opera at the Metropolitan in New York City, how much is a ticket?" or "Is there a handicap entrance to Candlestick Park?" There is actually a game you can play on the Internet where players post questions like this and see who can answer them. Trying to track down information like this is a great way to practice your Internet skills and learn about new sources of information. As you explore the Internet in the next seven units, keep track of your topics and questions and see how many of them you can answer.

INDEPENDENT
CHALLENGE 2

The Internet is changing and growing so quickly that in the short few months it takes this book to be published, parts of it may already be out of date. Internet expansion has attracted intense media attention from newspapers, magazines, television, and radio. Research and report on the expansion of the Internet and the benefits and problems that have come up.

To complete this independent challenge, consider the following questions as guidelines:

I What new services are being added to the Internet? How does this affect services already available?

2 Which government agencies or departments have gone on-line? How does this affect legislative issues and governmental security?

3 How has increased user volume on the Internet affected its ability to function? What problems are associated with this phenomenal growth, and what solutions do Internet experts see in sight?

4 What are the issues surrounding the regulation of what is posted on the Internet? Can you find information, for example, about lawsuits relating to commercial vendors trying to sell products over the Internet?

5 In what ways do you think the Internet will make a difference in your life?

UNIT 2

OBJECTIVES

▶ Understand parts of
an e-mail message

▶ Send an e-mail
message

▶ View and maintain
a message list

▶ Reply to a message

▶ Understand mailing
lists

▶ Understand
netiquette

▶ Use Listserv

▶ Subscribe to a
mailing list

▶ Use mailing lists

Using ELECTRONIC MAIL

*T*he most common activity on the Internet is the sending and receiving of electronic mail, or e-mail. In this unit you will learn how to use the mailer that comes with the UNIX operating system. A **mailer** is a program that you use to work with e-mail. After exploring the different features of the standard UNIX mailer, you'll learn how to join a **mailing list**, a group of Internet users who share a common interest and communicate with each other through e-mail. ▶ Olivia Sanchez, a MidWest University student in occupational therapy (OT), wants to learn to use e-mail to communicate with other OT students and the larger OT community. She begins by experimenting with sending and receiving mail messages.

Understanding parts of an e-mail message

An electronic mail, or **e-mail**, message is simply a message sent electronically from one host to another. Vast numbers of e-mail messages are transmitted daily across the Internet. These messages can be personal, business-related, research-related, or informational. They can be messages between people who have never met but who share a common interest. For information on sending an e-mail message, see the related topic "E-mail addresses" in this lesson. Before you send your first e-mail message in the next lesson, take a look at a sample e-mail message to learn its fundamental parts. Dr. Simpson, the chair of the occupational therapy department, uses e-mail regularly to communicate with her students and colleagues. Dr. Lenore Simpson sends good news to Olivia Sanchez over the Internet. Figure 2-1 shows the basic parts of the e-mail message Dr. Simpson sent to Olivia.

Header

The header tells you who sent the message, and when, the route of the message, its subject, and other information about the transmission.

Fields

Within the header are various fields that contain specific information about the message. Table 2-1 lists the most common fields you are likely to see when you send and receive e-mail. For the message that Olivia received, you can see from the Date field that this message was received on Thursday, September 17, 1995, and from the Subject field that the subject of the message was "Congratulations."

Body

The body is the central substance of the message; the text composed by the sender.

Signature

Many e-mail programs allow the sender to automatically append a text message, called a signature, to every message sent. Dr. Simpson, for example, has a signature that provides information about her office address and phone number as well as her office hours. This signature appears at the end of every message she sends.

FIGURE 2-1: Parts of an e-mail message

Fields

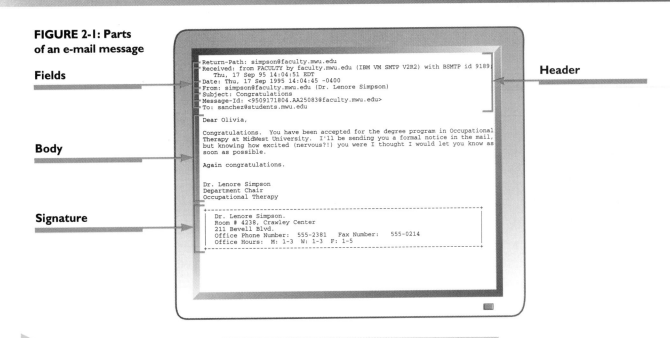

Header

```
Return-Path: simpson@faculty.mwu.edu
Received: from FACULTY by faculty.mwu.edu (IBM VM SMTP V2R2) with BSMTP id 9189;
    Thu, 17 Sep 95 14:04:51 EDT
Date: Thu, 17 Sep 1995 14:04:45 -0400
From: simpson@faculty.mwu.edu (Dr. Lenore Simpson)
Subject: Congratulations
Message-Id: <9509171804.AA25083@faculty.mwu.edu>
To: sanchez@students.mwu.edu

Dear Olivia,

Congratulations.  You have been accepted for the degree program in Occupational
Therapy at MidWest University.  I'll be sending you a formal notice in the mail,
but knowing how excited (nervous?!) you were I thought I would let you know as
soon as possible.

Again congratulations.


Dr. Lenore Simpson
Department Chair
Occupational Therapy

+--------------------------------------------------------------+
| Dr. Lenore Simpson.                                          |
| Room # 4238, Crawley Center                                  |
| 211 Bevell Blvd.                                             |
| Office Phone Number:  555-2381    Fax Number:   555-0214     |
| Office Hours:  M: 1-3  W: 1-3  F: 1-5                        |
+--------------------------------------------------------------+
```

Body

Signature

E-mail addresses

In order to send electronic mail you must know the recipient's e-mail address. Typically this consists of the recipient's user name, the @ symbol, and the domain name of the host on which he or she has an account (review the previous unit if you aren't sure what these items are). You do not need to specify parts of the domain name that you have in common with your recipient. For example, if your e-mail address is jones@students.mwu.edu and the person to whom you are sending e-mail has the address thompson@faculty.mwu.edu, you need only specify the address thompson@faculty–the mwu.edu part of the address will be inferred by the mail server.

TABLE 2-1: Common fields appearing in the header

FIELD NAME	DESCRIPTION
Return-Path	The route the message takes to get to you
Received	The host or hosts through which the message is routed
Date	Date the message is sent
From	Person who sends the message
Subject	Message topic, entered by the sender
Message-Id	Internal number that identifies the message to the hosts that transfer the message
To	Person to whom the message is addressed
Cc	List of others who receive a "carbon copy" of the message (Dr. Simpson sent the message in Figure 2-1 only to Olivia, so no Cc field appears there)

Sending an e-mail message

UNIX has its own mailer, the UNIX Mail program, that lets you send and receive e-mail. The UNIX Mail program is available to most Internet users, though many universities have additional mailers that are more user-friendly. You'll use the UNIX Mail program now and will be introduced to a different mailer, Pine, in the next unit. The related topic "E-mail command switches" in this lesson tells you about some of the options you have when using the UNIX Mail program. Now that you've seen what an e-mail message looks like, try sending one using the UNIX **mail** command, which is used both to send and view your e-mail messages. To ensure that you receive some e-mail, your first task will be to send mail to yourself. ▶ Olivia Sanchez, the newest member of MidWest University's Occupational Therapy program, decides to send a message to herself as a means of learning how to use e-mail. Follow along with Olivia, but enter your own name and address instead of hers when instructed. In the steps, the text you are to type appears in bold. Anything that requires you to enter information for your own situation appears in bold italics. Olivia's entries, appearing in quotation marks in the substeps, show what one user might type.

1 Connect to your Internet host and log on to your account as discussed in Unit 1
  Be sure the UNIX command prompt appears.

2 Type **mail *user*** at the UNIX command prompt, where *user* is the e-mail address of the individual to whom you are sending mail (in this case your own user name), then press **[Enter]**
  Because Olivia is sending mail to herself, she doesn't need to type more than her user name as the address (as shown in Figure 2-2). If she was sending e-mail to a different user on another Internet host, she would need to type the entire e-mail address rather than just a user name. The UNIX mailer then prompts her for a subject.

3 Type a short description of the subject of the message, then press **[Enter]**
  Since this is just a test message, Olivia types "Test Message" as the subject of the message.

4 Type the body of your message, pressing **[Enter]** when you get to the end of each line
  Olivia types "This is a test message of UNIX mail" as her message body. If you make a mistake, press [Backspace] and then correct the typing error. Once you press [Enter] and go to a new line, you cannot change the previous line without using a text editor.

5 When finished with the message, press **[Enter]** to go to a new line, type **[.]** (a period), then press **[Enter]** again
  The period tells the UNIX Mail program that you are finished composing the message. Olivia's message in Figure 2-2 is just a single line. The UNIX Mail program may then prompt you for additional information, depending on how your site's system administrator has configured the mailer.

6 Respond to each prompt by either entering appropriate text or leaving the field blank, then press **[Enter]**
  The UNIX mailer prompts Olivia with Cc: to ask if she wants to send a copy of her message to other users. Oliva presses [Enter] to leave the Cc: field blank. After you have responded to the final prompt, you should find yourself back at the UNIX command prompt.

FIGURE 2-2: Sending a **UNIX** mail message

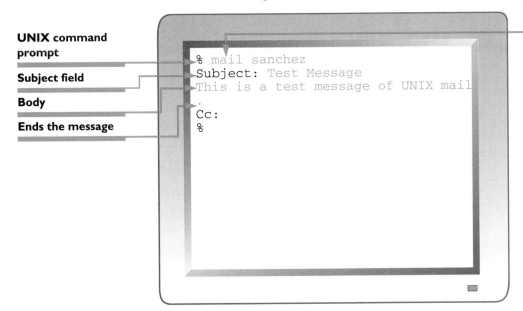

UNIX command prompt

Subject field

Body

Ends the message

Mail command, followed by recipient's address

```
% mail sanchez
Subject: Test Message
This is a test message of UNIX mail
.
Cc:
%
```

E-mail command switches

The UNIX Mail program uses switches so you can set values of different parameters. You can avoid being prompted for a subject, for example, by using the -s switch. In this way, Olivia could have sent the message in Figure 2-2 by typing "mail -s 'Test Message' sanchez" at the command prompt. UNIX would not prompt her for a subject, and her next step would be to type the body of the message. As another example, if you want to know what route your message took through several Internet hosts, use the -v switch by typing "mail -v sanchez" at the UNIX command prompt. This can be helpful if a message is returned to you as undeliverable.

QUICK **TIP**

To cancel a message, enter the key combination [Ctrl][C] (press and hold down the [Ctrl] key and then press the letter [C] with [Ctrl] still held down) at any point within the body of the letter.

TROUBLE?

When typing the body of your message, be sure to press [Enter] before you reach the end of a line. Even though UNIX automatically wraps text to the next line, it will return an error message when it has wrapped too much text (about 256 characters).■

Viewing and maintaining a message list

Now that Olivia has sent e-mail to herself, she can check to see whether she has any mail waiting. The UNIX command to check for the presence of mail is the same command used to send mail: type "mail" at the UNIX command prompt. UNIX displays the contents of your mailbox (your message list) and precedes new messages with an N and unread messages with a U. Messages appearing in the list without a prefix have already been read. UNIX uses the **>** symbol to point to the most recent message in the mailbox. The UNIX mail prompt, the **&** symbol, appears at the end of the list. After this prompt you can type special UNIX mailer commands, some of which are shown in Table 2-2, to handle and review your mail. Note that most UNIX mail commands are lowercase; be sure to type them exactly as shown. For information on maintaining additional mailboxes, see the related topic "Folders" in this lesson.

▶ Olivia views the contents of her mailbox. Your mailbox may contain only the message you sent yourself in the previous lesson. In that case, just view that message.

1 Connect to your Internet host and log on to your account as discussed in Unit 1 if you have not already done so
   Be sure the UNIX command prompt appears.

2 Type **mail** at the UNIX command prompt, then press **[Enter]**
   UNIX lists your messages and displays the & prompt. To read a message, you type the message number and press [Enter], and the UNIX mailer displays that message's contents. Olivia's mailbox, shown in Figure 2-3, contains four messages. She decides to read the third message, from a fellow student with the user name "griffith."

3 Type the number of the message you want to read then press **[Enter]**
   Olivia wants to read the third message, so she types "3" at the UNIX mail prompt. The mailer displays the contents of message 3, as shown in Figure 2-4.

4 When finished viewing messages, press **[q]** to quit UNIX Mail
   The mailer indicates how many messages remain in your mailbox (4 in Olivia's case, as shown in Figure 2-4) and returns you to the UNIX command prompt.

TABLE 2-2: Common UNIX mail commands

COMMAND	NAME	DESCRIPTION
?	help	Displays list of mail commands
d *message list*	delete	Deletes specified messages in the mailbox
e *message list*	edit	Edits messages in the mailbox using the default UNIX text editor
folder *filename*	folder	Switches to a different mailbox folder
p *message list*	print	Prints the messages in the message list
s *message list foldername*	save	Saves the message in the list to a folder
u *message list*	undelete	Undeletes previously deleted or specified mail message

FIGURE 2-3: UNIX message list

Old messages

Unread messages

Indicates most recent message

UNIX mail prompt

Status of mail box

New message

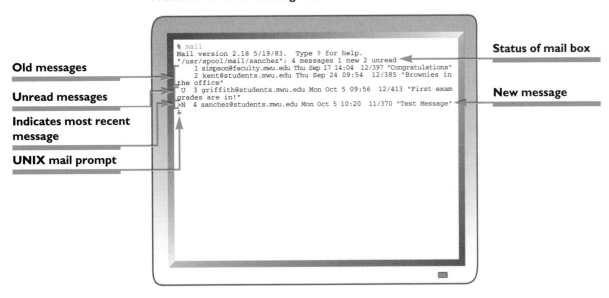

FIGURE 2-4: Viewing a message

UNIX mail prompt

Quits UNIX Mail

UNIX command prompt reappears

Type number of message you want to read

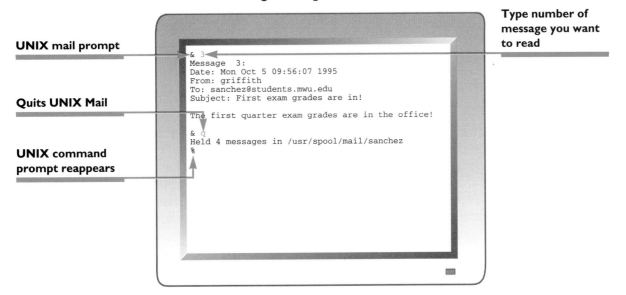

Folders

You can maintain more than one mailbox or **folder**. You might want to use one mailbox for personal messages and another for homework, for example. Using UNIX mail commands, you can move the messages in your active mailbox to another folder. For example, to place messages 2, 4, and 6 in a new folder called "personal," type "s 2 4 6 personal" at the UNIX mail prompt & and press [Enter]. If the personal folder does not yet exist, this command creates it for you. Once this folder exists, you can switch to it by typing, "folder personal" at the UNIX mail prompt. If you want the UNIX mail command to open a particular folder instead of the default folder, use the -f switch. For example, typing "mail -f personal" at the UNIX command prompt starts the UNIX Mail program using the personal folder as the new default.

TROUBLE?

If you forget the UNIX mail commands, press [?] at the UNIX mail prompt or type "man mail" at the UNIX command prompt to get a listing of commands and their meanings.■

Replying to a message

A quick way to reply to a mail message is to enter the **r** or **R** command at the UNIX mail prompt. If you want to reply only to the person who sent the message, use the R command. If you want to reply to the sender as well as any other users who received the original message, use the r command. On some systems, these commands may be reversed, so you should view the description of your mailer's commands by pressing [?] at the mail prompt. Using the R command automatically places the sender's e-mail address in the To: field of the header. The r command places the addresses of all who received the message in the To: field. You can designate groups of recipients using aliases; see the related topic "Aliases" in this lesson for more information. ▶ Olivia decides to use the R command to reply to message 3, the message about the first quarter grades that have just been posted. As before, you should go through these steps with a message of your own.

1 Connect to your Internet host and log on to your account as discussed in Unit 1 if you have not already done so
   Be sure the UNIX command prompt appears.

2 Start the UNIX mailer by typing **mail** at the UNIX command prompt, then press **[Enter]**
   UNIX lists your messages, then the UNIX mail prompt, &, appears.

3 Type the number of the message to which you want to reply at the UNIX mail prompt, then press **[Enter]**
   Olivia types "3" since she wants to respond to message 3.

4 Press **[R]** to reply to the message, then press **[Enter]**
   The UNIX mailer automatically enters the sender's e-mail address in the To: field and uses the subject from the original message prefaced by the word "Re:" (that is, regarding).

5 Type the body of the message you want to send, pressing **[Enter]** after each line
   Olivia types "How do the grades look?" as the body text.

6 Press **[Enter]** after the last line of the body text, press **[.]** (a period), then press **[Enter]** again to send the message

7 If the UNIX mailer prompts you for more header information, type whatever text you think appropriate, pressing **[Enter]** after each header
   The mailer prompts Olivia with the Cc: prompt, asking whether she wants to send a copy of this message to another user. Since she does not, Olivia presses [Enter]. When you are finished with the header fields, UNIX Mail sends the message.

8 Press **[q]** to exit UNIX Mail
   Again you return to the UNIX command prompt. Figure 2-5 shows the entire session.

FIGURE 2-5: Replying to an e-mail message

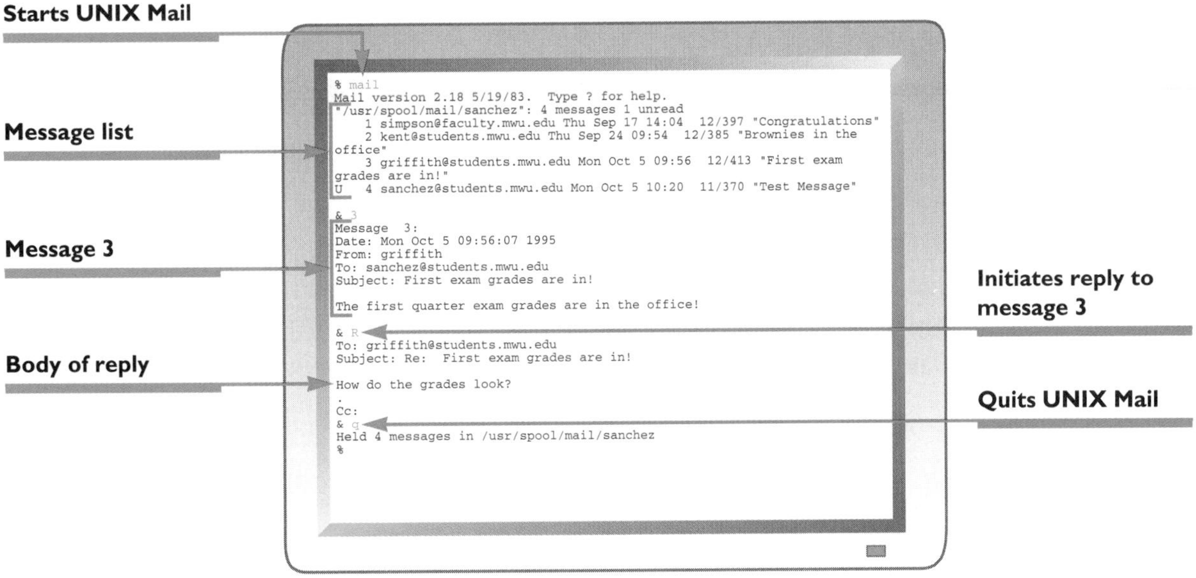

Starts UNIX Mail

Message list

Message 3

Body of reply

Initiates reply to
message 3

Quits UNIX Mail

```
% mail
Mail version 2.18 5/19/83.  Type ? for help.
"/usr/spool/mail/sanchez": 4 messages 1 unread
    1 simpson@faculty.mwu.edu Thu Sep 17 14:04  12/397 "Congratulations"
    2 kent@students.mwu.edu Thu Sep 24 09:54  12/385 "Brownies in the
office"
    3 griffith@students.mwu.edu Mon Oct 5 09:56  12/413 "First exam
grades are in!"
U   4 sanchez@students.mwu.edu Mon Oct 5 10:20  11/370 "Test Message"

& 3
Message  3:
Date: Mon Oct 5 09:56:07 1995
From: griffith
To: sanchez@students.mwu.edu
Subject: First exam grades are in!

The first quarter exam grades are in the office!

& R
To: griffith@students.mwu.edu
Subject: Re:  First exam grades are in!

How do the grades look?
.
Cc:
& q
Held 4 messages in /usr/spool/mail/sanchez
%
```

Aliases

You can reduce the need to remember complex e-mail addresses by using aliases.
An **alias** is a name that represents an e-mail address or a group of e-mail addresses.
To create an alias you have to create or edit a file in your home directory called
".mailrc." If you are not sure how to create and edit text files, talk to your instructor
or system administrator. In the .mailrc file, Olivia Sanchez might add the line "alias
friends hilton kent griffith" to define an alias for three of her friends. She can now
send mail to the alias "friends" as a substitute for the e-mail addresses: hilton,
kent, and griffith. An alias that stands for several e-mail addresses is also known
as a **distribution list**.

QUICK **TIP**

Delete messages
you don't need with
the d command
(as described in
Table 2-2 in the
previous lesson).

Understanding mailing lists

The related topic in the previous lesson, "Aliases," discussed using a single word to stand for a long e-mail address or for many e-mail addresses. Now imagine you have a large group of people who share a common interest, like Olivia's field of occupational therapy (OT). This group could easily share e-mail messages about OT experiences if each user in the group created an alias representing the e-mail messages of all other members of the group. However, as members of the group leave and new ones join, each member would have to update his or her alias. If the group expands, this becomes increasingly difficult. To partially alleviate this problem, a single member of the group could agree to maintain the member list. This is essentially how mailing lists work. A **mailing list** is a list of users who share a common interest. The person responsible for maintaining the member list is called the **moderator**. Users who participate in the list are called **subscribers**: they send e-mail to the moderator who forwards it to all the other subscribers. Sometimes the moderator has the additional task of screening the messages for content before sending them. Some mailing lists are maintained by software programs called **list servers** that automate the adding and subtracting of members and the forwarding of mail messages, as shown in Figure 2-6. One of the more popular mailing list programs is called **Listserv**. The related topic "Mailing lists and Bitnet" in this lesson gives more information on the history of mailing lists.

▶ Each of the many mailing lists available on the Internet has a name associated with it. For example, the mailing list INDIA-L facilitates discussion about the Indian subcontinent. Other examples of Internet mailing lists follow (you'll learn how to join lists like these in upcoming lessons).

■ **bikecommute** offers information on improving bicycling conditions in urban and suburban areas. It originated in Silicon Valley but doesn't limit membership to that area.

■ **WRITERS** is for aspiring and professional writers. In addition to discussing writing issues, it also features announcements of workshops, conferences, and publication opportunities.

■ **folk-dancing** gives you information on where folk-dancing groups and clubs meet and welcomes discussion on anything having to do with folk-dancing.

■ **immune** serves as a support group for people dealing with the symptoms of immune-system breakdowns. Family members and friends are welcome, as well as medical and disability professionals.

■ **SWIP-L** originated with members of the Society for Women in Philosophy and welcomes those involved in the field of feminist philosophy.

■ **JOBPLACE** is not a "want ads" forum but a place to go to learn about self-directed job searches and to discuss job placement issues.

FIGURE 2-6: How a list server operates

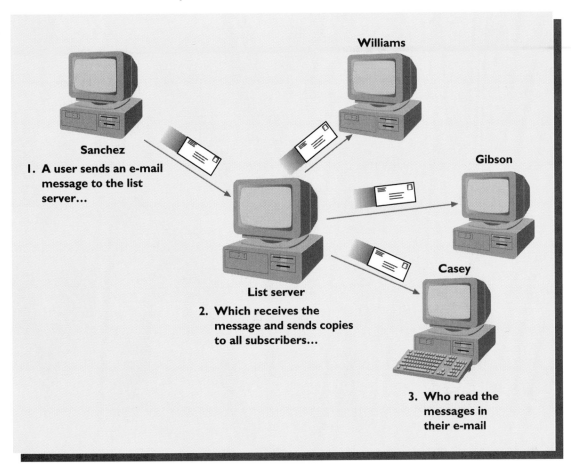

Williams

Sanchez

1. A user sends an e-mail message to the list server...

Gibson

List server

2. Which receives the message and sends copies to all subscribers...

Casey

3. Who read the messages in their e-mail

Mailing lists and Bitnet

The source of many of the worldwide mailing lists is a network called **Bitnet**. Bitnet began in 1981 as a network separate from the Internet with the purpose of keeping faculty members from different universities in touch with each another. Today Bitnet reaches over 1,300 educational institutes and contains thousands of mailing lists. On many Internet hosts, you can reach Bitnet through a machine that acts as a gateway between the two networks. The mailing address often tells you whether a computer is on Bitnet. For example, the address smith@portal.bitnet means that a user named smith has an account on the Bitnet host named "portal."

Understanding netiquette

Before joining an Internet mailing list, you should first be aware of the rules of Internet behavior, commonly called **netiquette**, that govern interaction on the Internet. In joining a mailing list, you are dealing with people you have never met and may never meet, so the Internet provides a bit of anonymity in your inter-actions with other users. Some users take advantage of this anonymity by indulging in unnecessarily insulting language (commonly called **flames**). In addition, the Internet community is made up of people whose Internet experiences vary widely. Some Internet users are "old hands" who may not appreciate new users (sometimes called **newbies**) pestering them with questions. Behavior on the Internet is mostly a matter of common sense (always post "thank you" messages when you receive help, and so on), but there is no Internet police squad enforcing the laws of netiquette. If you blatantly break a law, you may be surprised by the ferocity of other users' responses. This book offers the following set of basic netiquette guidelines for using mailing lists and includes specialized tips on netiquette throughout the book in the margins (for example, note the netiquette tip on the opposite page):

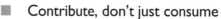

■ **Contribute, don't just consume**
Remember that the Internet is largely composed of volunteers. If you only take and never give, you are not adding to the diversity that makes the Internet as rich as it is.

■ **Be sure to spend some time with a new group**
Read their messages and catch the flow of conversation before you contribute.

■ **Minimize clutter on the Internet**
Think twice before you fire off a message and keep your message short and to the point. This is also called "not wasting bandwidth."

■ **Avoid advertising on the Internet**
It is a largely noncommercial environment, and users will not appreciate having to wade through commercial messages when they settle in to read their e-mail.

■ **Be polite**
Although some mailing lists seem to exist solely for the pleasure of a good argument, most users prefer to keep dialog on a friendly level.

■ **Learn the language**
See Table 2-3 for information on a few terms currently in use on the Internet (but be aware that, like any slang, these terms won't be around forever, and new ones will take their place). Another way of expressing ideas or emotions is with "smileys" or "emoticons." For more information, see the related topic "Smileys" in this lesson.

TABLE 2-3: Sampling of Internet acronyms

TERM	MEANING
BRB	Be Right Back
BTW	By The Way
FAQ	Frequently Asked Question
IMHO	In My Humble Opinion
MOTOS	Member Of The Opposite Sex
ROTFL	Rolling On The Floor Laughing
WRT	With Respect To

Smileys

You probably won't have to be on the Internet very long to start seeing strange symbols popping up at the end of messages, like **:-)**. Turn your head sideways to the left to see that the three symbols **:-)** look like a smiley face. These symbol combinations are called **smileys** or **emoticons**: typographical representations of body language. On the Internet no one can see your face when you communicate, so if you are saying something that could be misinterpreted, when you meant it to be friendly, include a smiley. For example, you might say, "You mean you're actually going to be on time for once **:-)**?" Table 2-4 shows some common smileys.

TABLE 2-4: Common smileys

TYPED SMILEY	MEANING
:-)	smile
:-D	laugh
;-)	wink
:-(	frown
:-X	my lips are sealed
%-)	I've been working too hard

NETIQUETTE

The Internet works because everyone is expected to share ideas. Once you've spent some time on the Internet, make sure to help out newer members just as you were helped. ■

Using Listserv

You can use **Listserv** to help find a mailing list on a particular topic. You send commands in the body of an e-mail message to a network host running the Listserv program. The results of the command are then sent back to you through e-mail. ▶ Olivia Sanchez of MidWest University would like to subscribe to a mailing list on sign language. To find whether such a list exists, she connects to a computer running Listserv. There are many such servers on the Internet: the one she uses has the e-mail address listserv@listserv.net. Go through the steps with a topic of your own, replacing any italicized text with entries relevant to your topic.

I   Type **mail *listserv*** at the UNIX command prompt to start the UNIX Mail program where *listserv* is the e-mail address of the mailing list server you want to connect to, then press **[Enter]**
Olivia types "mail listserv@listserv.net" at the UNIX command prompt. You can use the same address if you want, or you can use one suggested by your instructor.

2   When prompted for a subject, press **[Enter]** to leave the Subject: field blank
Do not include any text in the subject header.

3   Type **list global / *topic*** in the message body where *topic* is a word describing the subject you're interested in, then press **[Enter]**
Do not type anything else since the list server can only read commands and will try to interpret anything you type as a command. Users who have signatures appended to their e-mail messages should be sure to delete them. Olivia types "global / sign" in the body of her message.

4   Send the e-mail message by pressing **[.]** (a period) on a separate line and then pressing **[Enter]**, leaving all other mail header fields blank
When you have sent the mail message, you are returned to the UNIX command prompt. Figure 2-7 shows the entire session. It may take awhile for Listserv to return an answer to your request.

5   Start the UNIX Mail program, then read any messages sent to you by the list server using techniques discussed in previous lessons
Figure 2-8 shows Olivia's e-mail message, which echoes back her command and tells her that the list server is processing her request; yours will look different depending on the server you accessed. This message lets Olivia verify that she has written the command correctly. Later she receives a second message shown in Figure 2-9, which gives the results of her command. (This figure shows only a selection of the mailing list Olivia received.) Again, your message will look different depending on the topic you chose. Olivia's message indicates that there are a number of mailing lists whose descriptions include the word "sign," two of which seem dedicated to issues regarding sign language: SLLING-L and TERPS-L. In the next lesson, follow Olivia as she becomes a subscriber of the SLLING-L mailing list.

6   Press **[q]** after the UNIX mail prompt to return to the UNIX command prompt when you are done reading your messages

FIGURE 2-7: Mail message sent to Listserv

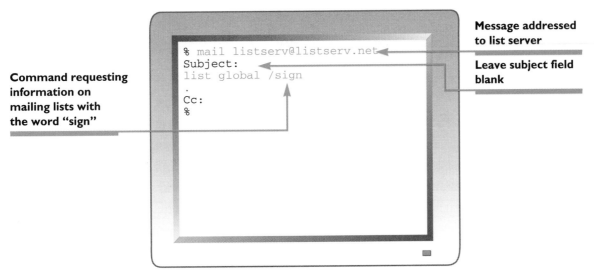

Command requesting information on mailing lists with the word "sign"

Message addressed to list server

Leave subject field blank

```
% mail listserv@listserv.net
Subject:
list global /sign
.
Cc:
%
```

FIGURE 2-8: Notification that Listserv command is being processed

Information Olivia requested in a separate message

Technical information about the transmission

Echo of the command Olivia sent

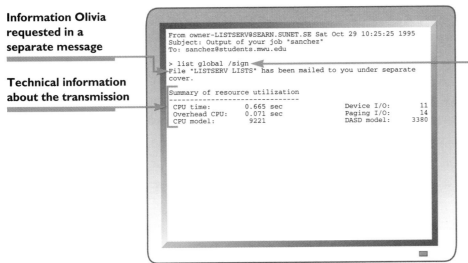

```
From owner-LISTSERV@SEARN.SUNET.SE Sat Oct 29 10:25:25 1995
Subject: Output of your job "sanchez"
To: sanchez@students.mwu.edu

> list global /sign
File "LISTSERV LISTS" has been mailed to you under separate
cover.

Summary of resource utilization
--------------------------------
CPU time:       0.665 sec        Device I/O:      11
Overhead CPU:   0.071 sec        Paging I/O:      14
CPU model:      9221             DASD model:      3380
```

FIGURE 2-9: Results of Listserv command

e-mail address for the mailing list

Name of the mailing list

Sign language mailing lists

Description

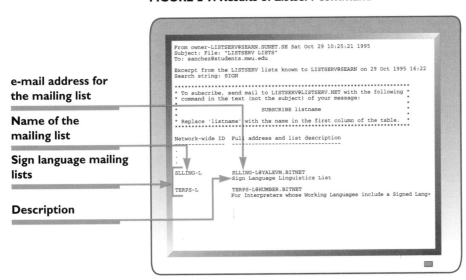

```
From owner-LISTSERV@SEARN.SUNET.SE Sat Oct 29 10:25:21 1995
Subject: File: 'LISTSERV LISTS'
To: sanchez@students.mwu.edu

Excerpt from the LISTSERV lists known to LISTSERV@SEARN on 29 Oct 1995 16:22
Search string: SIGN

*******************************************************************
* To subscribe, send mail to LISTSERV@LISTSERV.NET with the following *
* command in the text (not the subject) of your message:          *
*                    SUBSCRIBE listname                           *
* Replace 'listname' with the name in the first column of the table. *
*******************************************************************

Network-wide ID   Full address and list description
---------------   --------------------------------
.
.
.
SLLING-L          SLLING-L@YALEVM.BITNET
                  Sign Language Linguistics List

TERPS-L           TERPS-L@HUMBER.BITNET
                  For Interpreters whose Working Languages include a Signed Lang+
```

QUICK TIP

If you want to a get a list of all mailing lists, send the command "list global" to a list server such as the one located at Listserv@Listserv.net. Be warned however, that the list you receive will be extremely large.■

TROUBLE?

If the list server finds no match for the search word you entered, try another related word or request a list of all list servers to search for the appropriate mailing list.■

Subscribing to a mailing list

In the previous lesson, the list server sent Olivia information on the mailing list, SLLING-L, which she decides to join. If you have been going through the steps with a topic of your own, you should also have a mailing list that you want to join. You become a subscriber by sending an e-mail message to a list server with the command **SUBSCRIBE** *listname* in the body of the message (case is not important in Listserv commands). Often you will have to include your name in the command so that it reads "SUBSCRIBE *listname firstname lastname*." Once you become a subscriber, you can send other commands to the mailing list, some of which you'll learn about in the next lesson. To unsubscribe from a mailing list once you've subscribed, see the related topic "Unsubscribing from a mailing list" in this lesson.
▶ Olivia subscribes to the SLLING-L list. Try subscribing to a mailing list that you found in your own search from the previous lesson.

1 Connect to your Internet host and log on to your account as discussed in Unit 1 if you have not already done so
   Be sure the UNIX command prompt appears.

2 Start the UNIX mail program by typing **mail** *listserv* at the UNIX command prompt (where *listserv* is the e-mail address of the list server you want to send the command to) and press **[Enter]**
   Olivia types "mail listserv@listserv.net" to send a command to the list server with the address listserv@listserv.net. You should send your message to the list server you accessed in the previous lesson.

3 As before, leave the Subject: field blank and press **[Enter]** to proceed to the message body

4 Type **SUBSCRIBE** *listname firstname lastname* as the message body, where *listname* is the e-mail address of the list server and *firstname lastname* is your first and last name; then press **[.]** (a period) in a separate line and press **[Enter]** to send the message
   Olivia types the command "SUBSCRIBE SLLING-L Olivia Sanchez" in the body of her message, as shown in Figure 2-10. You should type the name of the mailing list you found in the previous lesson, and enter your own name. When you send the message, be sure to leave the header fields blank, and be sure there is no other text in the message. Once the message is sent, the UNIX mailer returns you to the UNIX command prompt. Olivia returns later to view her messages.

5 Read any messages sent to you from the list server using the techniques discussed in earlier lessons
   The first message Olivia receives, shown in Figure 2-11, tells her that her command has been processed. Later she receives a second message, part of which is shown in Figure 2-12, that informs her that her subscription to the SLLING-L list has been accepted and that gives her information on using the mailing list. Now that she's a subscriber, Olivia will start receiving mail messages from other subscribers on the list and be able to send messages of her own, as you will see in the next lesson. You should also have successfully subscribed to a mailing list at this point.

6 Quit the UNIX Mail program when you are done reading your messages

FIGURE 2-10: E-mail message subscribing to the SLLING-L list

Olivia's subscription request

Mailing list name

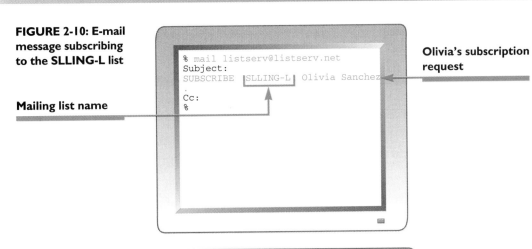

```
% mail listserv@listserv.net
Subject:
SUBSCRIBE  SLLING-L  Olivia Sanchez
.
Cc:
%
```

FIGURE 2-11: Response of the Listserv on the status of Olivia's command

```
From owner-LISTSERV@SEARN.SUNET.SE Sat Oct 29 11:09:36 1995
Subject: Output of your job "sanchez"
To: sanchez@students.mwu.edu

> SUBSCRIBE SLLING-L Olivia Sanchez
Your request is being forwarded to LISTSERV@YALEVM.

Summary of resource utilization
-------------------------------
CPU time:        0.286 sec        Device I/O:        2
Overhead CPU:    0.028 sec        Paging I/O:        8
CPU model:       9221             DASD model:     3380
```

FIGURE 2-12: Information on the SLLING-L list

Instructions on sending messages vs. sending commands

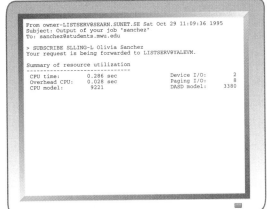

```
From owner-SLLING-L@YaleVM.YCC.Yale.Edu Sat Oct 29 11:09:49 1995
Subject:    You are now subscribed to the SLLING-L list
To: Olivia Sanchez <sanchez@students.mwu.edu>
Reply-To: SLLING-L-Request@YALEVM.CIS.YALE.EDU
X-Lsv-Listid: SLLING-L

Sat, 29 Oct 1995 12:08:50

Your subscription to the SLLING-L list (Sign Language Linguistics List)
has been accepted.

To send a message to all the people currently subscribed to the list, just send
mail to SLLING-L@YALEVM.CIS.YALE.EDU.  This is called "sending mail to the
list", because you send mail to a single address and LISTSERV makes copies for
all the people who have subscribed. This address (SLLING-L@YALEVM.CIS.YALE.EDU)
is also called the "list address". You must never try to send any command to
that address, as it would be distributed to all the people who have subscribed.
All commands must be sent to the "LISTSERV address", LISTSERV@YALEVM.BITNET (or
LISTSERV@YALEVM.CIS.YALE.EDU).
```

QUICK TIP

Be sure to save the welcoming message sent to you by the list server when you first subscribe to the list. It contains valuable information that you can use later, including how to unsubscribe.■

TROUBLE?

Don't subscribe to more than a few mailing lists at one time. The volume of mail messages can quickly overwhelm you.■

Unsubscribing from a mailing list

To unsubscribe from a mailing list you send an e-mail message to a list server containing the command UNSUBSCRIBE *listname* where *listname* is the name of the mailing list. If you only want to suspend the reception of mail messages but not leave the mailing list (for example, if you are leaving on vacation and don't want mail messages to pile up when you're gone), send the command SET *listname* NOMAIL to the list server. To start receiving mail again from the mailing list, send the command SET *listname* MAIL.

Using mailing lists

When you subscribe to a mailing list you usually will receive information on how the list operates, as Olivia did in Figure 2-12. You should look for two important addresses that you will need to participate in the mailing list: the **list server address**, or the e-mail address to which you send Listserv commands, and the **mailing list address**, also called the **list address**, the e-mail address to which you send mail messages to subscribers on the mailing list. These two addresses are different and you must not confuse them. Reading the Listserv information on the SLLING-L list in Figure 2-12 in the previous lesson, Olivia Sanchez learns that to send commands to the list server for the sign language mailing list she uses the address LISTSERV@YALEVM.BITNET (or LISTSERV@YALEVM.CIS.YALE.EDU; the two addresses are equivalent). Any messages sent to this address will be read and interpreted by the Listserv program. Table 2-5 shows a list of possible commands that she can send to the list server. For messages that Olivia wants other subscribers to receive, she should use the e-mail address SLLING-L@YALEVM.CIS.YALE.EDU (or the e-mail address she saw back in Figure 2-9, SLLING-L@YALEVM.BITNET; these two are equivalent). ▶ Olivia decides to send a mail message to other subscribers to get information on the history of sign language for the paper she is writing. She could also browse through old messages to see whether this topic has ever been treated on the SLLING-L mailing list; see the related topic "File Archives" in this lesson for more information.

1 Connect to your Internet host and log on to your account as discussed in Unit 1 if you have not already done so
Be sure the UNIX command prompt appears.

2 Type **mail** *mailing list address* at the UNIX command prompt, where *mailing list address* is the e-mail address of the mailing list, not the e-mail address of the list server, then press **[Enter]**
Olivia types "mail SLLING-L@YALEVM.CIS.YALE.EDU" at the UNIX command prompt to send an e-mail message to other subscribers of the SLLING-L list. You should type the mailing list address of the mailing list to which you subscribed in the previous lesson.

3 When prompted for a subject, type an informative subject title
Olivia types "Sign Language History" as her subject.

4 Type the message body, then send the message
Include any particular information or question you think would be pertinent to other subscribers of the mailing list. Olivia sends a message asking for information on the history of sign language, as shown in Figure 2-13. Within minutes this mail message is distributed to other members of the list. Perhaps another subscriber will have some good suggestions for her.

5 Quit the UNIX Mail program and return to the UNIX command prompt, then log out
Through e-mail, Olivia has discovered a way not only to keep in touch with her friend, but also to meet new colleagues.

FIGURE 2-13: Olivia's e-mail message, sent to all subscribers on the mailing list

Message body

Since this message is for subscribers, it is sent to mailing list

```
% mail SSLING-L@YALEVM.CIS.YALE.EDU
Subject: Sign Language History
Does anyone have any suggestions on good reference books on the
history of sign language?
                    Thank you.
.
Cc:
%
```

File archives

Listserv allows you to access mail messages that have been stored in file archives. The archives might include only the most useful messages, only the most recent, or perhaps the most frequently asked questions. You can search the file archives using Listserv search commands. You enter certain words or combinations of words representative of a topic (called **keywords**), like the "sign" word Olivia used earlier. When you enter a keyword and perform a search, Listserv shows you which archived messages contain your keyword. Exploring file archives is a useful aspect of Listserv that you should explore on your own. To get more information on which search commands you should use to search the file archives, send the command "INFO DATABASE" to the list server (some list servers may not recognize this command).

NETIQUETTE

Remember not to mix up the list server address with the mailing list address. Other subscribers will not appreciate having their mailboxes filled with your Listserv commands.■

TABLE 2-5: Common Listserv commands

COMMAND	DESCRIPTION
HELP	Obtains a list of commands
INDEX *listname*	Obtains a directory of files stored by the list server
LISTS GLOBAL /*string*	Obtains a list of mailing lists whose names or titles contains *string*
REVIEW *listname*	Obtains information about a list
SET *listname* MAIL/NOMAIL	Sets whether or not to receive mail from the list
STATS *listname*	Obtains statistics about a list
SUBSCRIBE *listname fullname*	Subscribes to a list or changes your name if you're already subscribed
UNSUBSCRIBE *listname*	Unsubscribes you from a list

CONCEPTSREVIEW

Label each of the elements shown in this figure.

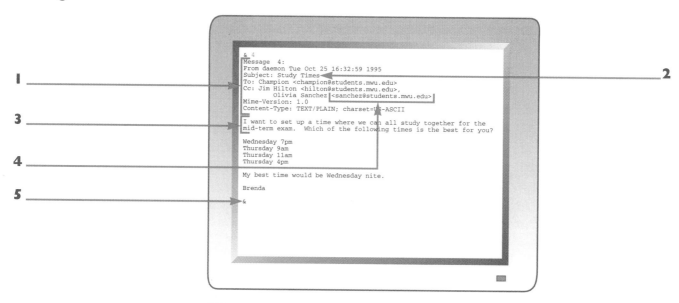

FIGURE 2-14

Match each of the statements with the term it describes.

6 The e-mail address to which you send mailing list commands

7 A file containing a list of e-mail messages

8 A name representing one or several e-mail addresses

9 The e-mail address to which you send messages intended for other mailing list subscribers

10 The part of an e-mail message containing information about the message

a. list address

b. header

c. alias

d. folder or mailbox

e. listserv address

Select the best answer from the list of choices.

11 Which of the following mail commands will create a mail message with the subject field "Meeting Times"?

a. mail -i "Meeting Times" carlson

b. mail -x "Meeting Times" carlson

c. mail -s Meeting Times carlson

d. mail -s "Meeting Times" carlson

12 What will be the e-mail address of a user whose user name is hilger and whose Internet domain name is english.msu.edu?

a. hilger@english.msu.edu

b. hilger.english.msu.edu

c. hilger&english.msu.edu

d. hilger@english@msu@edu

13 You have an account on a machine with the domain name econ.wash.edu and you want to send an e-mail message to a user on the same machine whose username is reichel. Which of the following is a legitimate address for you to use?

a. reichel

b. reichel@econ

c. reichel@econ.wash.edu

d. all of the above

14 What is the name of the file you have to edit to create an alias using the UNIX mailer?

a. mail.rc

b. .mailrc

c. alias.list

d. none of the above (the UNIX mailer does not support the use of aliases.)

15 If you want to temporarily suspend receiving e-mail from the mailing list EDUCAT-L, but still want to be a subscriber, which command should you send to the list server?

a. UNSUBSCRIBE EDUCAT-L

b. SIGNOFF EDUCAT-L

c. SET EDUCAT-L NOMAIL

d. SET EDUCAT-L STOPMAIL

16 If the list address of EDUCAT-L is educat-l@central.bitnet and the listserv address is listserv@central.bitnet, to where should you send a message requesting information on teaching whole language skills?

a. educat-l@central.bitnet

b. listserv@central.bitnet

c. Either will do since they're equivalent.

d. Both should be used so that the message will be processed by both machines.

17 When using the UNIX Mail program, what key combination must you type to abort sending the message?

a. [Ctrl][X]

b. [Ctrl][C]

c. [Ctrl][D]

d. !QUIT

18 Using the UNIX Mail program you decide you want to place messages 1, 3, and 8 in a folder named "joblist." Which command do you type to do this?

a. m 1 3 8 joblist

b. w 1 3 8 joblist

c. s 1 3 8 joblist

d. f 1 3 8 joblist

APPLICATIONS
REVIEW

1 Using the UNIX Mail program send a message from your machine to another user. Include a carbon copy of the message for yourself.

a. Log on to your Internet host and type "mail *username*" (where *username* is the name of your friend on the network).

b. Type an appropriate subject title.

c. Type the body of the message and press [.] (a period) on a separate line when finished.

d. Type your own e-mail address at the Cc: prompt to send a copy of the message to yourself.

2 View and respond to your mail messages.

a. Type "mail" at the UNIX command prompt.

b. Type the numbers of the messages you want to read.

c. Use the R command to respond to a message, then send it as you did in step 1.

d. Press [q] when you are done reading your messages to quit UNIX mail.

3 Create a folder called "personal" for personal e-mail messages.

a. Log on to your Internet host and type "mail" to begin the UNIX mailer.

b. Type "s *message list* personal" at the UNIX mail prompt (where *message list* is a list of messages that you want to place in the personal folder).

c. Press [q] to quit the default mailbox and then type "mail -f personal" to confirm that the personal folder has been created and contains your e-mail messages.

4 Create a distribution list for the UNIX mailer by editing the file .mailrc.

a. Using the text editor provided on your Internet host, create or edit the file .mailrc in your home directory (if you don't know how to use the text editor talk to your system administrator).

b. Type a new line in the file following the format:

alias *aliasname user1 user2 user3*

where *aliasname* is the alias and *user1, user2,* and *user3* are the e-mail addresses associated with that alias; include as many users as you want).

c. Exit the text editor and save the file.

5 Test whether the alias you created in the previous problem works by sending e-mail to the alias name.

a. Log on to your Internet host if you are not already logged on.

b. Type "mail *aliasname*" at the UNIX prompt to invoke the UNIX Mail program.

c. Enter an appropriate subject and body text, then send the message.

6 Using the Bitnet mail address listserv@listserv.net, find all the mailing lists that deal with education.

a. Using the UNIX Mail program (or another mailer if you prefer), address a mail message to "listserv@listserv.net."

b. Leave the subject header blank, but include in the body of the message the command: "LIST GLOBAL /educat."

c. Send the mail message.

d. Later you should receive a message from the listserv.net server. What mailing lists are mentioned?

7 Subscribe to a mailing list on a topic that interests you.

  a. Start the UNIX Mail program (or your own favorite mailer).

  b. Send the "LIST GLOBAL" command to a Listserv machine. Search for the name of a mailing list with a topic of interest.

  c. Send the command "SUBSCRIBE *listname firstname lastname*" to the list server to subscribe to the mailing list (where *listname* is the name of the mailing list).

8 Send a mail message to the subscribers on your mailing list.

  a. Type "mail *mailinglistaddress*".

  b. Type a subject.

  c. Type the body of the message, then send it.

INDEPENDENT
CHALLENGE 1

A useful feature that you can add to e-mail messages is a signature, a text message that appears at the tail end of every message you send. This text could include your full name, office phone number, office room number, and so forth. Other signatures (or **sigs** as they're called) contain favorite quotations or even pictures. Here's an example of a sig that a user might want to have placed at the end of each mail message he or she might send out.

Pat Carlson : Room 427 John Fisher Hall : Phone # 555-1282

To create a signature you must create a file called **.signature** in your home directory. To do this you must feel confident using your site's text editor; see your system administrator if you are not. To complete the independent challenge:

  1 Create and edit the file .signature in your home directory.

  2 Enter an appropriate signature that you would want to see listed on all your e-mail messages.

  3 Exit the editor.

The signature file is unfortunately not used by the UNIX Mail program. When you send commands to Listserv, for example, be sure you remove your signature so the server doesn't try to interpret the signature as a command.

INDEPENDENT
CHALLENGE 2

The last lesson in this unit included a related topic on file archives, collections of messages posted to the mailing list. Go back and read that related topic to review what a file archive is, and then try accessing the file archives associated with your mailing list to learn what topics have already been discussed by users of the mailing list.

To complete this independent challenge, you must be a subscriber to a mailing list that has a file archive. Not all do. Your instructor may have ideas on which mailing lists you could join to be sure you succeed in this independent challenge.

  1 Send the command "INFO DATABASE" to the list server of your mailing list. The list server will send you information on the commands you can use to search a Listserv database.

  2 Read through the material on searching the file archives and formulate a search of your own for your mailing list. Here are the sample commands Olivia Sanchez could have sent to the list server to search for the word "history" in the file archives of the SLLING-L mailing list:

```
//
Database Search DD=Rules
//Rules DD *
Search history in SLLING-L
Index
/*
```

If you want to try this set of commands on your own mailing list, simply replace the word "history" with your own keyword and the mailing list SLLING-L with your own mailing list.

  3 If the search is successful, the list server will return an index of archived mail messages with item numbers identifying each message. You can then use the database commands of the list server to retrieve those specific files. For example, Olivia Sanchez receives a list of archived messages. Two of these messages interest her, items 4192 and 4195. To retrieve these messages, she mails the following command to the list server:

```
//
Database Search DD=Rules
//Rules DD *
Search history in SLLING-L
Print all of 4192 4195
/*
```

  4 Viewing the index for your own search, pick out some item numbers that interest you and, using the preceding commands, have the list server mail the contents of those messages to your account.

UNIT 3

OBJECTIVES

▶ Understand Pine

▶ Compose a message using Pine

▶ View messages using Pine

▶ Work with messages

▶ Attach files to messages

▶ Save an attached file

▶ Create and use folders

▶ Create and use an address book

▶ Create a distribution list

Managing
ELECTRONIC MAIL WITH PINE

*I*n the previous unit you used the UNIX Mail program to send and receive electronic mail messages. The standard UNIX Mail program, however, offers few tools that help users organize messages. As a result, mail programs with better e-mail-handling features are becoming increasingly popular, and one of the most common of these programs is Pine. ▶ Walter Hilbert, a member of the MidWest University Student Senate, has been using the UNIX Mail program, but his system administrator recommends Pine. Recently, he received an e-mail message asking him to create and facilitate a student volunteer corps to help staff a local homeless shelter. Walter realizes Pine's superior message organization features will make the administrative end of his work on this project much easier. ▶

Understanding Pine

Pine is a user-friendly mail program that was developed in response to the increasing demand for mail programs that handle e-mail more easily than the UNIX Mail program. In the previous unit you may have noticed that mail requires you to learn a set of sometimes obscure commands. Pine is only one of many alternative mail programs; the related topic in this lesson, "Other mailers and off-line mail readers," contains information on other mailer options. When you use Pine, you navigate menus that display lists of available options. A short description of each option also appears, so that usually you have all the information you need to choose an option that accomplishes an e-mail task. ▶ The MidWest University system administrator has recommended to Walter Hilbert, a new member of the MidWest University Student Senate, that he try using Pine instead of the more difficult UNIX Mail program. Walter starts Pine to take a look at its features.

1   Connect to your Internet host and log on to your account as described in Unit 1
The UNIX command prompt appears.

2   Type **pine** at the UNIX command prompt to start the Pine mail program
The Pine opening screen appears, as shown in Figure 3-1. Walter looks over the screen to familiarize himself with Pine's features, which are described in Table 3-1.

TABLE 3-1: Parts of the Pine opening screen

ELEMENT	DESCRIPTION
status bar	The **status bar** gives basic information on the status of the Pine program. This may include the version of Pine you are using, the current menu or the current folder (you'll learn more about folders in a later lesson), the number of messages remaining in the folder, or the percentage of the current message that has already been read. In Figure 3-1, the current folder is Inbox, and it contains 0 messages.
main menu	The **Main Menu**, a list of basic Pine options, appears in the **main display area**, the area between the status bar and the command list, when you first start Pine. To make a menu choice, you either highlight the menu item using the [↑] or [↓] key and then press [Enter], or you simply press the letter corresponding to the menu item you want. Unlike UNIX, Pine is not case-sensitive, so you can press, for example, either [C] or [c] to choose the Compose Message menu item. You can return to the Main Menu after completing any Pine task by pressing [M].
command list	The **command list** shows all commands available to the user for a particular task. The command list changes depending on what appears in the main display area. You choose commands from the command list in the same way you choose menu items: simply press any highlighted letter to initiate a command.

FIGURE 3-1: Pine opening screen

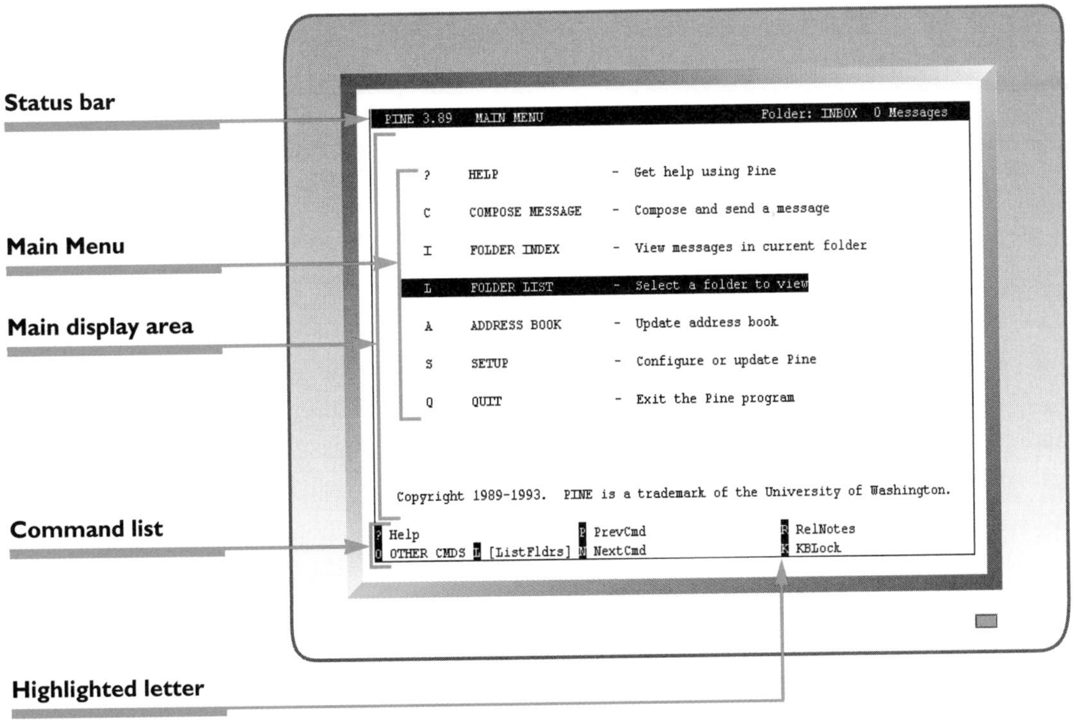

Status bar

Main Menu

Main display area

Command list

Highlighted letter

```
PINE 3.89    MAIN MENU                        Folder: INBOX   0 Messages

        ?     HELP            -  Get help using Pine

        C     COMPOSE MESSAGE -  Compose and send a message

        I     FOLDER INDEX    -  View messages in current folder

        L     FOLDER LIST     -  Select a folder to view

        A     ADDRESS BOOK    -  Update address book

        S     SETUP           -  Configure or update Pine

        Q     QUIT            -  Exit the Pine program



        Copyright 1989-1993.  PINE is a trademark of the University of Washington.

 ? Help              P PrevCmd                    R RelNotes
 O OTHER CMDS L [ListFldrs] N NextCmd             K KBLock
```

Other mailers and off-line mail readers

There are a variety of software packages besides Pine that make sending and receiving mail easier. For example, your site may be using Elm, a mailer that works much like Pine in that it creates a user-friendly interface for the UNIX mail commands. UNIX is often installed with a program called **mh** (for mail handler), which makes handling mail files easier. If you access your e-mail from a personal computer or Macintosh, you may be using an off-line mail reader. **Off-line mail readers** differ from mailers in that the mail is not actually sent to your computer as it comes across the Internet, but rather to an Internet host that stores all your mail until you are ready to read it. You then use the off-line mail reader to query the Internet host for new mail, and then transfer that mail to your computer, usually using a modem. Some common off-line mail readers include Eudora and Pegasus Mail.

TROUBLE?

If you can't start Pine, your site might not have it installed and you may have to skip this unit. Check with your system administrator to see if Pine could be made available, or ask if there is an alternative to the UNIX Mail program. ■

Composing a message using Pine

Pine has several features that make it easy to write and edit your messages. To compose a message, you choose the Compose Message menu item from the Main Menu. This opens the Compose Message screen (the name of the screen appears in the status bar). The command list changes to display commands that facilitate composing a message; Table 3-2 lists and describes some of these commands. Notice that the command keys in Table 3-2 are preceded by the ^ symbol. This indicates that you use a key combination to initiate the command. In Pine, the ^ symbol stands for [Ctrl], so ^X means that you press and hold [Ctrl], and press the letter [X] at the same time. See the related topic "Context sensitive key combinations" in this lesson for more information on using Pine key combinations. As you did with the UNIX Mail program, your first task with Pine will be to compose and send an e-mail message to yourself, so that you have some mail waiting when you try to read a message in the next lesson. ▶ Walter Hilbert experiments by composing a message to himself using Pine.

STEPS

1 **At the Pine opening screen, press [C] to start composing a message**
The Compose Message screen appears. The four fields at the top comprise the mail header, which you fill in to give Pine the information it needs to send your message. The cursor is blinking at the first of the four fields, the To: field, after which you type the address of the person to whom you are sending mail.

2 **Type your own e-mail address in the To: field, then press [Enter]**
Walter types "hilbert" since he is sending the message to himself. Pine automatically fills in complete information (the user's full name and complete e-mail address) on hilbert in the To: field.

3 **Press [Enter] to leave the Cc: field blank**
If Walter wanted to send this message to other members of the Student Senate, he could enter their e-mail addresses in the Cc: field.

4 **Press [Enter] to leave the Attchmnt: field blank**
If you wanted to attach a file to your message, you could enter its name here, and Pine would send it along with your message. You'll try this in a later lesson in this unit.

5 **Type Pine Test Message in the Subject: field and press [Enter]**
The information you type in the Subject: field identifies the message contents to the recipient. When you press [Enter], Pine moves the cursor into the Message Text area.

6 **Type This is a test message from the Pine Mail program. in the Message Text area, as shown in Figure 3-2**

7 **Press [Ctrl][X] to send the message, then press [Y] when Pine asks whether you want to send the message**
You could press [N] instead of [Y] to cancel sending the message. After sending the message Pine returns you to the Main Menu screen. Walter decides to quit Pine for now. He'll check back for his messages later.

8 **Press [Q] to quit Pine, then press [Y] to confirm**
You return to the UNIX command prompt. A message may appear telling you that you have new mail (which you should have since you just composed a message to yourself). You can log out if you are ready to end your session, or you can continue to the next lesson.

FIGURE 3-2:
Completed Compose
Message screen

Mail header

Message Text area

Compose Message command list

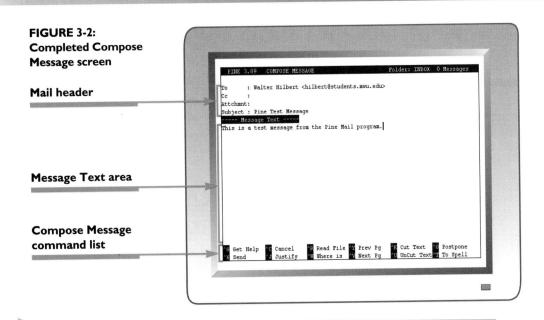

```
PINE 3.89   COMPOSE MESSAGE                    Folder: INBOX  Q Messages

To      : Walter Hilbert <hilbert@students.mwu.edu>
Cc      :
Attchmnt:
Subject : Pine Test Message
----- Message Text -----
This is a test message from the Pine Mail program.|




^G Get Help   ^C Cancel     ^R Read File   ^Y Prev Pg   ^K Cut Text   ^O Postpone
^X Send       ^J Justify     ^W Where is    ^V Next Pg   ^U UnCut Text ^T To Spell
```

Context sensitive key combinations

Pine's key combinations change their meaning depending on the contents of the main display area. For example, [Ctrl][T] runs Pine's spell checker when you are working with the body of the message, but when you are specifying what, if any, files to attach to your e-mail message, [Ctrl][T] allows you to browse the contents of your directories. If you are not sure of the effect of a certain key combination, check the command list descriptions at the bottom of the Pine screen.

QUICK **TIP**

If you want to send the same message to multiple users, you can type their e-mail addresses in the To: field, separated by commas.■

TABLE 3-2: Commands available on Compose Message screen

COMMAND	KEYSTROKES	DESCRIPTION
Cancel	^C	Cancel composing a message and return to the Main Menu
Cut Text	^K	Cut marked text or delete the current line
Get Help	^G	Get help on Pine's commands for composing a message
Mark Text	^^	Set a mark
Next Page	^V	Move to the next page in the message
Prev Pg	^Y	Move to the previous page in the message
Read File	^R	Insert a text file into the body of the message
Send	^X	Send current mail message
Spell	^T	Start Pine's built-in spell checker
Uncut Text	^U	Restore previously cut text

Viewing messages using Pine

Pine helps you organize your mail messages into **folders**, which are storage locations for related messages. When you first start Pine, you are automatically assigned three folders: the Inbox folder, the sent-mail folder, and the saved-messages folder. Later in this unit you will learn how to create your own folders. Pine automatically places incoming e-mail messages into the Inbox folder. When you've read the messages in the Inbox folder, you can place them in another folder or you can delete them. See the related topic "Deleting messages" for more information. When you want to view the contents of a folder, you use the Folder Index screen. The commands available to you in the Folder Index screen appear in the command list, and Table 3-3 lists some of these commands. ▶ Walter Hilbert returns to Pine to view his latest e-mail messages. You can check your messages along with Walter; you should have at least one, if you completed the previous lesson.

1 Type **pine** at the UNIX command prompt and press **[Enter]** to start Pine
   The Pine Main Menu appears. Notice that the third command is [I] for Folder Index. Select this command to view the messages in the current folder.

2 Press **[I]** to view the messages in the Inbox folder
   The Folder Index screen opens, displaying Walter's message list, as shown in Figure 3-3. Walter has two new messages: the test message he sent to himself and a new message from a colleague. New messages are identified by an N prefix.

3 Use the **[↑]** or **[↓]** key to highlight the message you want to read, then press **[Enter]**
   Since Walter already knows the contents of his test message, he decides to view first the contents of the message from David Shapiro regarding the homeless shelter. He presses [↓] once and then presses [Enter], and the text of David's message appears on the Message Text screen, as shown in Figure 3-4. The contents of your message will, of course, be different. The status bar indicates the percentage of the message that has been read and gives the message number (in Walter's case, message 2). David is asking for Walter's help in coordinating a student volunteer corps for a local homeless shelter. In the next lesson, Walter replies to David's message.

TABLE 3-3: Some of the commands available on the Folder Index screen

COMMAND	KEYSTROKE	DESCRIPTION
Delete	D	Mark the highlighted message for deletion
Export	E	Export the highlighted message to a text file
Forward	F	Forward the highlighted message to another user
Help	?	Get help on Pine's commands for maintaining a message list
Main Menu	M	Return to Pine's Main Menu screen
NextMsg	N	Highlight the next message in the folder
PrevMsg	P	Highlight the previous message in the folder

FIGURE 3-3: The Folder Index screen with two messages to Walter

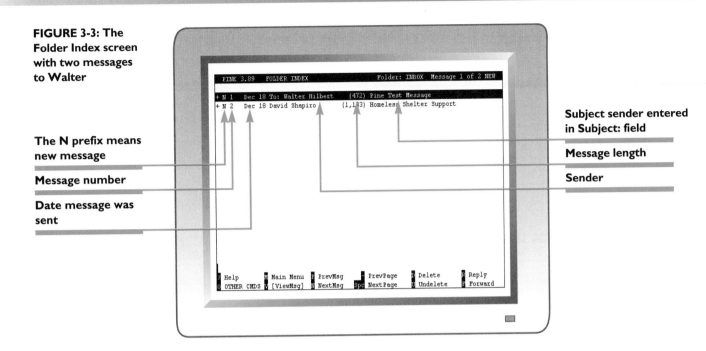

The N prefix means new message

Message number

Date message was sent

Subject sender entered in Subject: field

Message length

Sender

FIGURE 3-4: The Message Text screen for the message from David Shapiro

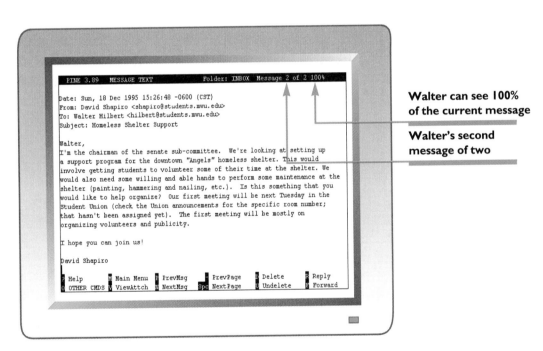

Walter can see 100% of the current message

Walter's second message of two

Deleting messages

Pine allows you to mark messages for deletion by pressing [D] in the Message Text or Folder Index screen, but does not permanently delete the messages until you **expunge**, or permanently remove, the messages from the folders. When you quit Pine, a prompt asks if you want to expunge the messages you've marked for deletion. As long as you have not expunged a message, you can always undelete it and work with it again. Deleting messages regularly helps keep your mail under control.

QUICK TIP

Press [$] to use the Sort command to sort the messages in your folder by subject, date, sender, or size.■

Working with messages

Using Pine, you can quickly and easily reply to a message, print its contents, or forward its contents to other users. Table 3-4 lists the Pine commands you can use while viewing the contents of an e-mail message. To print a message with Pine, either highlight the message in the Folder Index and press [Y] or press [Y] when you are viewing the contents of the message. Pine prompts you whether you want to print the message. You can always cancel the printing by pressing [N] after this prompt. You reply to a message using the same technique, but press [R] rather than [Y]. ▶ Walter is interested in helping with the committee's plans to support the homeless shelter, and he would like to bring the topic up with the Student Senate, which is meeting shortly. He takes advantage of Pine to print and then reply to David Shapiro's request. You can proceed through this lesson by using your own test message, if that is the only one you have, or by working with a different message on your list.

1   If necessary, start Pine and view the e-mail message with which you want to work

Walter is already viewing the message from David Shapiro.

2   Press **[Y]** to print the current message, then press **[Y]** again when Pine asks if you want to print the current message

Pine routes the message to the printer. If you can't locate the printer that prints your message, see your system administrator. If you are using Pine over a modem, you may need to press [Ctrl][L] when the printing is complete to re-display the current screen and command list. Now that Walter has the homeless shelter information in hard copy form, he is ready to reply to David's message.

3   Press **[R]** to reply to the current e-mail message

Pine asks whether you want to include the contents of the original message in your response.

4   Press **[Y]** to include the previous message contents

Walter presses [Y] to include the contents of the original message. You can leave the original contents out by pressing [N]. If you opt to include the original message contents, Pine places a > symbol before each line in the original message. The Compose Message Reply screen appears with the cursor blinking in the Message Text area. Note that Pine fills in the mail header fields for you with information from the original message.

5   Type the contents of your reply, press **[Ctrl][X]** to send it, then press **[Y]** to confirm sending the message

Walter types a quick response to the query, shown in Figure 3-5, and sends the message using the [Ctrl][X] key combination. After you send a reply, Pine returns you to the original message.

6   Press **[Q]** to quit Pine, then press **[Y]** to confirm quitting

Though Walter needs to quit Pine and hurry off to the Senate meeting, you could press [M] to return to the Main Menu screen and continue working with your new messages.

FIGURE 3-5:
Responding to
a message

> symbol marks
original message

Walter's reply

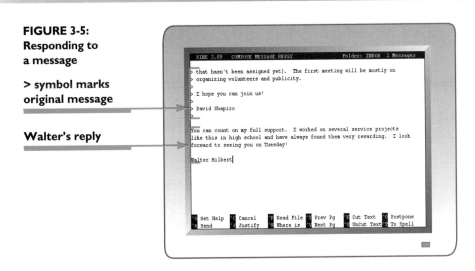

TABLE 3-4: Commands available on the Current Message screen

COMMAND	KEYSTROKE	DESCRIPTION
Delete	D	Mark the current message for deletion
Export	E	Export the current message to a text file
Forward	F	Forward the current message to another e-mail address
Help	?	Get help on Pine's commands for viewing message text
Index	I	Display the Folder Index for the current folder
Main Menu	M	Go to the Main Menu
NextMsg	N	Display the next message in the folder
NextPage	[Spacebar]	Display the next page of the message
PrevMsg	P	Display the previous message in the folder
PrevPage	–	Display the previous page of the message
Print	Y	Print the current e-mail message
Quit	Q	Quit Pine
Reply	R	Reply to the current message
Save	S	Save the current message to a folder
Undelete	U	Undelete (remove deletion mark)
ViewAttch	V	View attached file (if any)

QUICK **TIP**

If a message is longer than a single screen (also called a page), press [Spacebar] to view the next page and the hyphen key [-] to view the previous page.■

Attaching files to messages

For many years Internet users could send e-mail containing text only, which was a frustrating limitation for users who needed a quick way to send graphics or other non-text files. In recent years, however, new e-mail programs have been developed that allow users to attach files of any type to messages. One of the more common formats for attaching files is called **MIME** (Multipurpose Internet Mail Extensions). Versions 3.0 and above of the Pine mailer support this feature. The status bar of Pine indicates which version your site is using. If you are using an earlier version of Pine or an e-mail program that doesn't support file attachments, such as the standard UNIX Mail program, talk to your system administrator about upgrading your mail system to incorporate this feature. You can also insert text from a file directly into an e-mail message. See the related topic "Inserting a text file" in this lesson for more information. ▶ Work on the homeless shelter has been progressing steadily for Walter Hilbert. At the Student Senate meeting, Walter volunteered to create a flyer that the officers could post in the unions and volunteer centers advertising the need for student volunteers. Walter has created a word-processed document on his PC that includes graphics and special printer fonts. He uses Pine to send the document to other members of the homeless shelter committee for their comments. You can follow along by sending a message and attached file of your own to a friend or to yourself.

1   Start Pine and press **[C]** to compose a new message
Pine's Compose Message screen appears.

2   Type the e-mail address (or addresses) of the recipient(s) in the To: field, press **[Enter]**, type the addresses of those who should receive a copy in the Cc: field, then press **[Enter]**
Walter enters the e-mail addresses of other people on the committee in the To: field, as shown in the mail header in Figure 3-6.

3   Type the name of the file you want to attach to your message in the Attchmnt: field, then press **[Enter]**
You can enter multiple filenames separated by commas if you want to attach more than one file. Walter types "flyer.doc." Pine enters the complete name, path, and size of the file in kilobytes in the Attchmnt: field.

4   Complete the rest of the message by entering an appropriate subject in the Subject: field and entering appropriate text in the Message Text area, then press **[Ctrl][X]** and then **[Y]** to send the message
Walter completes the message, as shown in Figure 3-6.

5   Press **[Q]** and then **[Y]** to quit Pine
Walter quits Pine and logs out of UNIX; it's time for him to study for an exam he has tomorrow morning.

FIGURE 3-6: Composed message with file attachment

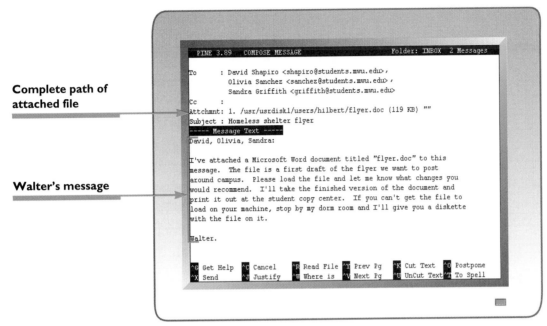

Complete path of attached file

Walter's message

Inserting a text file

Sometimes you may want to insert the contents of a text file directly into your e-mail message. You can do this in Pine by pressing [Ctrl][R] (R stands for read) while you are working in the Message Text area of the Compose Message screen. Pine prompts you for the name of the file you want to insert. After you enter it, Pine asks for confirmation and then inserts the file contents into the e-mail message. You can insert only text files in your message. If you want to add non-text information, you must attach the file to the message.

QUICK **TIP**

If you don't remember the name of the file you want to attach, press [Ctrl][T] in the Attchmnt: field to browse through the contents of your directories, then highlight the file you want to attach and press [Enter].■

Saving an attached file

When you receive a mail message that has an attached file, you can either view the file (if it is a text file) or save the file in one of your directories. In Pine, the e-mail message header displays attached files and their names. To work with attached files, you must be using Pine or another mail program that supports file attachment. The UNIX mailer, for example, will not handle attached files. You can also save mail messages as files. See the related topic "Exporting messages" in this lesson for more information. ▶ A few days have passed since Walter sent out his sample flyer. He has just received a message from David Shapiro with an attached file containing some suggested revisions to the document. To ensure that you have a message with a file attached, you can repeat the previous lesson, send a file to yourself, and then proceed through this lesson using that message.

1 **Start Pine and view the contents of the message with the attached file**
Walter starts Pine and views the mail message, as shown in Figure 3-7. Walter sees that in addition to the text of the mail message, there are two attached files, each preceded by an attachment number: sanchez.doc is number 2 and shapiro.doc is number 3. To save or view an attached file, use the [V] command.

2 **Press [V], enter the attachment number, then press [Enter]**
Walter presses [2] to view sanchez.doc when Pine asks which attachment he wants to view or save. See Figure 3-8. Pine then asks whether he wants to save or view the attachment. Since the attached file is not a text file, Walter saves it so he can view it later. You cannot view a non-text file in Pine. Instead, you must save it and then view it later using the appropriate software package. (In Walter's case, Microsoft Word.)

3 **Press [S] to save the attached file**
Walter presses [S], and Pine prompts him for the filename.

4 **Press [Enter] to save the attached file with the default filename**
Walter saves the file as sanchez.doc, as shown in Figure 3-9. Pine notifies him that the file has been saved to his directory and returns him to the mail message. Pine alerts you if you already have a file with that name and gives you the opportunity to enter a new name.

5 **Continue viewing or saving the files attached to the document**
Walter saves the second attached file, shapiro.doc, to his directory. He can now open these files in his word processor.

6 **Press [Q] to quit Pine, then press [Y]**

FIGURE 3-7: Mail message with file attachments

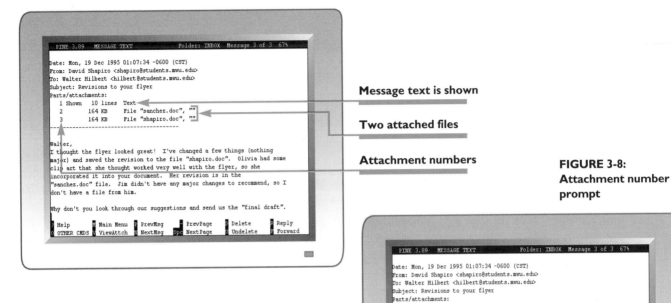

Message text is shown

Two attached files

Attachment numbers

FIGURE 3-8:
Attachment number
prompt

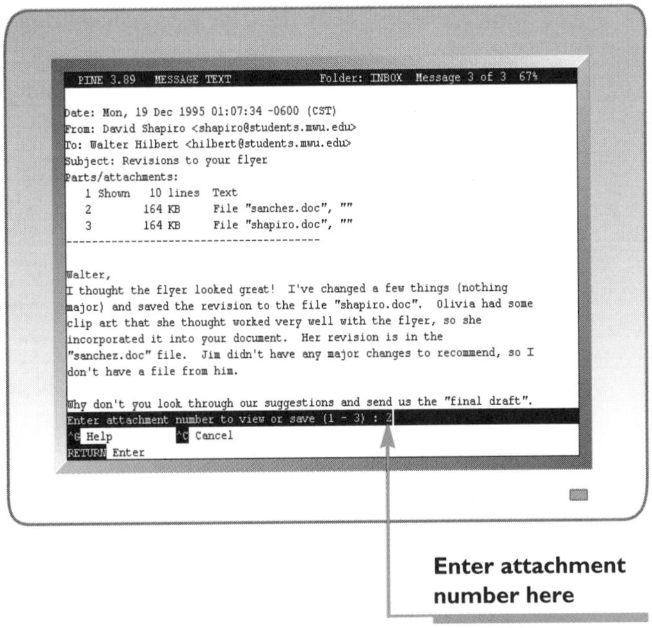

FIGURE 3-9:
Save file attachment
prompt

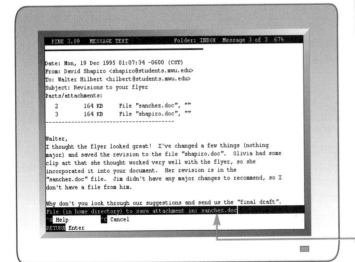

Enter attachment
number here

Enter file name here

Exporting messages

Occasionally, you will want to save a mail message to a text file. This is called **exporting**. To export the mail message, use Pine's export command by pressing [E] while viewing the contents of a mail message. Don't confuse exporting a mail message with saving a mail message. Saving a mail message simply involves placing the message in a different folder within Pine.

Creating and using folders

In the previous lessons Pine has simply placed incoming messages in a single folder, the Inbox folder. As the number of messages in the Inbox increases, you may find it difficult to locate a particular message. With Pine you can organize your mail by placing messages sharing a common topic into the same folder. Table 3-5 lists some of the commands in Pine's Folder List screen that you can use to create and edit your customized folders. ▶ Walter has received several messages about the homeless shelter project. He decides to create a new folder and place all mail pertaining to the shelter project in that folder. You should have at least three messages if you have created test messages as directed in this unit, so you can follow along with Walter by placing them in an appropriate folder.

1 **Start Pine and press [L] at the Main Menu screen to display the Folder List screen**
Walter's folder list appears, as shown in Figure 3-10. He has only the three folders Pine originally assigned him: Inbox, sent-mail, and saved-messages. He decides to add a fourth folder entitled "shelter".

2 **Press [A] (for add) then type the name of the new folder when prompted by Pine**
Walter presses [A] and gives the folder the name "shelter," as shown in Figure 3-11.

3 **Press [Enter] to accept the folder name**
The new folder appears in the main display area on the Folder List screen. Walter is now ready to move some of his messages into the shelter folder. To do so, he must first access the Folder Index for the Inbox folder.

4 **Press the appropriate arrow keys to highlight the Inbox folder, then press [Enter]**
Walter opens the Inbox folder and displays the list of messages, as shown in Figure 3-12. To save a message to a new folder, highlight the message in the index and press [S] (for save), then enter the name of the folder when prompted.

5 **Highlight the first message you want to move into a different folder, press [S], then type the name of the new folder and press [Enter]**
Walter highlights message 2 and presses [S]. He then types "shelter" as the name of the folder and presses [Enter]. Pine copies message 2 to the shelter folder and marks it for deletion from the Inbox folder. Continuing through the folder index, Walter saves all shelter-related mail messages to the shelter folder.

6 **Press [Q] to quit Pine, then press [Y] when Pine asks if you want to expunge the deleted messages from the Inbox folder**

FIGURE 3-10: Folder List screen

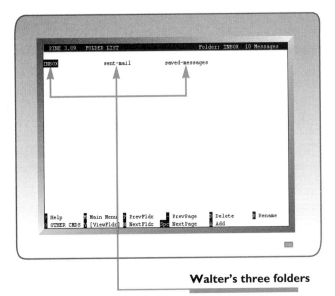

FIGURE 3-11:Prompt for a new folder

Walter's three folders

Folder name

**FIGURE 3-12:
Contents of
Walter's Inbox folder**

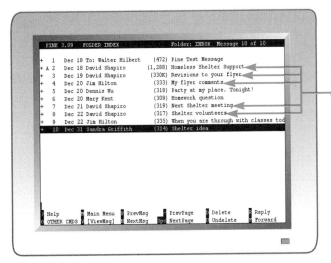

**Walter moves
these messages to
the shelter folder**

TABLE 3-5: Folder List screen commands

COMMAND	KEYSTROKE	DESCRIPTION
Add	A	Add a new folder to the list
Delete	D	Delete the highlighted folder
Help	?	Get help on Pine's commands for using a folder list
Main Menu	M	Return to Pine's Main Menu screen
NextFldr	N	Highlight the next folder in the list
PrevFldr	P	Highlight the previous folder in the list
Rename	R	Re-name the highlighted folder
View	V	View the contents of the highlighted folder

Creating and using an address book

You may find long electronic mail addresses difficult to remember. For addresses you use often, you can create an **alias**, a word that is easy to remember that takes the place of the long address. Use Pine's address book feature to create such an alias. The **Address Book** is an index of e-mail addresses, user descriptions, and aliases. Table 3-6 shows a list of commonly used Address Book commands. ▶ Walter Hilbert has a friend at South Central College who has had extensive experience in setting up volunteer organizations. Walter decides to ask her for advice about the shelter project, but he first wants to add her e-mail address to Pine's Address Book and create an alias for her. You can add e-mail addresses that you use frequently to your Address Book.

1 Start Pine, then press **[A]** at the Main Menu to display the Address Book screen

2 Press **[A]** to add an entry to the Address Book

3 Type the last and first name of the person whose address you are adding, then press **[Enter]**
Walter types "Lorenzo, Carmen". Pine prompts the user for a one-word nickname for the new entry.

4 Type an alias, then press **[Enter]**
Walter types "Carmen" as a one-word alias for Carmen Lorenzo. Pine prompts Walter for the complete e-mail address of the new Address Book entry.

5 Type the e-mail address, then press **[Enter]**
Walter types "lorenzo@admin.gschool.scc.edu" for Carmen Lorenzo's e-mail address. Pine adds Carmen Lorenzo to Walter Hilbert's Address Book, as shown in Figure 3-13. The next time Walter wants to send mail to Carmen Lorenzo he can use the alias Carmen in place of the longer e-mail address lorenzo@admin.gschool.scc.edu.

FIGURE 3-13: Address Book with new entry

Walter's Address
Book entry

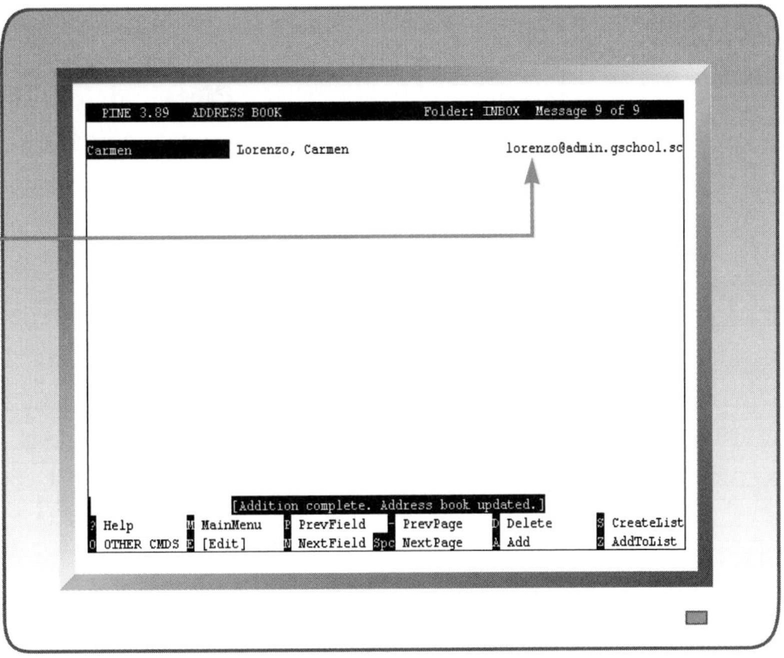

TABLE 3-6: Commands available on the Address Book screen

COMMAND	KEYSTROKE	DESCRIPTION
Add	A	Add a new entry to the Address Book
AddToList	Z	Add an entry to a distribution list
CreateList	S	Create a distribution list
Delete	D	Delete the highlighted entry from the Address Book
Help	?	Get help on Pine's Address Book commands
Main Menu	M	Return to Pine's Main Menu screen
NextField	N	Highlight the next entry in the Address Book
PrevField	P	Highlight the previous entry in the Address Book
Print	Y	Print the contents of the Address Book

QUICK **TIP**

To compose a message using the Address Book quickly, highlight the Address Book entry and press [C] (for compose).■

Creating a distribution list

In your Pine Address Book, an alias can stand for a single e-mail address or for several e-mail addresses, called a **distribution list**. Distribution lists are useful when you want to send the same mail message to several users at once without having to type the mail addresses of all the recipients. The related topic "Modifying a distribution list" in this lesson gives you more information about updating a list once you've created it. ▶ The effort to recruit volunteers for the shelter has been a success. Walter's next job will be to coordinate the efforts of the volunteers. He decides to create a volunteer distribution list so that he can regularly notify everyone of meeting times, scheduling information, and duty rosters. You can follow along by creating a distribution list of friends.

1   Start Pine if it's not already running and press **[A]** at the Main Menu to display the Address Book screen

2   Press **[S]** to create a new distribution list, enter an appropriate description for the list, then press **[Enter]**
Walter presses [S] to create a distribution list and types "Shelter Volunteers" for the list description. Pine prompts him for a one-word alias for the distribution list.

3   Type a one-word alias and press **[Enter]**
Walter types "volunteers" as the alias for the distribution list. Pine prompts you for the e-mail addresses of members of the distribution list.

4   Type the first address, press **[Enter]**, type the second address, press **[Enter]**, and continue until you have added all addresses to the distribution list

5   Press **[Enter]** on a blank line when you are finished adding list entries
Walter enters the e-mail addresses of the shelter volunteers. Pine updates the Address Book to show the contents of the Shelter Volunteers distribution list, as shown in Figure 3-14. Because all of the members of Walter's distribution list are at MWU, he doesn't need to type their domain names. The next time Walter wants to send mail to the shelter volunteers, he can address the message to the alias named "volunteers" and Pine will send the message to all members on the list.

6   Press **[Q]** to quit Pine, then press **[Y]**

FIGURE 3-14: Shelter Volunteers distribution list

Students on the
Shelter Volunteers
distribution list

```
   PINE 3.89   ADDRESS BOOK                 Folder: INBOX  Message 9 of 9

Carmen            Lorenzo, Carmen            lorenzo@admin.gschool.sc

volunteers        Shelter Volunteers         DISTRIBUTION LIST:
                                             czieweiski
                                             davidman
                                             davis
                                             griffith
                                             sanchez
                                             shapiro
                                             wei




               [Addition of list volunteers complete. Address book updated.]
? Help        M MainMenu   P PrevField    - PrevPage    D Delete      S CreateList
O OTHER CMDS  E [Edit]     N NextField  Spc NextPage    A Add         Z AddToList
```

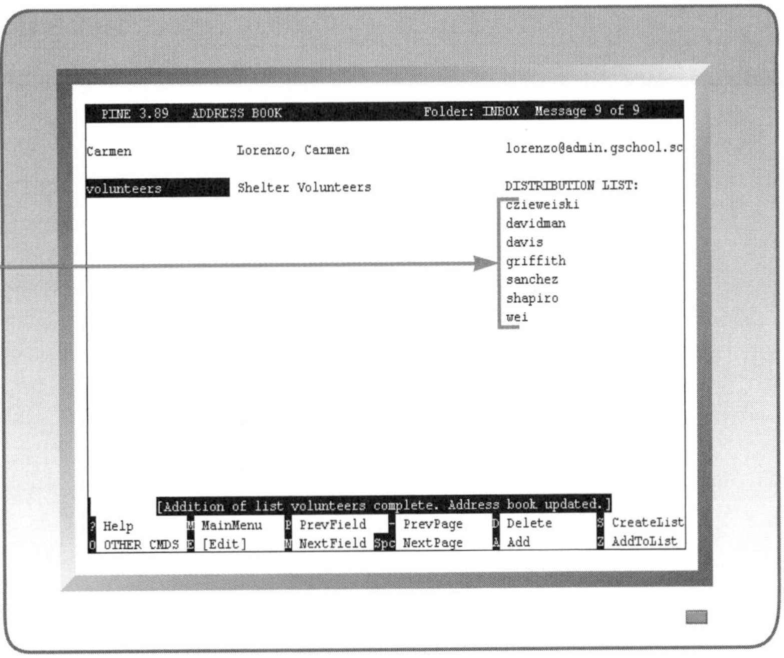

Modifying a distribution list

You can easily modify a distribution list after you've created it. To add new entries
to a distribution list, highlight the distribution list and press [Z] to invoke the
AddToList command. To modify the e-mail addresses in a distribution list, highlight the individual entry and press [E] to invoke the Edit command. To remove
a distribution list or an individual entry, highlight the list or entry and press [D].

CONCEPTSREVIEW

Label each of the elements shown in this figure.

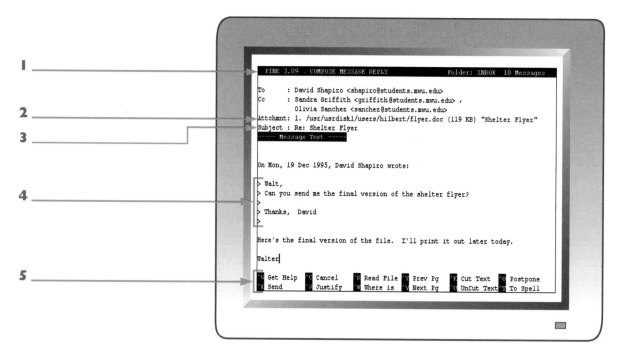

```
 PINE 3.89 · COMPOSE MESSAGE REPLY              Folder: INBOX  10 Messages

To      : David Shapiro <shapiro@students.mwu.edu>
Cc      : Sandra Griffith <griffith@students.mwu.edu> ,
          Olivia Sanchez <sanchez@students.mwu.edu>
Attchmnt: 1. /usr/usrdisk1/users/hilbert/flyer.doc (119 KB) "Shelter Flyer"
Subject : Re: Shelter Flyer
----- Message Text -----


On Mon, 19 Dec 1995, David Shapiro wrote:

> Walt,
> Can you send me the final version of the shelter flyer?
>
> Thanks,  David
>

Here's the final version of the file.  I'll print it out later today.

Walter

^G Get Help  ^C Cancel   ^R Read File ^Y Prev Pg  ^K Cut Text   ^O Postpone
^X Send      ^J Justify   ^W Where is  ^V Next Pg  ^U UnCut Text ^T To Spell
```

FIGURE 3-15

Match each of the statements with the term it describes.

6 A popular e-mail program that makes sending and receiving files easier

7 A file containing a list of e-mail messages

8 A name representing several e-mail addresses

9 A program usually on a PC or Macintosh that transfers mail messages from a network host

10 One of the popular conventions used for sending non-text files through electronic mail

a. MIME

b. Distribution list

c. Off-line mail reader

d. Folder

e. Elm

Select the best answer from the list of choices.

11 To compose a new mail message
   a. Press [C] at the Main Menu
   b. Type compose at the Main Main
   c. Press [N] at the Main Menu
   d. All of the above

12 By default, Pine stores all incoming mail to the
   a. New folder
   b. Incoming folder
   c. Saved-message folder
   d. Inbox folder

13 You can use Pine's Address Book for

   a. Creating e-mail aliases

   b. Creating a list of commonly used e-mail addresses

   c. Creating distribution lists

   d. All of the above

14 To send a graphics file through e-mail with Pine

   a. Verify the recipient is using an e-mail program that supports MIME

   b. Attach the graphics file by specifying the name of the file in the Attchmnt: field of the mail message

   c. Both of the above

   d. None of the above; Pine can only send text, not graphics

15 To save a copy of a mail message to a text file

   a. Press [S] (for save) while viewing the contents of the message

   b. Press [E] (for export) while viewing the contents of the message

   c. Press [W] (for write) while viewing the contents of the message

   d. All of the above are correct

16 To move a mail message to another folder, go to the Folder Index containing the message and

   a. Press [M] (for move) and enter the name of the new folder

   b. Press [E] (for export) and enter the name of the new folder

   c. Press [S] (for save) and enter the name of the new folder

   d. Press [W] (for write) and enter the name of the new folder

17 To print the contents of an e-mail message

   a. Press [P] (for Print) while viewing the contents of the message

   b. Press [Y] while viewing the contents of the message

   c. Press [L] (for list) while viewing the contents of the message

   d. All of the above will work

APPLICATIONS
REVIEW

1 Using the Pine program, send a message to another user. Include a carbon copy of the message for yourself. Then read your messages.

   a. Log in to your Internet host and type "pine" to start the Pine program.

   b. Press [C] to compose a new message.

   c. Enter the e-mail address of the recipient in the To: field.

   d. Type your own e-mail address in the Cc: field.

   e. Type the text of the message and press [Ctrl][X] when you are ready to send the message.

   f. Read the message by pressing [I] from the Pine Main Menu.

   g. Press [Q] to quit Pine and return to the UNIX command prompt.

2 Send a message to another user with an attached file.

   a. Start Pine by typing "pine" at the UNIX command prompt.

   b. Press [C] to compose a new message.

   c. In the Attchmnt: field, enter the name of the file you want to attach.

   d. Complete the rest of the mail header including the e-mail address of the user.

   e. Write the message body including a description of the attached file. Press [Ctrl][X] to send the message.

   f. Press [Q] to quit Pine and return to the UNIX command prompt.

3 Save a file attached to a message (if you cannot get another user to send you mail, send a message to yourself).

   a. Start Pine by typing "pine" at the UNIX command prompt.

   b. Press I to go to the Inbox Folder Index and select the message with the attached file.

   c. Press [V] to view the attached file, then enter the attachment number of the file.

   d. Press [S] to save the attached file and accept the default filename.

   e. Press [Q] to quit Pine and return to the UNIX command prompt.

4 Create a folder called "personal" to store your personal e-mail messages.

 a. Log in to your Internet host and type "pine" to start the Pine program.

 b. Press [L] to display the Folder List screen.

 c. Press [A] to add a new folder and type "personal" for the folder name.

 d. Press [Q] to quit Pine and return to the UNIX command prompt.

5 Create a distribution list of other users in your class.

 a. Log in to your Internet host and type "pine" to start the Pine program.

 b. Press [A] to display the Address Book screen.

 c. Press [S] to create a distribution list.

 d. Enter a description for the distribution list and give the list an alias.

 e. Enter the e-mail address of other users in your class.

 f. Press [Q] to quit Pine and return to the UNIX command prompt.

6 Test whether the distribution list you created in the previous problem works by sending e-mail to the distribution list alias.

 a. Log in to your Internet host and type "pine" to start the Pine program.

 b. Press [C] to compose a new message.

 c. Enter the distribution list alias in the To: field.

 d. Complete the rest of the message and header fields, then press [Ctrl][X] to send the message to other users on the list.

 e. Press [Q] to quit Pine and return to the UNIX command prompt.

INDEPENDENT
CHALLENGE 1

You can get a copy of Pine software upgrades while using Pine itself. You request an upgrade and it connects you to a mail server that lets you access software upgrades and technical notes. The software files are attached to the mail messages so you will have to save the attached files to one of your directories. Pine also comes in a PC version for personal computers that have Internet access. Read the appropriate mail messages to learn how to install the new version of Pine on your system.

To complete this independent challenge:

1 Start Pine.

2 Choose Setup from the Main Menu.

3 Press [U] for update. A list of messages appears, some covering technical notes and others accompanying different versions of the Pine software. The Subject: field tells you what version comes with each message. For example, one of the Subject: fields might say, "PC-Pine 3.91 for Windows 3.1," so Windows users would retrieve this message.

4 Select the message number you want.

5 Retrieve the attached file and use it to upgrade your Pine version. This might involve simply replacing an existing (older) version of the file. Ask your instructor if you aren't sure how to complete this step.

INDEPENDENT
CHALLENGE 2

In Unit 2 you accessed a list server to join a mailing list. Since most members of mailing lists consult the lists regularly, it is helpful to have an alias for the mailing list address and the list server address. Create two such aliases for the mailing list you joined, one for the list server program to which you send commands and the other for the mailing list address to which you send mail intended for other subscribers.

To complete this independent challenge:

1 Locate the addresses of both the mailing list address and list server address.

2 Start Pine, then press [A] at the Main Menu to display the Address Book screen.

3 Press [A] to add an entry to the Address Book, type an entry that describes the mailing list address (for example, "Parents of twins support group mailing list address"), press [Enter], type a one-word nickname (for example, "twins"), press [Enter], type the complete e-mail address, then press [Enter].

4 Repeat step 3 for the list server address.

5 Press[Q] to quit Pine, then press [Y] to confirm.

UNIT 4

OBJECTIVES

▶ Understand Usenet news

▶ Find newsgroups with trn

▶ Subscribe to a newsgroup

▶ Work with the article selection list

▶ Read newsgroup articles

▶ Post articles to Usenet

Joining
INTEREST GROUPS WITH USENET

*I*n Unit 2, you saw how Olivia Sanchez used e-mail's mailing list capabilities to communicate with users from all over the world who shared a common interest in sign language. In this unit you'll look at another application that brings people with common interests together – Usenet. **Usenet** is an Internet tool that allows users to meet and discuss a wide variety of topics. Usenet functions in many ways like a mailing list; interested users subscribe to Usenet, select the topic they're interested in, and then exchange messages with other subscribers on that topic. Of all the Internet tools you'll learn about, Usenet may be the most popular. To some people, Usenet *is* the Internet. ▶ Stewart Raymer, a MidWest University music student and classical guitar aficionado, explores Usenet to find a forum in which he can exchange ideas with other music students on the Internet. ▶

Understanding Usenet news

Usenet is made up of over 5,000 discussion groups called **newsgroups**. Each newsgroup focuses on a single topic, such as rock climbing, the history of the Civil War, or the literary works of Chaucer. As you can imagine, with so many newsgroups, just about every conceivable topic is covered. In Usenet terminology, messages sent to newsgroups are called **articles,** and the act of sending an article is called **posting**. Like many Internet tools, Usenet operates on the client/server model. See the related topic "The History of Usenet" in this lesson for information on how Usenet got started. In order to use Usenet you need a client software application called a **newsreader** installed on your Internet host that lets you post and read newsgroup articles. There are many different types of newsreaders; the most common UNIX newsreaders are **rn**, **trn**, **tin**, and **rtin**. This unit uses trn; if your host is running a different one, you may find slight differences as you proceed through the lessons. Your instructor can help you identify the commands that differ between trn and your newsreader. A special server, called a **news server**, stores and manages the articles that newsreaders post to the newsgroup. Every time you read an article, your newsreader is retrieving the article from a news server. ► As shown in Figure 4-1, news servers share their articles with other news servers on the network, so an article that Stewart Raymer posts from MidWest University may eventually be made available to a newsreader in Hong Kong. Of course Olivia's messages sent to the mailing list in Unit 2 also reached a worldwide audience, and you may be wondering how newsgroups are different from the mailing lists you've already worked with. Consider these important points:

■ **Article selection**
With mailing lists you receive all the messages sent to the list server whether they interest you or not. Newsreaders allow you to select only the articles you want to read.

■ **Interface**
To use mailing lists you only need an e-mail program, a standard UNIX application. With Usenet you need a newsreader (not all sites have one installed) and access to a news server that supports your network host (not all servers do).

■ **Topics**
Usenet covers a larger variety of topics than mailing lists, and many of the messages that appear in mailing lists also appear in Usenet newsgroups. Using Usenet, you thus have access to a wider discussion forum.

■ **Article organization**
Many Usenet newsreaders sort articles by content, which makes it easier for you to follow the ebb and flow of a discussion on a particular issue. Mailing lists send you the messages unsorted.

■ **Article storage**
Usenet articles are saved on the news servers. You view these articles with the newsreader, saving a copy to your account only if you want to. Messages from mailing lists are automatically placed in your mailbox where you have to delete them if you don't want a permanent copy.

FIGURE 4-1: Structure of Usenet

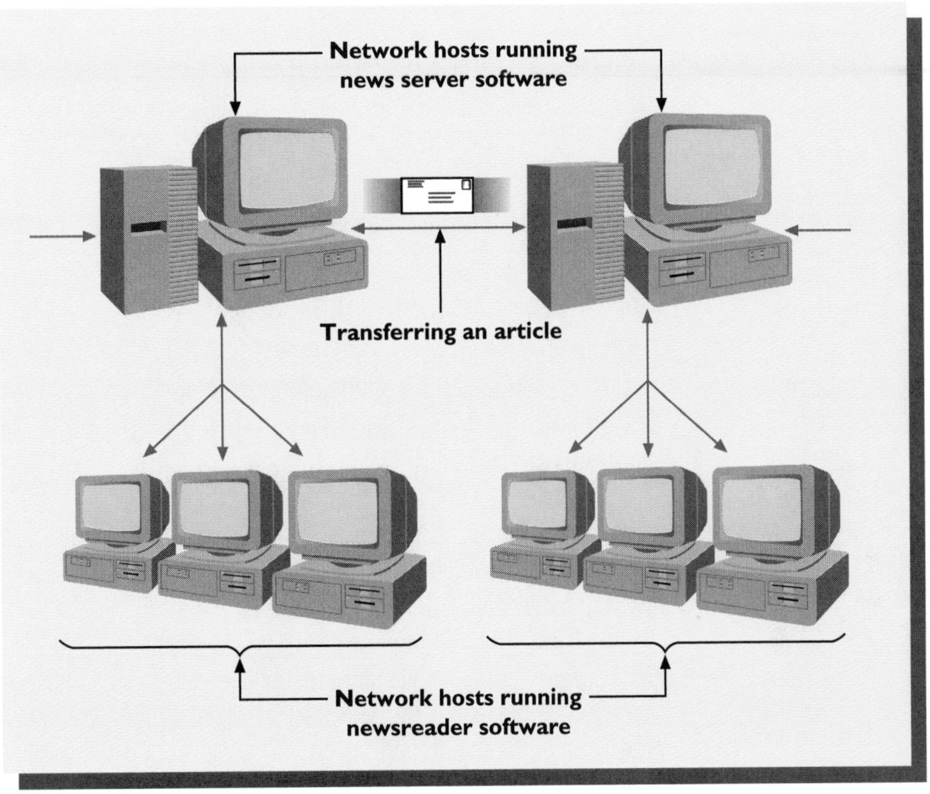

Network hosts running
news server software

Transferring an article

Network hosts running
newsreader software

The History of Usenet

Usenet was developed in 1979 as an electronic bulletin board in order to share messages between the University of North Carolina and Duke University. In a short time other sites joined in, and the explosion of the Internet resulted in a similar increased use of Usenet. There are currently more than 10,000 Usenet sites with more than two million participants. Like much of the Internet, Usenet relies on volunteerism and cooperation. There is no single Usenet system administrator. Instead, there are many administrators who are each responsible for their own news servers. They work in cooperation with other system administrators. While there is a set of accepted conventions, there is no central authority.

Finding newsgroups with trn

Newsgroup names are defined based on a hierarchy, or set, of common categories. Figure 4-2 shows a small part of this hierarchy. The newsgroup dealing with college football, for example, is called "rec.sport.football.college." Each level of the hierarchy is separated by a dot. The first level is the general category to which a topic belongs. For example, newsgroups that begin with "rec" deal with recreation. Table 4-1 shows a selection of other general categories. Within the recreational topic category are newsgroups that deal with sports ("sport"), hobbies, art, music, and so on. Within the sport category is the football category, while within that category you find the college category. ▶ Stewart Raymer of MidWest University is interested in subscribing to a classical guitar newsgroup using trn. Follow along with Stewart, but choose a topic of your own.

1 **Type trn at the UNIX command prompt and press [Enter]**
Depending on your system's configuration, you may see a welcoming message, such as the one Stewart receives in Figure 4-3. Stewart is automatically subscribed to a newsgroup for new users called "news.announce.newusers" and is told that he has 28 unread articles in that newsgroup. The newsreader at your site may automatically subscribe you to all 5000+ newsgroups, in which case you should refer to the related topic "Unsubscribing to all newsgroups" in this lesson. Stewart uses the **l** command, which lists all newsgroups on a topic that one can select, to search for a classical music newsgroup.

2 **Type l *topic*, and press [Enter] where *topic* describes the topic you're interested in**
Stewart types "l classical" at the "read now?" prompt. You should type your own topic after "l" using a single word. The trn newsreader lists four newsgroups that include the word "classical" in their name. Stewart notes that one of them, rec.music.classical.guitar, appears to deal with classical guitar. In the next lesson, he will subscribe to this newsgroup.

3 **Press [Enter] to return to the "read now?" prompt**
The trn newsreader again prompts Stewart as to whether he wants to read articles from the newusers newsgroup. From this prompt he can subscribe to a newsgroup or search for other newsgroups.

TABLE 4-1: Common Usenet news categories

CATEGORY	DESCRIPTION	EXAMPLE
alt	Alternative newsgroups of many different types	**alt.politics.usa.republican** for discussions about Republicans
bit	Usenet postings of Bitnet mailing lists (list servers)	**bit.listserv.cinema-l** for the cinema Listserv mailing list
news	Discussion about Usenet itself	**news.groups** for discussion and lists of newsgroups
rec	Discussion about recreational activities	**rec.arts.poems** for the posting of poems
sci	Scientific discussions	**sci.space.shuttle** for information on the Space Shuttle program

FIGURE 4-2:
Selected newsgroup categories in the newsgroup hierarchy

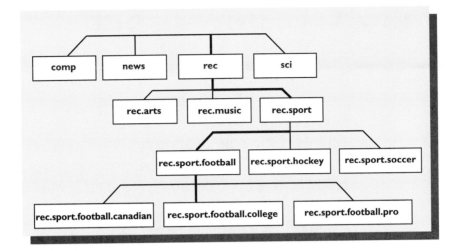

FIGURE 4-3:
Searching for a newsgroup using trn

Command to start trn newsreader

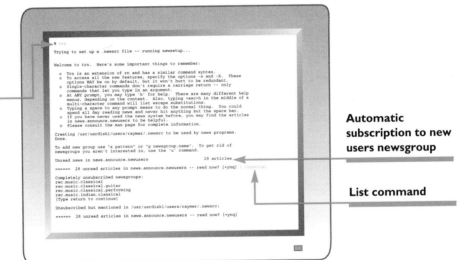

Automatic subscription to new users newsgroup

List command

Unsubscribing from all newsgroups

Some sites automatically subscribe new users to all Usenet newsgroups (over 5,000). Unfortunately trn does not have a command for unsubscribing to all newsgroups at once, and unsubscribing one at a time is laborious. To unsubscribe from all newsgroups, you use a text editor to modify the file .newsrc that contains configuration information for trn. The most common UNIX text editor is called **vi** (consult your site's documentation to learn how to use it; if your site doesn't have vi, ask your instructor about using text editors to search and replace text). To edit your .newsrc file using vi and unsubscribe from all newsgroups, follow these instructions *precisely*.

1   If you're in trn, press [q] at the "read now?" prompt and press [Enter] to return to the UNIX command prompt

2   Type vi .newsrc at the UNIX command prompt to open your .newsrc file in vi

3   Type :%s/:/!/ (no spaces between characters) and press [Enter] to replace every occurrence of a ":" in the file with a "!"

4   Type :wq and press [Enter] to write (w) the changes to the file and quit (q) the vi text editor

QUICK TIP

To view a listing of all the Usenet newsgroups your news server supports, type "newsgroups" at the UNIX command prompt and press [Enter].■

TROUBLE?

If your site doesn't use trn, see your instructor about the corresponding commands you should use for your newsreader.■

Subscribing to a newsgroup

In the previous lesson you saw how to use trn to search for newsgroups that cover particular topics. In this lesson you'll learn how to subscribe to a newsgroup. Newsreader commands exist on three levels: (1) the **newsgroup selection level**, in which you search for or select newsgroups (as in the previous lesson); (2) the **article selection level**, in which you choose which articles to view; and, (3) the **paging level**, at which you either read or post a specific newsgroup article. As you go from one level to another within your newsreader (say from choosing a newsgroup to viewing a list of articles posted to that newsgroup), you have a different set of command options. In the previous lesson you were left at the command prompt, "28 unread articles in news.announce.newusers--read now? [+ynq]." At this prompt you can type any of the newsgroup selection level commands listed in Table 4-2. If there are no newsgroup articles to read, the newsgroup selection level command prompt is "End of newsgroups--what next? [npq]." Once again you may respond with any of the newsgroup selection level commands in Table 4-2. ▶ Stewart Raymer, having discovered the name of a newsgroup name devoted to the discussion of classical guitar music, decides he wants to subscribe to rec.music.classical.guitar. He will use one of the newsgroup selection level commands to do this. Follow along with your own newsgroup (your instructor might suggest newsgroups for you to join if you didn't find one in the previous lesson).

1 If you have not already started your newsreader and found a newsgroup that you are interested in, repeat the previous lesson so you are at the newsgroup selection level command prompt [+ynq]

Stewart is already at the command prompt, "read now? [+ynq]." The "+ynq" in brackets represents four of the commands (view, yes, next, and quit) available to you in Table 4-2.

2 Type **g** *newsgroup* where *newsgroup* is the name of the newsgroup you want to go to, and press **[Enter]**

Stewart types "g rec.music.classical.guitar" to go to the rec.music.classical.guitar newsgroup, as shown in Figure 4-4. You should enter the name of the newsgroup you are interested in. The newsreader then prompts you as to whether you want to subscribe, if you are not already a subscriber.

3 Press **[y]** to subscribe

If you decided not to subscribe, you would press [n]. After you press [y], the newsreader then asks you where you want to place the newsgroup within your list of subscribed groups, giving you the options [$^.Lq]. Pressing [^] places the newsgroup at the beginning of the list so that the next time you run trn, it will be the first newsgroup you see. Typing [$] puts it at the end of your subscription list. You can use the h command described in Table 4-2 to get help on the other options.

4 Press **[^]** so that the newsgroup you are subscribing to will appear first the next time you start trn

The trn newsreader tells you how many articles are currently unread and asks whether you want to view the articles in the new newsgroup. You'll learn about viewing the list of articles in the next lesson. There are 4630 unread articles for the classical guitar group.

FIGURE 4-4: Subscribing to a newsgroup

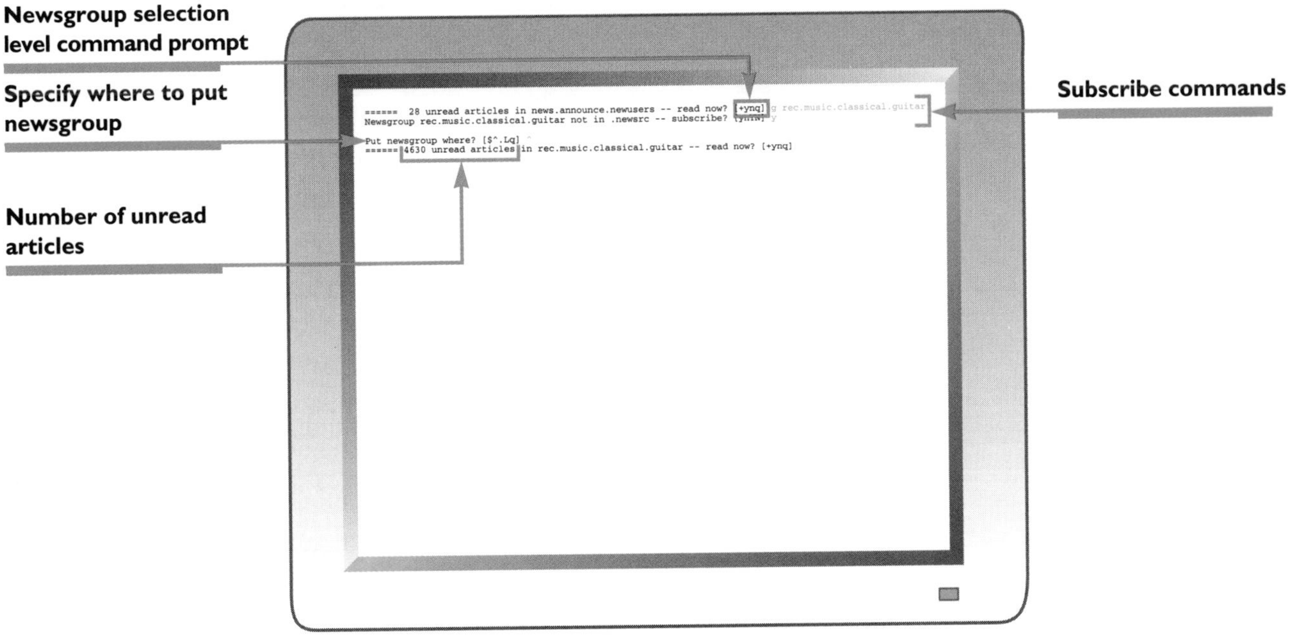

Newsgroup selection
level command prompt

Specify where to put
newsgroup

Number of unread
articles

Subscribe commands

```
======  28 unread articles in news.announce.newusers -- read now? [+ynq] g rec.music.classical.guitar
Newsgroup rec.music.classical.guitar not in .newsrc -- subscribe? [ynYN] y
Put newsgroup where? [$^.Lq]
======4630 unread articles in rec.music.classical.guitar -- read now? [+ynq]
```

TABLE 4-2: Common trn newsgroup selection level commands

COMMAND	DESCRIPTION
$	Go to the last subscribed newsgroup
+	View the article list in the current newsgroup
^	Go to the first subscribed newsgroup with unread messages
g newsgroup	Go to a newsgroup with the name newsgroup (you will be prompted to subscribe if you are not a subscriber)
h	Display help screen
l topic	List unsubscribed newsgroups containing topic
L	List newsgroups and their positions on your newsreaders
n	Go to the next subscribed newsgroup
p	Go back to the previous subscribed newsgroups
q	Quit trn
y	Respond "yes" to the newsgroup selection prompt
u	Unsubscribe from the currently selected newsgroup

QUICK TIP

To unsubscribe from
a newsgroup, press [u]
when trn prompts you
to read articles in that
newsgroup.■

TROUBLE?

Commands in trn are
case-sensitive; press-
ing [L] means some-
thing different than
pressing [l].■

Working with the article selection list

Once you've subscribed to a newsgroup, you can select the articles that you want to read by working with the article selection list, a sorted list of subject headings for articles in that newsgroup. This list appears when you use the **+** command (for "view") at the newsgroup selection level command prompt. The trn newsreader **threads** the articles; that is, it sorts the articles by the subject headings. That way, as you read articles from other users and the responses to those articles, you can follow the thread of a single discussion. Not all newsreaders have this feature, so you should check with your instructor to see if your newsreader supports threading. When viewing the article list, you are placed in the article selection level of trn, where the commands available to you, shown in Table 4-3, are different from those you used in the previous lesson. ▶ Stewart views the article selection list so he can see which threads are available to him in the classical guitar newsgroup. Follow along with your own newsgroup articles. Note that articles posted to a newsgroup are kept only for a certain length of time.

1   Be sure you are at the "read now [+ynq]" prompt for your newsgroup, as at the end of the previous lesson

2   Press [+] to view the list of articles
The trn newsreader responds by first threading the unread articles in the newsgroup. Note that the unread articles are less than the 4630 quoted. This is because most of the unread articles have already expired and been removed by the news server, leaving only 100. Once trn has sorted these 100 articles into threads, it moves you to the article selection level and displays the article list. The article list is displayed on a screen called a **page**, and its information is displayed in four columns, as shown in Figure 4-5. To select a thread, you press its letter. Some letters are missing since they represent trn article selection commands (for example, the letter "c" stands for the "mark all articles as read" command, so it is not assigned a thread). In many cases the article list will not fit onto one screen or page, so trn extends the list across multiple pages. The status line at the bottom of the page indicates what percent of the article list has been displayed. In Figure 4-5, 16% of the article list has been displayed, leaving 84% still to be viewed.

3   Press the letter of the thread you want to read
Much of Stewart's knowledge of classical guitar has been self-taught. The "d" thread, "Learning w/o a teacher," intrigues him, so he presses [d] to select this thread for later viewing. A "+" sign appears next to the letter "d," as shown in Figure 4-5. You should press the letter of the thread that interests you. If you want to select more than one thread, press the corresponding letters, one at a time, and watch as the "+" sign appears before each one. You can also press [>] to view the threads on the next page or pages. In the next lesson, you learn to read the articles in the thread or threads you have chosen.

FIGURE 4-5: Article list

Press +

Prompt

Plus sign indicates thread has been selected

Article list

1st column: article threads

2nd column: person who posted article

3rd column: number of articles in each thread

4th column: thread subject title

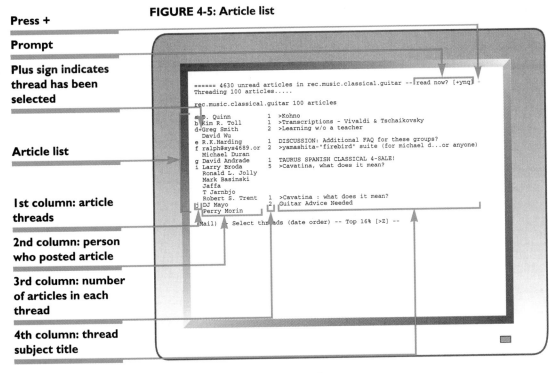

```
====== 4630 unread articles in rec.music.classical.guitar -- read now? [+ynq]
Threading 100 articles.....

rec.music.classical.guitar 100 articles

a D. Quinn           1  >Kohno
b Kim R. Toll        1  >Transcriptions - Vivaldi & Tschaikovsky
d+Greg Smith         2  >Learning w/o a teacher
  David Wu
e R.K.Harding        1  DISCUSSION: Additional FAQ for these groups?
f ralph@sys4689.or   2  >yamashita-"firebird" suite (for michael d...or anyone)
  Michael Duran
g David Andrade      1  TAURUS SPANISH CLASSICAL 4-SALE!
i Larry Broda        5  >Cavatina, what does it mean?
  Ronald L. Jolly
  Mark Basinski
  Jaffa
  T Jarnbjo
  Robert S. Trent    1  >Cavatina : what does it mean?
  DJ Mayo            2  Guitar Advice Needed
  Perry Morin

(Mail) -- Select threads (date order) -- Top 16% [>Z] --
```

TABLE 4-3: Common trn article selection level commands

COMMAND	DESCRIPTION
/topic	Select all article threads containing *topic*
<	Go back to the previous page of article threads
>	Go to the next page of article threads
[Enter]	Start reading all selected threads (if no threads are selected start reading the current thread)
c	Mark all the articles in the newsgroup as read
h	Display help screen
letter	Select the article thread identified by *letter* (if the thread is already selected, typing *letter* deselects the thread)
N	Go to the next newsgroup with unread news
n	Go to the next article thread
P	Go back to the previous newsgroup with unread news
p	Go back to the previous article thread
q	Quit current newsgroup

QUICK **TIP**

To select article threads whose subject titles include a specific word, use the /topic command where *topic* is the word you want to search for.■

TROUBLE?

When selecting article threads, pay attention to case. Pressing [n] is different than pressing [N].■

Reading newsgroup articles

Once you've selected all the article threads that you're interested in from the article list, as you did in the previous lesson, you can start to read them by pressing [Enter]. This moves you to the paging level, the level at which you either read or post a specific newsgroup article. Table 4-4 displays some of the commands available at the paging level. After you've read the first article, you use the **n** command to move to the next unread article and trn removes the article you just finished with from the article list. If you want a permanent copy of an article, use the **s** command to save the article to a text file in your account. You can then view the file using the UNIX **more** command (see Unit 1). ▶ Stewart reads the articles in the thread, "Learning w/out a teacher," which he marked at the end of the previous lesson. Follow along and read the articles you selected.

I   Be sure trn is running and that you've selected some article threads to read from the article list, as described in the previous lesson

2   Press **[Enter]** to view the articles you've marked
For Stewart, the first article in the "Learning w/out a teacher" thread appears, as shown in Figure 4-6. Notice the header fields at the top of the article. They are similar to those found on e-mail messages. In Figure 4-6, the subject is "Learning w/o a teacher." Next comes the address of the sender, followed by the distribution of the article, which in this case was sent to all news servers in the world. Finally, the header shows the date the article was posted, the organization or news server that posted the article to other servers, and the number of lines in the article. Notice that a number of lines within the message body are preceded with a ">" symbol. This indicates that those lines were quoted from a previous post. They let you follow the flow of the discussion thread even if you missed a prior article.

Since the article cannot fit onto a single screen, trn indicates at the bottom of the screen that 47% of the article has been viewed. To move to the next page, you use the [Spacebar].

3   Press **[Spacebar]** to view the next screen or page of the article if it does not all fit on one screen
The rest of the article appears, shown in Figure 4-7. When you reach the end of an article, you have several options. For example, you can press [n] to go the next unread article in the thread, [q] to quit the newsgroup, [h] to view other paging level command options, or you can post a response to this article. You can also re-read the article using the key combination [Ctrl][R]. Stewart decides to post a message to the newsgroup before moving on. You'll see how to do this in the next lesson.

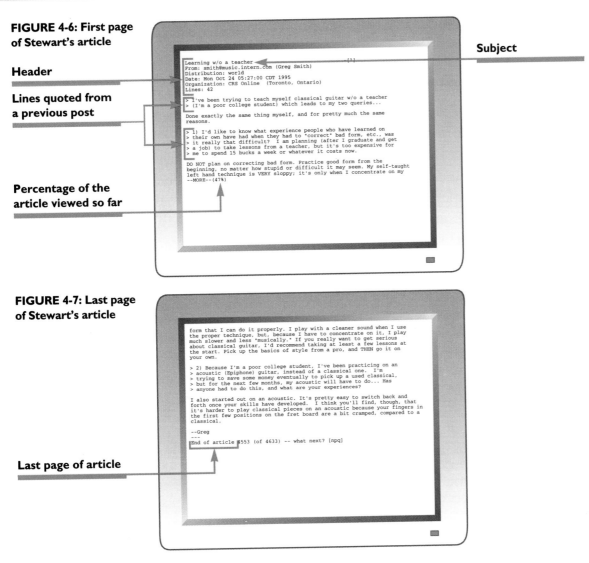

FIGURE 4-6: First page of Stewart's article

Subject

Header

Lines quoted from a previous post

Percentage of the article viewed so far

```
Learning w/o a teacher                          [1]
From: smith@music.intern.com (Greg Smith)
Distribution: world
Date: Mon Oct 24 05:27:00 CDT 1995
Organization: CRS Online  (Toronto, Ontario)
Lines: 42

> I've been trying to teach myself classical guitar w/o a teacher
> (I'm a poor college student) which leads to my two queries...

Done exactly the same thing myself, and for pretty much the same
reasons.

> 1) I'd like to know what experience people who have learned on
> their own have had when they had to "correct" bad form, etc., was
> it really that difficult?  I am planning (after I graduate and get
> a job) to take lessons from a teacher, but it's too expensive for
> me to spend 15 bucks a week or whatever it costs now.

DO NOT plan on correcting bad form. Practice good form from the
beginning, no matter how stupid or difficult it may seem. My self-taught
left hand technique is VERY sloppy; it's only when I concentrate on my
--MORE--(47%)
```

FIGURE 4-7: Last page of Stewart's article

```
form that I can do it properly. I play with a cleaner sound when I use
the proper technique, but, because I have to concentrate on it, I play
much slower and less "musically." If you really want to get serious
about classical guitar, I'd recommend taking at least a few lessons at
the start. Pick up the basics of style from a pro, and THEN go it on
your own.

> 2) Because I'm a poor college student, I've been practicing on an
> acoustic (Epiphone) guitar, instead of a classical one.  I'm
> trying to save some money eventually to pick up a used classical,
> but for the next few months, my acoustic will have to do... Has
> anyone had to do this, and what are your experiences?

I also started out on an acoustic. It's pretty easy to switch back and
forth once your skills have developed.  I think you'll find, though, that
it's harder to play classical pieces on an acoustic because your fingers in
the first few positions on the fret board are a bit cramped, compared to a
classical.

--Greg
---
End of article 4553 (of 4633) -- what next? [npq]
```

Last page of article

TABLE 4-4: Common trn paging level commands

COMMAND	DESCRIPTION
+	Go back to the newsgroup article list
<	Go to the previously selected article thread
>	Go to the next selected article thread
[Spacebar]	View the next page of the article
b	Go back one page in the article
c	Mark all articles in the newsgroup as read
[Ctrl][R]	Redisplay the current article
h	Display help screen

QUICK **TIP**

With trn, you can enter paging level commands at any time at the paging level, even in the middle of viewing an article.

Posting articles to Usenet

Once you have read through some of the articles in a newsgroup, you might be ready to post one of your own. Posting is done at the paging level of trn, so in order to post an article you must first be reading one. You can either post a follow-up message to the article you are reading, send a response directly to the person who posted the article through e-mail (bypassing Usenet entirely), or post an article to the newsgroup on a completely new topic. You can limit your post to local distribution or to news servers throughout the world. You can also post to several newsgroups at once (this is known as **cross-posting**). Table 4-5 shows the commands you use to post articles. ▶ Stewart decides to start a new thread on finding guitar tutors in the Denver area. Follow along by posting an article to the newsgroup you've joined.

STEPS

1 **Be sure you are reading an article within trn**
In the previous lesson, Stewart has just finished reading the first article of a thread on learning guitar without a tutor. He decides to post an article asking about tutors in Denver.

2 **Press [f] (you must use lowercase), then press [y] and press [Enter] when asked if you are starting an unrelated topic**

3 **Type a short descriptive title for the article you're about to post in response to the trn subject title prompt, then press [Enter]**
Stewart types "Tutors in Denver." Next, trn prompts you for the distribution. You can type "world" for worldwide distribution (the default, or preset, option), "na" for North American distribution, or "usa" for United States distribution.

4 **Type the distribution you want, press [Enter], then press [y] and press [Enter] to verify that you want to send the article to Usenet when prompted**
Since Stewart realizes only people in the United States are likely to be aware of classical guitar teachers in Denver, he decides to limit the distribution to "usa."

5 **Press [Enter] to skip sending a text file when prompted and then press [Enter] to accept the system's default text editor if prompted**
On MidWest University's computer, the default text editor is vi. You may have a different editor. Stewart's text editor displays the header fields shown in Figure 4-8. Some will already be filled in based on your responses to trn's earlier prompts, and you can fill in others (like Summary or Keywords) using your text editor. Enter the body of your article after the last field (usually the Cc: field).

6 **Enter your message using the system's text editor**
Stewart types a message regarding classical guitar tutors in the Denver area.

7 **When finished entering your message, exit your system's default text editor**
See your instructor if you aren't sure how to exit your text editor. You return to trn, where you can press [s] to send the message, [l] to review the article, [e] to return to your text editor, and [a] to abort sending the article.

8 **Press [s] to send your message, and then press [q] to quit the newsgroup. Press [q] again to exit trn**
You are returned to trn's paging level. After viewing all the articles you're interested in, you can press [q] to quit the newsgroup. Pressing [q] again at trn's newsgroup selection level prompt returns you to the UNIX command prompt, at which point you can log out.

FIGURE 4-8: Stewart's post

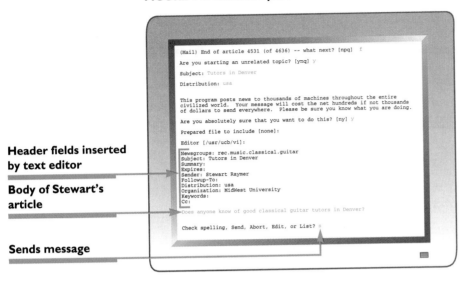

Header fields inserted by text editor

Body of Stewart's article

Sends message

TABLE 4-5: Common trn commands to send articles

COMMAND	DESCRIPTION
r	Send an e-mail message to the author of the article
R	Send an e-mail message to the author of the article, including the text of the article
f	Post a follow-up article, or a new article to the newsgroup
F	Post a follow-up article to the newsgroup, including the text of the original article in the post

NETIQUETTE

When you respond to an article, quote as sparingly as possible from the article to which you are responding to keep your message short. Many newsreaders do not let you post a message unless there is more new material than quotes.■

QUICK **TIP**

When you are finished viewing articles, remove the remaining articles that don't interest you by pressing [c] (for catch-up) within the article selection or paging level.■

CONCEPTSREVIEW

Label each of the elements shown in this figure.

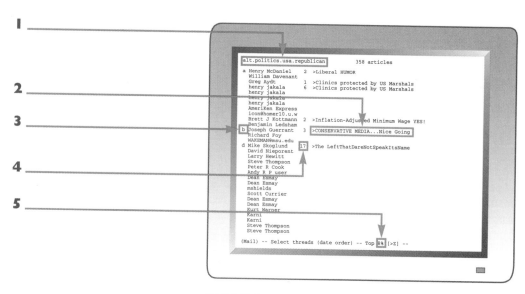

FIGURE 4-9

Match each of the statements with the term it describes.

6 The part of trn in which you view and select article threads

7 The computer that stores and manages newsgroup articles

8 The part of trn in which you subscribe to newsgroups

9 The part of trn in which you view and post newsgroup articles

10 A group of newsgroup articles organized by subject header

11 Software that lets you view and post articles to different Usenet newsgroups

a. thread

b. paging level

c. newsreader

d. article selection level

e. newsgroup selection level

f. news server

Select the best answer from the list of choices.

12 If you want to participate in a discussion about books by the writer Stephen King, in which Usenet category would you expect to find the appropriate newsgroup?

a. soc

b. alt

c. sci

d. rec

13 If you want to find a Usenet newsgroup that deals with health-care reform, which command should you type to begin your search?

a. l health

b. g health

c. f health

d. ? health

14 An advantage that Usenet has over mailing lists for discussing issues is:

    a. Usenet messages can be organized into article threads so that discussions can be easily followed.

    b. Using Usenet the user can pick and choose which articles he or she wants to view.

    c. Usenet offers a greater variety of discussion groups.

    d. All of the above

15 To mark all articles in a newsgroup as read so that they do not appear the next time you view the newsgroup, which command should you use at the article selection level?

    a. C

    b. c

    c. q

    d. Any of the above

16 To post a follow-up response to a newsgroup that includes the text of the article you're reading, which command should you use?

    a. F

    b. f

    c. r

    d. R

17 If EDUCAT-L is a Bitnet mailing list whose messages can also be found in a Usenet newsgroup, in which newsgroup category would you expect to find it?

    a. sci

    b. alt

    c. bit

    d. soc

18 Within trn's article selection level, which command should you use to select all threads with the word "clinton" in their subject headers?

    a. g clinton

    b. f clinton

    c. ? clinton

    d. /clinton

19 To respond to the posting of an article privately through e-mail rather than publicly through Usenet, including the text of the article in your response, which command should you use at trn's paging level?

    a. r

    b. R

    c. f

    d. F

20 To display help within trn, which command should you use?

    a. H

    b. h

    c. q

    d. Any of the above

21 Cross-posting is:

    a. the act of distributing an article to several geographic locations, such as North America and South America

    b. a newsgroup found in the alt newsgroup category

    c. the act of distributing an article to several different newsgroups

    d. the act of posting an article containing inflammatory language

APPLICATIONS
REVIEW

1 Start your newsreader, then find all the newsgroups in Usenet that deal with a topic of your interest or one that your instructor suggests (this review uses the trn newsreader).

    a. Type "trn" to start the trn newsreader.

    b. Type "l *topic*" (where *topic* is the word describing the topic you are interested in) at the newsgroup selection level prompt.

    c. Select a newsgroup from among those that are listed that you would like to join.

2 Subscribe to the Usenet newsgroup you found in the previous step.

    a. Be sure your newsreader is running and you are at the newsgroup selection level prompt.

    b. Type the command "g *newsgroup*" where *newsgroup* is the name of the newsgroup that you've selected.

    c. Press [y] to subscribe, and [^] to place the newsgroup at the beginning of your newsgroup list.

3 View the article list for a selected newsgroup and select threads of interest.

  a. Be sure your newsreader is running and that you have subscribed to a newsgroup.

  b. Go to the newsgroup you found in the previous exercise using the "g /*newsgroup*" command if you are not already there.

  c. Press [+] to view the article list for the newsgroup.

  d. Press the letters associated with threads that interest you. Press [>] to move to the next article list page, and press [<] to move to the previous page if you want to navigate the article list.

4 Read the articles in the threads you selected.

  a. Be sure your newsreader is running and that you have marked the threads you want to read.

  b. Press [Enter] to start viewing the selected articles.

  c. Press [Spacebar] to read the rest of an article that has more than one page and [n] to go to the next article.

5 Post a new article to the newsgroup you are working with.

  a. Be sure you are at the paging level of the trn newsreader and are viewing one of the newsgroup articles as described in the previous step.

  b. While viewing one of the articles, press [f] to forward a response to the newsgroup.

  c. When prompted by trn, press [y] to indicate that you are starting a new thread. Also indicate the planned distribution for the article. Limit the distribution to "usa."

  d. Using your site's text editor, write an article for the newsgroup.

  e. Exit the text editor and return to trn.

  f. To send the article to the newsgroup press [s].

INDEPENDENT
CHALLENGE 1

When reading articles in a newsgroup you may find some article threads that you have no interest in having constantly appear. You can have the newsreader "kill" these threads before they ever get put in your article list. To kill off annoying or uninteresting threads, you use the "K" command. Try experimenting with limiting the threads in the newsgroups you subscribe to. To complete this independent challenge:

1 Start your newsreader (in this example, trn).

2 Go to the article list for your selected newsgroup (in trn, this is the "g *newsgroup*" command).

3 Select an article from the thread that you want to kill (in trn, you press the article thread letter).

4 While viewing the article at the paging level of trn, press K to add the thread title to your newsreader's kill file. From this point on, whenever trn loads the article list for this newsgroup, it removes this thread automatically.

INDEPENDENT
CHALLENGE 2

You can use trn to search the subject titles of newsgroup articles for particular text strings by typing "/*topic*" where *topic* is the word you are searching for at the article list prompt. Typing this command at trn's article selection level selects all the articles with the word *topic* in their subject headers. You can also do more specific searches. For example:

/*topic*/a	searches through the body of the article for the word *topic*
/*topic*/h	searches through the article header for the word *topic*
/*name*/f	searches for articles from users named *name*

Experiment with searching for subject titles. To complete this independent challenge:

1 Start the trn newsreader.

2 View the article list for one of the newsgroups you're interested in.

3 Use "/*topic*/a" to search through the articles for the occurrence of the word *topic*.

4 Note which articles are selected. Pressing [Enter] at this point moves you to trn's paging level where you can view the contents of these selected articles.

Using the search command, you can quickly scan through a newsgroup for articles that cover specifics topics. However, if there are a lot of articles posted to the group, you might find that searching through entire articles for a specific text string can be very time-consuming.

UNIT 5

OBJECTIVES

▶ Telnet to other machines

▶ Suspend Telnet

▶ Obtain files using FTP

▶ Navigate FTP directory trees

▶ Download a text file

▶ Download multiple files

▶ Receive a binary file

▶ Suspend an FTP session

Connecting
WITH TELNET AND FTP

*A*lthough communication is, as you have seen, a crucial aspect of the Internet, another one of its equally powerful aspects is the capability to access files all over the world instantly through tools like Telnet and FTP. Telnet lets you log on to other machines to get information. For example, if you're planning a vacation in France, you can connect to a computer in Paris that features weather bulletins. FTP is the process you use to retrieve files stored on other network hosts and transfer them to your account. Imagine being able to retrieve a travel guide to Paris hotspots written by the students who live there. For those involved in scholarly or medical research, the degree of easy access to the work of other experts in a given field is unprecedented in the history of science. ▶ In this unit you will follow MidWest University undergraduate Mary Alvarez as she uses Telnet and FTP to prepare term papers for two classes: an essay on Shakespeare's *Henry V* for her introductory literature class, and a research paper on *The Federalist Papers* for a course in constitutional law. ▶

Telneting to other machines

Telnet, an Internet tool that you use to log on to other remote Internet hosts, lets you work on a computer halfway around the world almost as easily as you would on one across the room. For example, some universities offer Telnet access to on-line catalogs of the campus library holdings. Computers across the globe let users view reports on local weather conditions; others help investors keep track of the latest fluctuations in the stock market. Some computers provide several services. You can tell the remote host which service you want by specifying the **port number** that identifies the service program, as explained in the related topic "Port numbers" in this lesson. To use Telnet, you must either have an account on the remote host or you must use a host that offers a public or **guest account** to Internet users. Table 5-1 lists some of the popular Internet public-access hosts. Remember, however, that because the Internet is in a state of constant change, some of these sites may have changed. Your instructor can give you current information on the most useful Telnet sites. ▶ Mary Alvarez has just started her *Henry V* paper. She wants to include information from the sources that Shakespeare drew upon for his play and would like to check the library's holdings to see what source material is available. She uses Telnet to connect to the library's computer and check the on-line card catalog.

1 Obtain the domain name of a Telnet site from your instructor or use one of those listed in Table 5-1

As a MidWest University student, Mary has access to the MWU on-line library catalog; its Telnet address is nls.mwu.edu. (This is a fictional example; you must use a different Telnet address.)

2 Connect to your Internet host and log on to your account as described in Unit 1

The UNIX command prompt appears.

3 Type **telnet *hostname*** at the UNIX command prompt, where *hostname* is the name of the network host you want to connect to, then press **[Enter]**

Mary types "telnet nls.mwu.edu." The library computer responds with the welcome screen shown in Figure 5-1. Your screen will undoubtedly look different, depending on the host you are telnetting to.

4 If necessary, type the login name for the host and the password to connect to the machine

The MWU library computer does not request a login name or a password, but on other computers you might have to know the guest account login name and password. Table 5-1 includes this information for the listed sites, which your instructor can update and augment as necessary. Now that she is connected to the library host, Mary can search the catalog for books on sources of Shakespeare's *Henry V*.

FIGURE 5-1:
Logging onto MWU's
library catalog

telnet command

Welcome screen

Domain name
of remote host

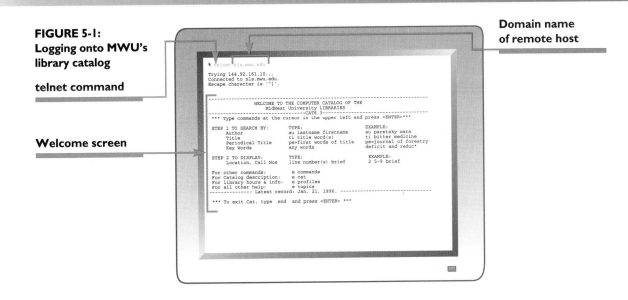

Port numbers

A single network host can provide many services, each of which is assigned a port number. When you want to access a particular service on a host that offers more than one service, you attach the service's port number to the Telnet command. For example, the weather report service offered by downwind.spri.umich.edu in Table 5-1 has a port number 3000 as part of its address. Including the port number 3000 in the Telnet command tells this host to initiate the weather report server and not some other program on the host. The standard port number is 23. If you do not include a port number in your Telnet command, this is the port number that is assumed by the remote host.

TABLE 5-1: A few popular telnet sites

RESOURCE	TO CONNECT	LOGIN AND PASSWORD
Library of Congress Offers access to the Library of Congress on-line catalog	telnet **locis.loc.gov**	No login or password required
NASA Space Link Contains a database of NASA-related materials, news, and educational services	telnet **spacelink.msfc.nasa.gov**	No login or password required
Washington University Services Offers information on a variety of network services: library catalogs, public databases, and data on universities	telnet **library.wustl.edu**	Login: services No login or password required
Weather Reports Offers up-to-date weather reports for locations in the United States or around the world	telnet **downwind.sprl.umich.edu 3000**	No login or password required

Suspending Telnet

As you work on remote hosts you may occasionally need to return to your own machine, perhaps to check your mail or to verify the contents of a file. With Telnet, you can "escape" to your own machine without losing your connection to the remote host by entering the appropriate escape character. When Mary logged on to the remote MWU library host, the welcome screen (shown in Figure 5-1 in the previous lesson) told her that the escape character for the host is **^**]. The caret symbol ^ stands for the [Ctrl] key and the] symbol is the right bracket, so the escape character is the key combination [Ctrl][Right bracket]. Once you return to your own machine's telnet command prompt, you can enter any one of the commands listed in Table 5-2. The **z** command suspends the Telnet session and returns you to your local machine's UNIX command prompt. To return to the remote host from UNIX, you use the **fg** command (for "foreground"). If you work on your own machine for too long, however, you might find that the remote host has disconnected you, in which case you simply log back on. ▶ While Mary is logged on to the campus library computer, she decides to send an e-mail message to a colleague. You should still be logged on to a Telnet site from the last lesson, so follow along with her and send an e-mail message to a friend or your instructor. If you are having trouble logging on to a Telnet host, see the related topic "Terminal types" in this lesson.

STEPS ▶

1 Be sure you are connected to a remote machine as described in the previous lesson

2 Work with the remote host to obtain the information you want
Mary manages to locate a reference work on Shakespeare's sources, shown in the first part of Figure 5-2. She knows she has to work late and hopes her friend Debbie, who is planning on spending the day in the library, can pick up the book for her. She suspends her session to e-mail her request to Debbie.

3 Press **[Ctrl][Right bracket]** to suspend the connection to the remote machine and return to the telnet command prompt on your local machine

4 Press **[z]** at the telnet prompt to suspend Telnet and access the UNIX command prompt on your local machine

5 Send an e-mail message to a friend from your local machine
Mary sends an e-mail message to her friend Debbie asking her to pick up the book from the library, as shown in Figure 5-2. When Mary is done, she returns to the library computer.

6 Type **fg** and press **[Enter]** at the UNIX command prompt to return to the remote host
UNIX returns Mary to the library computer at the point where she left it.

7 When you are finished working with the remote host, log out to return to your local UNIX prompt
The logout procedure varies from host to host; Mary, for example, types the word "end" to quit the library catalog host.

FIGURE 5-2: Working with a remote host

Information on the book Mary wants

Mary's e-mail message on her local machine

Current Telnet screen reappears

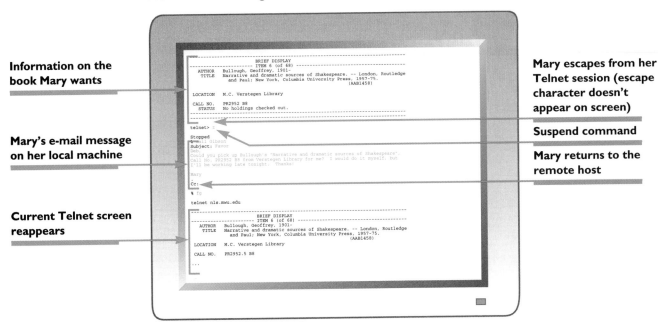

Mary escapes from her Telnet session (escape character doesn't appear on screen)

Suspend command

Mary returns to the remote host

Terminal types

Some hosts prompt you for a terminal type when you try to telnet to them. The terminal type tells the remote host how to interpret your keystrokes. The most common type, and the one you'll probably want to enter if you're working on a UNIX system, is "VT100." Using the incorrect terminal type might result in a display of unreadable characters on your screen. If you're not sure what type of terminal you're using, type "echo $TERM" at the UNIX command prompt, and UNIX will display your terminal type.

QUICK TIP

If you want to learn more about Telnet commands, type "man telnet" at the UNIX command prompt.■

TROUBLE?

If you're having trouble connecting to a service, use the nslookup command to obtain the machine's IP address (discussed in Unit 1) and use the IP address instead of the domain name in the Telnet command.■

TABLE 5-2: Telnet commands

COMMAND	DESCRIPTION
?	Returns a list of possible Telnet commands
[Enter]	Returns you to the remote host to which you are connected
close	Closes the current connection and disconnects you from the remote machine
display	Shows the current operating parameters for your Telnet session
open	Connects you to a remote host from within Telnet
quit	Exits you from the Telnet program
z	Suspends your Telnet session and returns you to your local machine

Obtaining files using FTP

You can transfer information that you find on remote hosts to your account using FTP. **FTP** stands for "File Transfer Protocol" and is an Internet service that lets you copy files from an Internet host to your account. As with Telnet, there are a few restrictions: you must either have an account on the remote machine or that machine must have a guest account. Sites that allow this kind of open access are called **anonymous FTP servers** since the login name for individuals accessing the site's files is "anonymous." Table 5-3 shows a list of some popular ones from which you can access files of many different types. See the related topic "File types" in this lesson for more information. ▶ Mary Alvarez is rushing to finish her paper on Shakespeare's *Henry V*. She knows she could speed up her work if she had the text of the play in electronic form: she could then search the document and find all the occurrences of the word "honour," for example. She's been told that a file containing the complete text of the play can be found on the Internet, so she uses FTP to connect to the host where the file is located.

1 Type **ftp *domain name*** at the UNIX command prompt, where *domain name* is the FTP site you are accessing, then press **[Enter]**
Mary types "ftp terminator.rs.itd.umich.edu" at the UNIX prompt to connect to the anonymous FTP server located at terminator.rs.itd.umich.edu. This one of the actual sites that feature complete texts of Shakespeare's plays. Your instructor might suggest other sites to which you can connect.

2 Type your account name at the Name prompt if you have an account on the FTP site; or, if this is an anonymous FTP site, type **anonymous** and press **[Enter]**
The FTP server prompts Mary for her user name and gives a default name of "Alvarez" (Mary's user name). You will see your own user name when you try to use FTP. Mary types "anonymous" to replace "Alvarez" since she does not have an account on this host, which is open to public use.

3 Type your password at the Password prompt; if this is an anonymous FTP site, type your complete e-mail address
Mary types "alvarez@students.mwu.edu" as the password. The command prompt, ftp, appears, indicating that the remote FTP server is ready to receive commands. Figure 5-3 shows the entire session so far. Note that Mary's password entry does not appear on the screen as a security measure.

FIGURE 5-3: Connecting to an anonymous FTP site

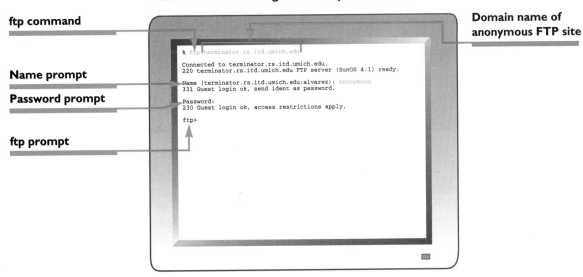

ftp command

Name prompt

Password prompt

ftp prompt

Domain name of
anonymous FTP site

```
% ftp terminator.rs.itd.umich.edu
Connected to terminator.rs.itd.umich.edu.
220 terminator.rs.itd.umich.edu FTP server (SunOS 4.1) ready.
Name (terminator.rs.itd.umich.edu:alvarez): anonymous
331 Guest login ok, send ident as password.
Password:
230 Guest login ok, access restrictions apply.

ftp>
```

File types

The types of files you can receive using FTP fall into two classes: text files and binary files. **Text files** (also called **ascii files**), are, as you would expect, files composed exclusively of text, with no graphics or formatting. **Binary files** are either executable files, such as software programs, or files that require a specialized software package in order to view, such as word-processed documents, spreadsheets, pictures, sound, or video. The process you use to transfer text files differs slightly from the one used for binary files, as you'll see later in this unit.

TABLE 5-3: Popular anonymous FTP sites

LOCATION	DESCRIPTION
archive.umich.edu	Software archives for UNIX, PC, and Macintosh computers
ftp.cica.indiana.edu	Software archives for UNIX machines and PCs
ftp.cwru.edu	Full text of U.S. Supreme Court decisions
ftp.microsoft.com	Device drivers and technical support files for Microsoft products
ftp.sura.net	Basic information on Internet tools such as mail, newsgroups, and anonymous ftp; useful for beginning Internet users who want to learn more
nic.funet.fi	Electronic documents for major works of literature; software files for the Macintosh, UNIX, and PCs
rtfm.mit.edu	Information about the Internet, including tutorials and software about newsreaders
wuarchive.wustl.edu	Software archives for UNIX, PC, and Macintosh computers

NETIQUETTE

When you connect to an FTP or Telnet site you are working on someone else's computer. Don't slow down the machine with frivolous and time-consuming file transfers during working hours.■

Navigating FTP directory trees

Once you have gained access to an FTP server, you usually have to move around the directory structure to find the file you want. Figure 5-4 shows the commands you use to navigate FTP server directories. Like UNIX commands, FTP commands are case-sensitive. If you're not sure what has been stored on the FTP server, look for a README file, as discussed in the related topic "Readme files" in this lesson.

▶ Mary Alvarez has connected to the FTP server that contains the complete text of Shakespeare's plays, and now she must go to the directory containing the appropriate file.

1 Connect to an FTP server if you haven't done so already
2 Type **ls -F** at the ftp command prompt to display the home directory
Mary sees that a shakespeare subdirectory exists on the FTP server (subdirectories are indicated by the / appended to their names). See the first part of Figure 5-4. Mary moves to that subdirectory.
3 Type **cd** *directory*
Mary types "cd shakespeare" to move to the shakespeare subdirectory.
4 Repeat steps 2 and 3 until you reach the subdirectory containing the file you want to retrieve
Mary types "ls -F" to show that the Shakespearean works are divided into subdirectories for tragedies, histories, comedies, and poetry. Mary types "cd histories" to move to the histories subdirectory, then types "ls -F" to see that the file she wants to retrieve is called kinghenryv. Figure 5-5 shows a schematic of the directory structure Mary navigated to find her file, which she transfers in the next lesson.

TABLE 5-4: Basic FTP commands

COMMAND	DESCRIPTION
!	Suspends FTP and sends you to the UNIX command prompt
?	Displays a list of all FTP commands
bye or quit	Terminates the FTP session and quits the FTP program
cd *directory*	Changes to the subdirectory named "directory"
close	Closes the connection with the FTP server but keeps you within the FTP program
lcd *directory*	Changes the current local directory to "directory"
ls or dir	Lists the contents of the current FTP directory. Typing ls -F lists the contents and indicates subdirectories with a backslash (/)
open	Connects to another remote FTP server
pwd	Displays the current working directory

FIGURE 5-4: Finding the file for *Henry V*

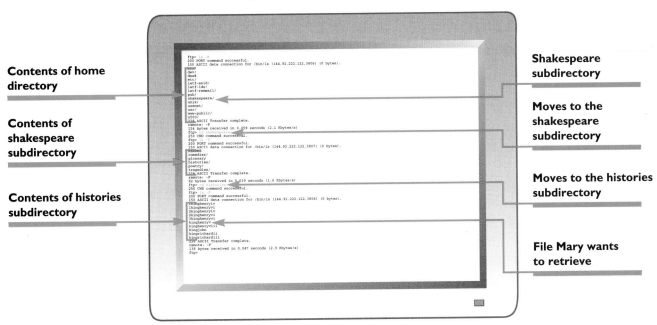

Contents of home directory

Contents of shakespeare subdirectory

Contents of histories subdirectory

Shakespeare subdirectory

Moves to the shakespeare subdirectory

Moves to the histories subdirectory

File Mary wants to retrieve

FIGURE 5-5: Schematic diagram of directory structure

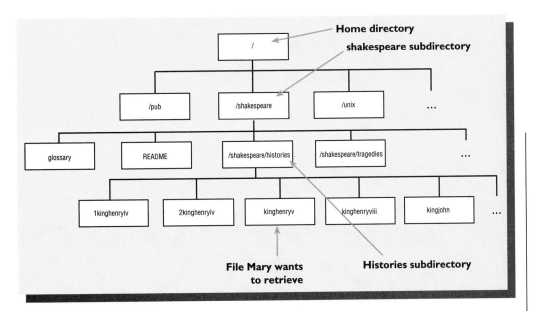

Home directory

shakespeare subdirectory

/

/pub   /shakespeare   /unix   ...

glossary   README   /shakespeare/histories   /shakespeare/tragedies   ...

1kinghenryiv   2kinghenryiv   kinghenryv   kinghenryviii   kingjohn   ...

File Mary wants to retrieve

Histories subdirectory

Readme files

Anonymous FTP sites usually have README files that contain information about the files available on the server. The README files are in text format, so you can easily read them. When retrieving files from an anonymous FTP server, the first file you may want to retrieve is the README file.

Downloading a text file

Once you've found the directory on the FTP server containing the file you're interested in, you can retrieve that file. This process is called **downloading**. By contrast, **uploading** is used when you want to place a file on the FTP server. If you have trouble keeping these two terms straight, think of uploading as sending a file *up and away* from your computer, and downloading as sending the file *down home* to your computer. When transferring files, you will have to keep track of the remote directory and the local directory. The **remote directory** is the directory on the FTP server that contains the files you want, whereas the **local directory** is the directory on your computer that will receive the files you download. The related topic "Local and remote directories" in this lesson discusses how to change your local directory so that you can send files to any directory in your account. Table 5-5 lists several FTP commands used to transfer files. ▶ Mary downloads the file containing the text of Shakespeare's *Henry V* to her local directory.

1   **If you are not already connected to an FTP server, connect to one and move to the directory containing the file you want to download**
Mary has already moved to the histories subdirectory containing the file she wants to retrieve.

2   **Type get *filename* at the ftp command prompt, where *filename* is the name of the file you want to download, then press [Enter]**
Mary types "get kinghenryv" at the ftp command prompt. As shown in Figure 5-6, the FTP server reports the size of the file to be transferred, which in Mary's case is over 150,000 bytes (commonly called 150k or 150 KB) and takes about 2 seconds to transfer. Depending upon the size of the file and how busy the site is, the transfer could take longer. If the file you're trying to download is too big to fit in your account, consider transferring a smaller file.

TABLE 5-5: FTP commands to transfer files

COMMAND	DESCRIPTION
ascii	Switches to ascii transfer mode to transfer ascii or text files
binary	Switches to binary transfer mode to transfer binary files
get *filename* [*newfile*]	Downloads a single file named *filename* to your local current directory; you can optionally give the file a new name called *newfile* in which you can also specify a path
mget *file1 file2 file3 ...*	Downloads the files named *file1*, *file2*, *file3* and so forth to your local current directory
mput *file1 file2 file3 ...*	Uploads the files named *file1*, *file2*, *file3* and so forth from your local current directory to the FTP server
put *filename* [*newfile*]	Uploads a single file named *filename* from your local current directory to the FTP server; you can optionally give the file a new name called *newfile*

FIGURE 5-6: Transferring the text of the *Henry V* play

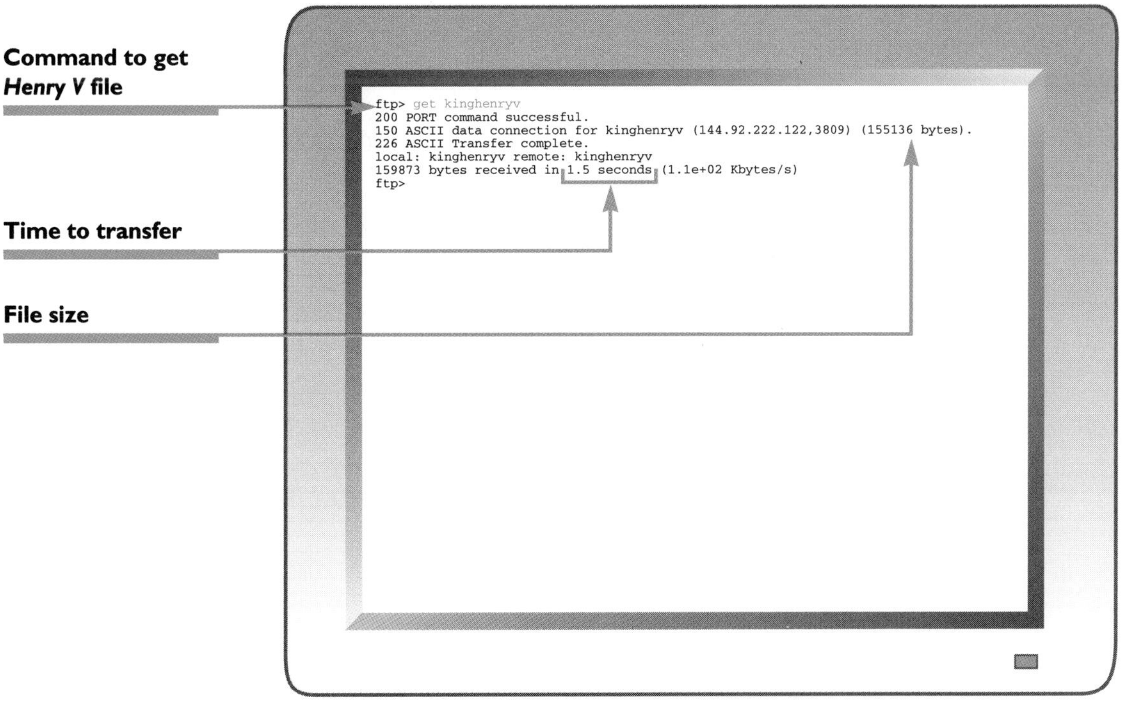

Command to get
Henry V file

Time to transfer

File size

```
ftp> get kinghenryv
200 PORT command successful.
150 ASCII data connection for kinghenryv (144.92.222.122,3809) (155136 bytes).
226 ASCII Transfer complete.
local: kinghenryv remote: kinghenryv
159873 bytes received in 1.5 seconds (1.1e+02 Kbytes/s)
ftp>
```

Local and remote directories

The local directory is the directory on your machine and the remote directory is the directory on the FTP server. The current local directory is usually the directory you were in when you first initiated your FTP session. By default, any files that you download go to the current local directory unless you specify a new location in the *newfile* part of the get command. If you want to change the current local directory, you can do so with the **lcd** command. In our example, Mary Alvarez could change the current local directory to /students/alvarez/english by typing "lcd /students/alvarez/english" at the ftp command prompt. Any files she transfers from the current FTP site will arrive in this subdirectory.

TROUBLE?

The get command will overwrite, without warning, any file in your current directory with the same name as the file you are downloading.■

QUICK **TIP**

If you want to view the contents of a text file without downloading the file to your local machine, type "get *filename* |more" at the ftp prompt.■

Downloading multiple files

If you want to download several files from an FTP server, you could type the get command several times, once for each of the files, or you could use the **mget** command described in Table 5-5. With the mget command you explicitly name the files you want by typing the command mget *file1 file2 file3* where *file1*, *file2*, and *file3* are three of the files you want (there is no limit, though, to the number of files you can specify). You can also download multiple files by using wildcards as described in the related topic "Wildcards" in this lesson. ▶ Mary Alvarez decides that she would also like to have the text for *Henry IV Part I* and *Henry IV Part II* for her paper. She can save a step by using the mget command.

1   If you are not already connected to an FTP server, connect to one and move to the directory containing the file you want to download

2   Type **mget *file1 file2 file3*** at the ftp command prompt (where *file1*, *file2*, *file3* (and so on) are the files you want to transfer), then press **[Enter]**
Mary Alvarez types "mget 1kinghenryiv 2kinghenryiv" at the ftp command prompt to get the text files of the plays *King Henry IV Part I* and *Part II* (since these text files are large, you might want to transfer files that are smaller and will not take up so much room on your account). The FTP server prompts her on whether or not she wants to download each of the files.

3   Press **[y]** to download each file when prompted, then press **[Enter]**
The FTP server reports the size of each file and the amount of time each takes to transfer. Mary Alvarez's two files are around 150 KB each and take about 3 seconds total to transfer. See Figure 5-7.

4   Type **quit** and press **[Enter]** at the ftp command prompt to exit your FTP session and close the connection to the FTP server
Mary types "quit" and is returned to the UNIX command prompt.

FIGURE 5-7: Transferring two files at once

Command to get two files

Prompts for transferring the files

Quit command

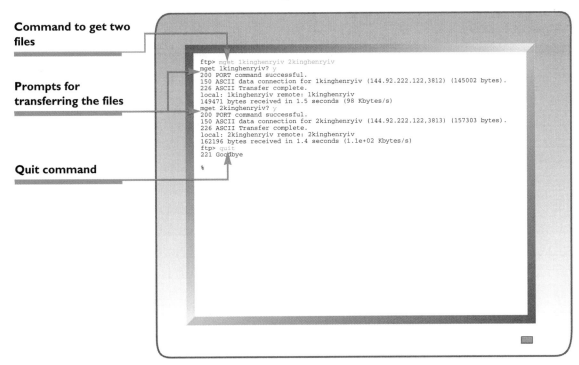

```
ftp> mget 1kinghenryiv 2kinghenryiv
mget 1kinghenryiv? y
200 PORT command successful.
150 ASCII data connection for 1kinghenryiv (144.92.222.122,3812) (145002 bytes).
226 ASCII Transfer complete.
local: 1kinghenryiv remote: 1kinghenryiv
149471 bytes received in 1.5 seconds (98 Kbytes/s)
mget 2kinghenryiv? y
200 PORT command successful.
150 ASCII data connection for 2kinghenryiv (144.92.222.122,3813) (157303 bytes).
226 ASCII Transfer complete.
local: 2kinghenryiv remote: 2kinghenryiv
162196 bytes received in 1.4 seconds (1.1e+02 Kbytes/s)
ftp> quit
221 Goodbye

%
```

Wildcards

You can specify multiple files through the use of **wildcards**, special symbols that UNIX recognizes as standing for any symbol or set of symbols. The most common wildcard is the asterisk (*), which stands for any set of symbols. For example, if Mary Alvarez had wanted to transfer the plays King Richard II and King Richard III, she could type "mget kingrichardii kingrichardiii", or she could have used the wildcard command mget kingr*, which would download all files starting with the letters *kingr*. Another commonly used wildcard is the question mark symbol (?), which stands for any single symbol. If Mary Alvarez wanted the three Henry VI files, she could have typed "mget 1kinghenryvi 2kinghenryvi 3kinghenryvi", or she could have used the wildcard command mget ?kinghenryvi. Wildcards are commonly used with UNIX commands, such as ls. For example, to list only those files starting with the letter k, type "ls k*" at the UNIX command prompt.

QUICK **TIP**

If you want to bypass the prompt when using the mget command, type the command "prompt" before using mget (type prompt again to turn prompting back on).■

TROUBLE?

If files are taking a long time to transfer, you might want to try again when traffic on the network is not so high.■

Receiving a binary file

Up to now, you've been transferring text files. You can also transfer binary files using FTP, which include, for example, software programs, graphic images, sound, or video clips. You first tell the FTP server that you are transferring a binary file by typing "binary" at the ftp command prompt. If you want to send an ascii or text file afterwards, type "ascii" at the ftp command prompt so that the FTP server treats all subsequent files as text. Once you set the transfer type to binary, you use the same FTP commands to transfer the file. Another type of binary file is a **compressed file**, which has been compacted to take up less space and allow for quicker transfer. See the related topic "Compressed files" in this lesson for more information. ▶ Mary Alvarez is taking a course on constitutional law and wants to use the Internet to find a transcript of *The Federalist Papers*. Her instructor told her that this file is stored on the FTP server located at mrcnext.cso.uiuc.edu.

1 **Connect to the FTP server containing the file you want to download**
Mary types "ftp mrcnext.cso.uiuc.edu" at the UNIX command prompt. Since this is an anonymous FTP site, she logs on as "anonymous" and gives her e-mail address as the password.

2 **Change to the subdirectory that contains the file you want**
Mary has already learned that the file is located in /pub/etext/etext91 and is called feder16, so she types "cd pub/etext/etext91" at the ftp command prompt.

3 **List the files in the subdirectory to verify the existence of the file you want**
Mary types "dir feder*" at the ftp command prompt to list the files starting with the letters *feder* (see the previous lesson for a review of wildcards). She uses the dir command so that she can get information on the size of each file as well as the name. There are two feder16 files: a feder16.txt and a feder16.txt.Z. The feder16.txt file is a text file version of *The Federalist Papers* while the feder16.txt.Z is a compressed binary version of the same file. Note that the compressed version is 458 KB in size, about ⅓ the size of the uncompressed file. Mary decides to download the compressed version (again, you may want to transfer a smaller file if disk space is a problem).

4 **Type binary at the ftp command prompt and press [Enter] to switch to binary mode for transferring files**

5 **Transfer the binary file (or files) of interest**
Mary types "get feder16.txt.Z" at the ftp command prompt to download the compressed version of *The Federalist Papers* to her local machine.

6 **Type ascii to switch the transfer mode back to ascii**
The files are now in Mary's local account, and the ftp command prompt awaits her next command.

FIGURE 5-8: Binary transfer of *The Federalist Papers*

Logging on

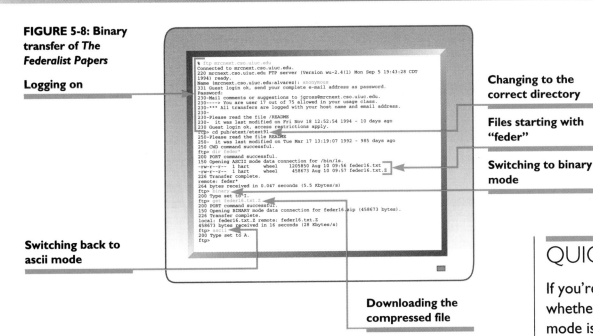

Changing to the correct directory

Files starting with "feder"

Switching to binary mode

Switching back to ascii mode

Downloading the compressed file

QUICK **TIP**

If you're unsure whether the transfer mode is set to binary or ascii, type "type" and press [Enter] at the ftp command prompt.■

TROUBLE?

If you get lost navigating through the directory tree structure of the FTP server, type "cd /" at the ftp command prompt to return to the home directory.■

Compressed files

In order to save space, many anonymous FTP servers compress the files they offer so that users can download them as quickly as possible. Once files are compressed, you need a software program to uncompress them. Table 5-6 shows some of the most common compression formats and how to uncompress them. Since the act of uncompressing a file might create several new files, you should place the compressed version into a separate directory before running an uncompression utility. The DOS and Macintosh utilities are not free and you should purchase them if you intend to use them.

TABLE 5-6: Compressed file formats

FILE FORMAT	OPERATING SYSTEM	SOFTWARE REQUIRED
filename.zip	DOS	To uncompress zip files you need the pkzip program, pkz204g.exe, available from the anonymous FTP server mirror.aol.com, located in the /mir01/CICA/pub/pc/starter directory. Once pkzip is installed, type "pkunzip *filename*.zip" at the DOS prompt.
filename.Z	UNIX	None. Type the command "uncompress *filename*.Z" at the UNIX command prompt.
filename.tar	UNIX	None. Type the command "tar -xvf *filename*.tar" at the UNIX command prompt.
filename.sit	Macintosh	To uncompress sit files you need the program stuffitlite3.5.sea.hqx, available from the anonymous FTP server mirror.aol.com, located in the /mir01/MICH/mac/uti/compression directory. Once Stuffit-Lite is installed you can drag compressed Mac files into the appropriate application to uncompress them.

Suspending an FTP session

As with Telnet, you can run UNIX commands on your local machine while your FTP session is active. Either type "!*command*" where *command* is the UNIX command you want to run on your local machine, or simply press [!] to return to the UNIX command prompt on your local machine. While you work on your local machine, you are still connected to the FTP site, but most FTP sites disconnect you automatically if you leave them idle for more than a few minutes. ▶ Mary Alvarez, having downloaded the compressed version of *The Federalist Papers*, returns to her local machine to uncompress the file using UNIX's uncompress command. She is delighted to find that she got the materials she needed to write her constitutional law paper without having to leave her desk. Mary realizes that as an Internet user she benefits from the work of others and hopes that she too will someday have files to make available on public servers. The related topic "Uploading files with FTP" tells you how to send files from your machine to a remote FTP server when you have something worth sharing with the rest of the Internet community.

1   Make sure that you are still connected to an anonymous FTP server and are at the ftp command prompt

2   Press **[!]** at the ftp command prompt to return to your local machine while still maintaining your FTP connection, then press **[Enter]**
The prompt changes to csh> letting Mary know that she is no longer working with FTP commands. Your prompt may be different.

3   Run any UNIX commands you want on your local machine
Mary types "uncompress feder16.txt.Z" to uncompress *The Federalist Papers* file that she downloaded in the previous lesson.

4   Type **exit** to return to the FTP session, then type **quit** to close the FTP server connection
Having uncompressed the file, Mary returns to the FTP server and then leaves the FTP session by typing "quit" to close the connection and exit the program. See Figure 5-9.

FIGURE 5-9: Suspending an FTP session

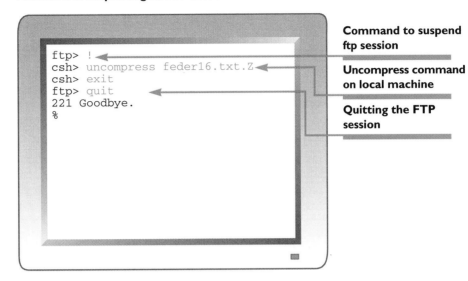

```
ftp> !
csh> uncompress feder16.txt.Z
csh> exit
ftp> quit
221 Goodbye.
%
```

Command to suspend
ftp session

Uncompress command
on local machine

Quitting the FTP
session

Uploading files with FTP

You can also use FTP's "send," "put," and "mput" commands to upload files from your machine to the FTP server. The only requirements for uploading are either that you have an account on the machine or, if the server is an anonymous FTP site, that it makes a directory open for any outside users. An open directory on an anonymous FTP site often has the name "uploads" or variants of that name. As a beginning Internet user you may not have any files to upload, but as you become more experienced you may find that you have some things that could be of interest to others. The Internet works only because people are willing to share their time, expertise, ideas, and files.

TROUBLE?

When downloading files from anonymous FTP sites you should have a virus-checking program review the new files for viruses. You can find virus checkers at many anonymous ftp sites, such as ftp.cica.indiana.edu.■

NETIQUETTE

Once you get the files you want from an anonymous FTP site, don't forget to log out. Others may be waiting to access the server.■

CONCEPTS REVIEW

Label each of the elements shown in this figure.

I _____

2 _____

3 _____

4 _____

5 _____

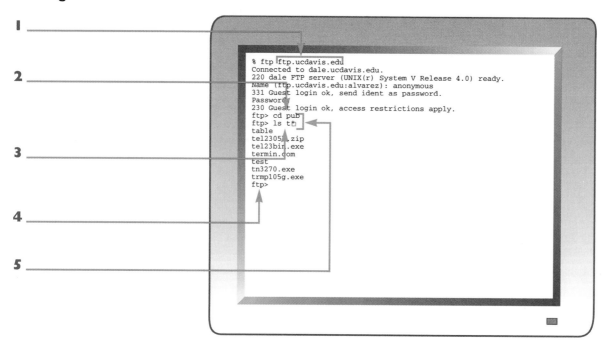

```
% ftp ftp.ucdavis.edu
Connected to dale.ucdavis.edu.
220 dale FTP server (UNIX(r) System V Release 4.0) ready.
Name (ftp.ucdavis.edu:alvarez): anonymous
331 Guest login ok, send ident as password.
Password:
230 Guest login ok, access restrictions apply.
ftp> cd pub
ftp> ls tb
table
tel2305.zip
tel23bin.exe
termin.com
test
tn3270.exe
trmp105g.exe
ftp>
```

FIGURE 5-10

Match each of the statements with the term it describes.

6 The protocol followed by Internet machines in transferring files

7 Video clips, graphics, or sound files are examples of this kind of file format

8 Text files are examples of this kind of file format

9 Use this login name when connecting to a public-access FTP site

10 The program used by Internet machines to connect to other Internet hosts

11 Commonly used login name for public-access Telnet sites

a. guest

b. ascii

c. FTP

d. binary

e. anonymous

f. Telnet

Select the best answer from the list of choices.

12 To escape from a remote machine during a Telnet session and return to the Telnet command prompt, type:

a. [Ctrl][Right bracket]

b. [!]

c. [Ctrl][c]

d. !quit

13 To suspend your Telnet session and escape to your local machine, type the following command at the telnet command prompt:

a. quit

b. close

c. [z]

d. stop

14 To return to your suspended Telnet session from your local machine, type

a. resume

b. fg

c. restart

d. Telnet

15 When connecting to a public-access FTP server, what login name should you use?

a. guest

b. newuser

c. your e-mail address

d. anonymous

16 To go to the /pub/dos/utilities subdirectory on an anonymous FTP server, which commands should you type?

a. cd pub/dos/utilities

b. cd Pub/Dos/Utilities

c. cd PUB/DOS/UTILITIES

d. any of the above

17 When connected to an FTP site, your current local directory is

a. The directory on your machine that was active when you initiated the FTP session

b. The directory on the FTP server you are presently working in

c. The directory returned by typing the "lcd" command at the ftp command prompt

d. The directory returned by typing the "pwd" command at the ftp command prompt

18 To view the contents of the "Index" file on the FTP server *without* downloading it to your machine, type

a. view Index

b. more Index

c. get Index |more

d. type Index

19 To view the contents of the Index file after downloading it to your machine, *without* quitting the FTP session, type

a. !more Index

b. !uncompress Index

c. !tar Index

d. (a & c are both correct)

20 Which one of the following files will *not* be downloaded by the command mget ?henry*?

a. 1henryvi

b. thehenryviplays

c. 2henry

d. henryvi123

21 Which of the following commands will not download the file 3henryvi?

a. mget 3?

b. get 3henryvi

c. mget 3*

d. recv 3henryvi

APPLICATIONS
REVIEW

Note that the servers in this review are currently active, but this may not always be the case. If you have problems with this review, see your instructor for other servers or files to practice with.

1 Access another machine using Telnet. For example, using the NASA Internet host at spacelink.msfc.nasa.gov, try to find information about the space probe Magellan. If this site doesn't work, your instructor could suggest a different one.

a. Type "telnet spacelink.msfc.nasa.gov."

b. Following the login instructions, log on to the system (the login name will probably be "guest").

c. Choose NASA projects from the menu.

d. Choose Planetary.Probes from the submenu.

e. Choose Magellan from the Planetary.Probes submenu.

f. View the 1992 fact sheet. What is Magellan's mission? On what date was it launched? What are the dates of its first mapping cycle?

2 Suspend your Telnet session to record your answers in a text editor.

  a. Press [Ctrl][Right bracket] to escape from the remote host.

  b. Press [z] and [Enter] at the telnet command prompt to suspend the Telnet session.

  c. Using your site's text editor, record your answers; then use the appropriate command to return to the UNIX command prompt.

  d. Type "fg" at the UNIX command prompt to return to the remote host.

  e. Log out of the remote host using the appropriate command.

3 Use FTP to retrieve a list of anonymous FTP servers.

  a. Type "ftp ftp.ucdavis.edu."

  b. Log on as "anonymous", and use your e-mail address as the password.

  c. Type "ls -F" to list the files and directories, then change to the /pub directory.

  d. Download the text file "FTP sites" to your local directory, then review it to find sites you might be interested in using.

4 Using FTP, retrieve a copy of *Hitchhiker's Guide to the Internet*, a popular text on using the Internet. Ask your instructor if you can't find the file at the suggested site.

  a. Use FTP to connect to mrcnext.cso.uiuc.edu.

  b. Log on as "anonymous", using your e-mail address as the password.

  c. Change to the /pub/etext/etext92 directory.

  d. Download the text file hhgi10.txt to your local directory and review it for information on the Internet.

5 Using FTP, retrieve the pkzip software used for uncompressing compressed files on the PC.

  a. Use FTP to connect to ftp.cica.indiana.edu.

  b. Log in as "anonymous", using your e-mail address as the password.

  c. Change to the /pub/pc/starter directory.

  d. Type "binary" to chnage the file transfer type to binary.

  e. Download the binary file pkz204g.exe to your local directory, and run it whenever you need to unzip files.

INDEPENDENT
CHALLENGE 1

In the next unit you'll work with an Internet tool called Gopher. You can get a sneak peek at Gopher by telnetting to the host consultant.micro.umn.edu and logging in with the name "gopher." Try connecting to this host. Gopher is designed like a menu tree. Using the arrow keys on your keyboard you can move a pointer to different menu options. Pressing [Enter] selects the menu option, pressing [u] moves you back up the menu tree and pressing [q] quits Gopher and ends your Telnet session. You can use Gopher to see which anonymous FTP servers are available from that host. See your instructor if you have problems with the steps. To complete this independent challenge:

  1 Telnet to the host at consultant.micro.umn.edu, then log on as "gopher."

  2 Select the menu item "Internet file server (ftp) sites/" and press [Enter].

  3 Select the menu item "Popular FTP sites via Gopher/" and press [Enter].

  4 Record the FTP lists in this menu.

  5 Press [q] to quit.

INDEPENDENT
CHALLENGE 2

If you don't have access to FTP you can still receive files from anonymous FTP servers using **ftpmail**, which works like a list server in that you send commands to a server in the body of your e-mail message. The server interprets the commands, performs an action, and sends you the results. One such server is located at the e-mail addresss ftpmail@decwrl.dec.com. To see how ftpmail works, try to get the Shakespeare file "loverscomplaint" from the anonymous FTP server located at terminator.rs.itd.umich.edu. To complete this independent challenge:

  1 Address an e-mail message to ftpmail@decwrl.dec.com.

  2 Type the following commands in the body of the message:

     connect terminator.rs.itd.umich.edu
     get /shakespeare/poetry/loverscomplaint
     quit

  3 Wait a few days, check your e-mail, and see if you get the text of Shakespeare's poem in an e-mail message from the ftpmail server.

UNIT 6

OBJECTIVES

▶ Use a Gopher client

▶ View text files

▶ Navigate Gopher

▶ Connect to other Gopher servers

▶ Use Gopher to access anonymous FTP servers

▶ Use Gopher to download a binary file

▶ Use Gopher to access Telnet sites

▶ Create bookmarks

Browsing
WITH GOPHER

A s you worked with Telnet and FTP in the previous unit, you may have found yourself overwhelmed by all the choices of Telnet sites and FTP servers. In its infancy, it was not difficult to keep track of Internet resources as there were relatively few sites and these were well-known. This is no longer the case. Beginning with this unit, you'll learn about some of the more popular tools that have been developed to cope with the flood of information available on the Internet. The first of these tools is **Gopher**, a program that organizes different Internet resources into easy-to-use menus. ▶ Dennis Wu is a new student at MidWest University who uses Gopher to learn more about MWU student organizations and the library system. ▶

Using a Gopher client

System administrators around the country have set up Internet hosts called **Gopher servers** that organize your access to other Internet resources. When you connect to a Gopher server, your computer is called a **Gopher client**. See the related topic "Gopher client software" in this lesson. One of the great advantages of Gopher over the tools you've used so far is its ease of use. Instead of having to remember commands, you simply start Gopher, which presents you with menus that list your options. You access an Internet resource by selecting it from the menu. ▶ Dennis Wu accesses the MWU Gopher server to find out about different student organizations.

STEPS ▶

1 Type **gopher** at the UNIX command prompt, then press **[Enter]**
Dennis's Gopher client program connects with MidWest University's Gopher server and displays an opening menu of items called a **page**. See Figure 6-1 (your site's opening menu will look different). The status line at the bottom-right of the screen indicates that this is the first page of one; a menu can have as many pages as necessary to display all the menu items. The **page title** gives the domain name of the Gopher server. This opening menu displays 16 possible items; a **pointer**, or arrow, points at the first one, the current menu item. You move the pointer to select the item you want. Selecting an item either accesses an Internet resource (such as another computer, an FTP site, or a text file) or displays a **submenu**, a menu that contains a new set of menu items. Gopher appends a [/] to menu items that open submenus.

2 Press **[↑]** or **[↓]** until the pointer points to a submenu item, then press **[Enter]**
Dennis selects item 5, a submenu containing the Registered Student Organization Directory. Gopher responds by displaying a new menu; the first of four pages is shown in Figure 6-2. Note that the page title changes from the name of the Gopher server to the title of the menu item you selected. Looking over the new menu, Dennis is interested in the Asian American Student Union, so he selects item 4 in Figure 6-2. This item has no additional characters appended to its item name, which means that it is a text file. Locate a text file in the menu you are looking at, and select it.

3 Press **[↑]** or **[↓]** until the pointer points to a text file, then press **[Enter]**
Gopher responds by opening the text file you selected; you'll learn more about how to view text files in the next lesson.

TABLE 6-1: Public access Gopher servers via Telnet

DOMAIN NAME	INSTRUCTIONS	DOMAIN NAME	INSTRUCTIONS
consultant.micro.umn.edu	log on as **gopher**	gopher.msu.edu	log on as **gopher**
ux1.cso.uiuc.edu	log on as **gopher**	infoslug.ucsc.edu	log in as **gopher**
panda.uiowa.edu	log on as **panda**		

FIGURE 6-1:
MWU's Gopher server opening menu

Gopher server domain name

Page title

Pointer

Opening menu

/ indicates a submenu

Dennis selects item 5

Status line

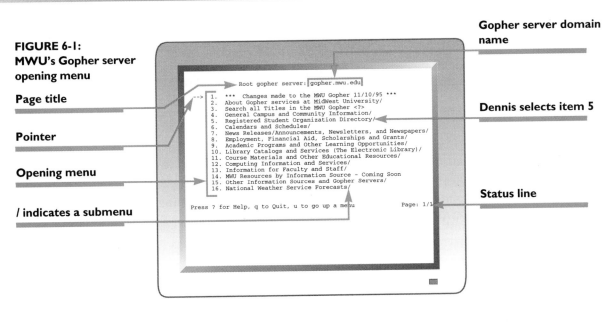

```
              Root gopher server: gopher.mwu.edu

-->  1.  *** Changes made to the MWU Gopher 11/10/95 ***
     2.  About Gopher services at MidWest University/
     3.  Search all Titles in the MWU Gopher <?>
     4.  General Campus and Community Information/
     5.  Registered Student Organization Directory/
     6.  Calendars and Schedules/
     7.  News Releases/Announcements, Newsletters, and Newspapers/
     8.  Employment, Financial Aid, Scholarships and Grants/
     9.  Academic Programs and Other Learning Opportunities/
    10.  Library Catalogs and Services (The Electronic Library)/
    11.  Course Materials and Other Educational Resources/
    12.  Computing Information and Services/
    13.  Information for Faculty and Staff/
    14.  MWU Resources by Information Source - Coming Soon
    15.  Other Information Sources and Gopher Servers/
    16.  National Weather Service Forecasts/

Press ? for Help, q to Quit, u to go up a menu          Page: 1/1
```

FIGURE 6-2:
Registered Student Organization Directory menu

Dennis selects item 4

Page title changes to show new menu name

First page of four pages of menu items

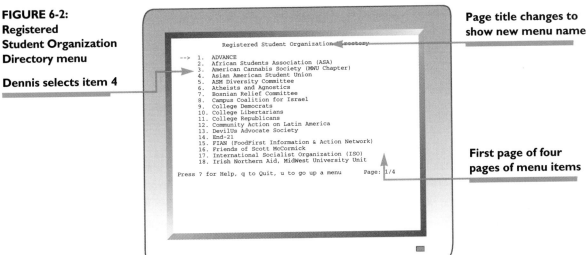

```
              Registered Student Organization Directory

-->  1.  ADVANCE
     2.  African Students Association (ASA)
     3.  American Cannabis Society (MWU Chapter)
     4.  Asian American Student Union
     5.  ASM Diversity Committee
     6.  Atheists and Agnostics
     7.  Bosnian Relief Committee
     8.  Campus Coalition for Israel
     9.  College Democrats
    10.  College Libertarians
    11.  College Republicans
    12.  Community Action on Latin America
    13.  DevilUs Advocate Society
    14.  End-21
    15.  FIAN (FoodFirst Information & Action Network)
    16.  Friends of Scott McCormick
    17.  International Socialist Organization (ISO)
    18.  Irish Northern Aid, MidWest University Unit

Press ? for Help, q to Quit, u to go up a menu     Page: 1/4
```

Gopher client software

There are several different Gopher client programs that you can use to access Gopher servers. The most common is **Gopher**, the software demonstrated in this book and used on UNIX machines. Some Gopher client programs offer a graphical interface to the Gopher menus. If your UNIX terminal uses X-Windows (a graphical user interface for UNIX) you may want to work with the Gopher client program Xgopher. If you are connected to the Internet with a PC, you can either use Wingopher if you are running Windows or PCGopher if you are running only DOS. Macintosh users with an Internet connection can try Macgopher or TurboGopher. You can download these programs from many of the popular anonymous FTP servers (for example, the anonymous FTP server at boombox.micro.umn.edu in the /pub/gopher directory).

TROUBLE?

If your university or institution does not support Gopher, you can still access a public Gopher server by using the skills you learned in the previous unit to telnet to one of the sites listed in Table 6-1.

Viewing text files

Of all Internet resources that offer information, the most common format is text files. Many institutions, like MidWest University, routinely make important text files available through their Gopher servers (for example, degree requirements, semester timetables, schedules of department guest lecturers, and so on). Having this type of information in text file format has many advantages, not the least of which is the ability to read the text file, print it, download it, or mail it to a colleague. Table 6-2 shows a list of common Gopher text file commands that you can use while viewing a text file. If you are accessing a Gopher client through Telnet, you won't be able to save or mail text files and will have to skip most of this lesson. ▶ Dennis Wu works with the text file on the Asian American Student Union, which he accessed in the previous lesson.

1 **Be sure you are viewing the text file you accessed in the previous lesson**
Figure 6-3 shows the text file Dennis selected from the Gopher menu. Dennis sees that only 43% of the text is displayed. If your text file has more than one page, press [Spacebar] to view the next page and press [b] to view the previous page.

2 **Press [Spacebar] to view the next page until 100% of the text file is displayed, if your text file has more than one page**
For Dennis, the remainder of the text file appears, as shown in Figure 6-4. The upper-right corner of the screen tells him that 100% of the text has now been displayed. Now try saving the text file you accessed (be sure you are still viewing the file).

3 **Press [s] to save the text to a file in your account, accept the default name or enter an appropriate name, and then press [Enter]**
When Dennis presses [s], Gopher prompts him for the name of the file, inserting the item name as the default, as shown in Figure 6-5. Dennis accepts the default name and saves the file. Now Dennis wants to mail a copy of the text to another new student he knows who might be interested. Be sure you are still viewing the file.

4 **Press [m] to mail the file, type the name of the recipient when Gopher prompts you for the e-mail address, then press [Enter]**
Dennis enters "ljwei@students.mwu.edu" when Gopher prompts him, as shown in Figure 6-6, to send the student union information to his friend L.J. Wei.

5 **Press [u] to return to the menu you used to access the text file**
Dennis returns to the Registered Student Organization Directory menu.

TABLE 6-2: Gopher text file commands

COMMAND	DESCRIPTION	COMMAND	DESCRIPTION
/ *text*	Searches for text string *text*	m	Mails text to an Internet user
?	Gets help on Gopher text commands	p	Sends text to your system printer
[Spacebar]	Moves to the next page	s	Saves text to a file
b	Moves to the previous page	u	Returns to the previous Gopher menu

FIGURE 6-3:
Asian American
Student Union
text file

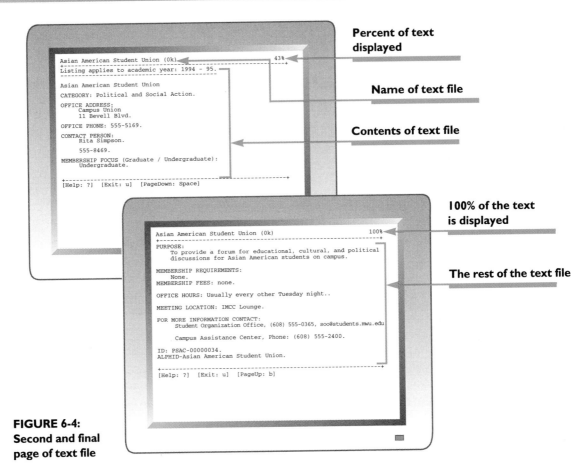

Percent of text
displayed

Name of text file

Contents of text file

FIGURE 6-4:
Second and final
page of text file

100% of the text
is displayed

The rest of the text file

FIGURE 6-5:
Saving a
text file

Save prompt

Default text file name

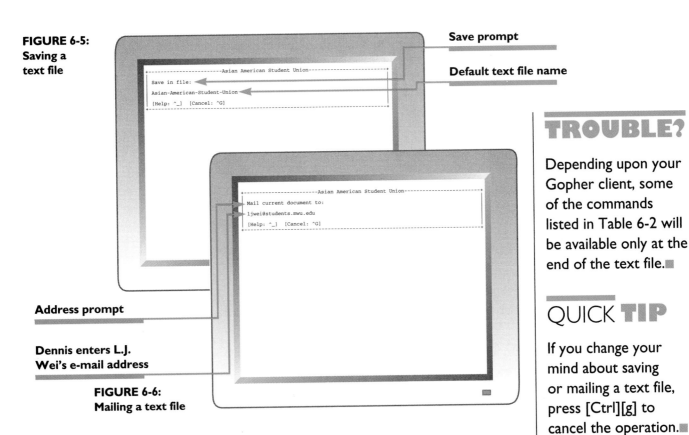

Address prompt

Dennis enters L.J.
Wei's e-mail address

FIGURE 6-6:
Mailing a text file

TROUBLE?

Depending upon your
Gopher client, some
of the commands
listed in Table 6-2 will
be available only at the
end of the text file.■

QUICK TIP

If you change your
mind about saving
or mailing a text file,
press [Ctrl][g] to
cancel the operation.■

Navigating Gopher

Once you know how to navigate Gopher menus, you can access almost any Internet resource available through Gopher. See the related topic "The origins of Gopher" in this lesson for information on Gopher's history. To navigate through the Gopher **menu tree**, the system of menus available on your Gopher server, you use the commands shown in Table 6-3. ▶ Dennis Wu, having finished working with the Asian American Student Union text file, goes back up the menu tree of the MidWest University Gopher server.

1 **Be sure you are at a Gopher menu, as at the end of the previous lesson**
Recall that Dennis's menu had 4 pages. If the menu you are at has only one page, skip step 2.

2 **Press [Spacebar] to view the next page of menus until you have viewed the entire menu, then press [b] until you are back to the first page**
Dennis presses [Spacebar] to view page 2 of the menus, as shown in Figure 6-7. He looks over all four pages, and then presses [b] to return to the first page of the Registered Student Organization Directory menu.

3 **Press [m] to go all the way back to the opening menu**
In the previous lesson you pressed [u] to go to the previous menu. Pressing [m] takes you all the way back to the opening menu, shown in Figure 6-8. Dennis has gone all the way back up to the top of the menu tree.

TABLE 6-3: Commands used to navigate Gopher menus

COMMAND	DESCRIPTION
[Enter], [→]	Displays currently selected item (indicated by the pointer)
u, [←]	Goes up a level in the menu tree
[↓]	Moves pointer down one line in the menu
[↑]	Moves pointer up one line in the menu
[>] , [+] , [Spacebar]	Moves to the next page of the menu
[<] , [-], b	Moves to the previous page of the menu
m	Goes to the opening menu
num	Displays item number *num*
/text	Searches for the text string *text* in the menu
n	Finds next occurrence of a prior search
S	Saves current menu to a file
?	Gets help on Gopher menu commands

FIGURE 6-7: Second page of Registered Student Organization Directory menu

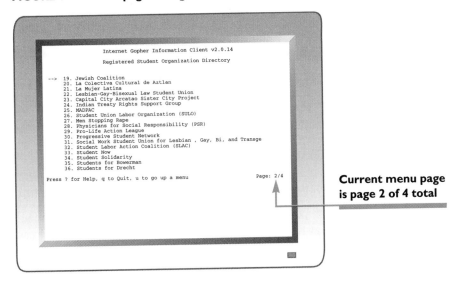

Current menu page
is page 2 of 4 total

FIGURE 6-8: Returning to MWU's opening menu

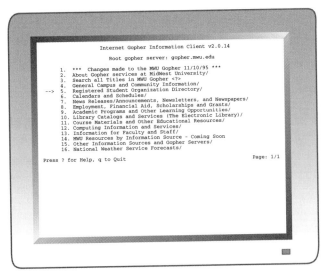

The origins of Gopher

Gopher was created in April 1991, appropriately enough, at the University of Minnesota—home of the Golden Gophers. The system was designed to help different campus departments make information available to the university community. The chief advantage of the system was that each department had control over its own Gopher server and the information it contained. To make the system easy for the students, they organized this information into easy-to-use and informative menus. Gopher caught on quickly, and there are now thousands of Gopher servers throughout the world. The University of Minnesota maintains the list of the worldwide Gopher servers.

QUICK **TIP**

Rather than using the arrow keys to point to an item and select it, type the item number, then press [Enter].■

Connecting to other Gopher servers

If Gopher had only provided access to local resources, such as the MidWest University's student group directory, it would not have become such an essential tool for Internet users. In fact, Gopher incorporates connections to other Gopher servers in its menu system, so you may find yourself on another server by simply making a menu choice. The network of different Gopher servers throughout the Internet is called **gopherspace**. As you'll see, you can navigate through gopherspace as easily as you can navigate through your local Gopher server's menus. You may not even know which Gopher server you are accessing when you select, for example, a menu item concerning federal documents. However, if you know the domain name of a Gopher server, you can access it directly (without having to navigate menus through gopherspace) by typing "gopher *domain name*" at the UNIX prompt where *domain name* is the name of the Gopher server. Table 6-4 shows a list of alternate Gopher servers that you can use instead of the server provided by your system administrator. ▶ Dennis Wu, having returned to the opening menu of MidWest University's Gopher server, now uses Gopher to connect to a Gopher server at the University of Minnesota, which he hopes to use to access an anonymous FTP site, as you will see in later lessons. Try accessing Minnesota's Gopher server yourself.

1 **Start your Gopher client if it is not already started and access the opening menu**
At the end of the previous lesson, Dennis had returned to MidWest University's opening menu. From the opening menu, he locates the menu item that gives him access to other Gopher servers (item 15 in Figure 6-8 shown in previous lesson). Try to find a similar menu item on your site's opening menu; it is often entitled, "Other Gophers and Information Sources," or variations of that title.

2 **Press the number of the menu item that offers access to other Gopher servers on the Internet, then press [Enter]**
Dennis selects item 15 on MWU's opening menu, "Other Information Sources and Gopher Servers/". A menu listing other Gopher servers appears, as shown in the first menu in Figure 6-9. If you do not see a menu listing other Gopher servers in the opening menu of your institute's Gopher server, talk to your instructor about connecting to other servers.

3 **Navigate through gopherspace to reach the Gopher server you want to access, such as the University of Minnesota**
Dennis presses [3] to select the menu item that lists midwestern Gopher servers; the second menu in Figure 6-9 appears. Paging through the menu, he discovers an entry for the University of Minnesota, the home of Gopher. Dennis then types "44" to select the University of Minnesota Gopher server. The opening menu for this server appears on the screen, as shown in the bottom menu of Figure 6-9. In the next few lessons, Dennis will use the Minnesota Gopher server to access an anonymous FTP server.

FIGURE 6-9: Three menu levels accessing the University of Minnesota Gopher server

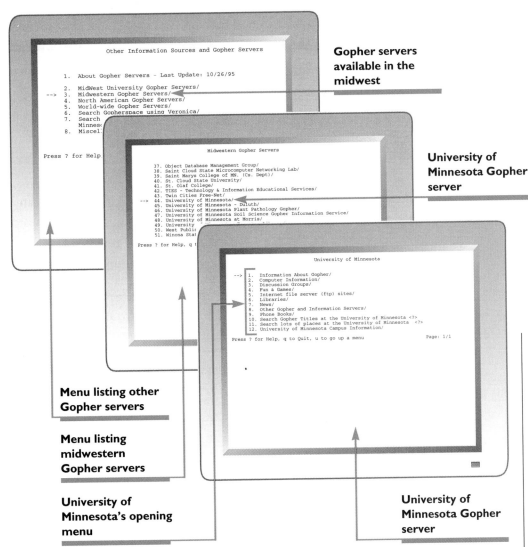

Gopher servers available in the midwest

University of Minnesota Gopher server

Menu listing other Gopher servers

Menu listing midwestern Gopher servers

University of Minnesota's opening menu

University of Minnesota Gopher server

TABLE 6-4: Domain names of some popular Gopher servers

DOMAIN NAME	DESCRIPTION
gopher.house.gov	Gopher server for the House of Representatives
gopher.senate.gov	Gopher server for the U.S. Senate
gopher.micro.umn.edu	University of Minnesota Gopher server, which offers connections to other Gopher servers, FTP sites, and public libraries
gopher.microsoft.com	Gopher server for the Microsoft Corporation, which offers bug fixes, technical support, and access to software updates
gopher.std.com	Gopher server for the commercial Internet provider World, which offers access to many public and commercial Internet sites
gopher.well.sf.ca.us	Gopher server for The WELL (The Whole Earth 'Lectronic Links)

QUICK TIP

If it is taking a long time to connect to a Gopher server, the network might be hung up, in which case you can press [Ctrl][c] to cancel your current Gopher session and try again later.■

TROUBLE?

If you can't find the University of Minnesota Gopher server by navigating menus, you can access it directly by typing "gopher *domain name*" at the UNIX prompt where *domain name* is the domain name of the Gopher server.■

Using Gopher to access anonymous FTP servers

In the previous unit you used anonymous FTP sites to access and download files. Gopher makes that process even easier by sending the FTP commands for you, saving you the trouble of memorizing the FTP command list. With Gopher you can view text files posted on the FTP server, download files, or upload files. You might also find that moving through the FTP server's directory tree is easier with Gopher since the commands to move through the FTP file tree are the same as those used in moving through the Gopher's menu tree. ▶ In the previous lesson, Dennis Wu accessed the Gopher server for the University of Minnesota. Dennis decides to investigate some FTP servers using Gopher, hoping that he can find and then download software that he can use to set up a Gopher client on his own Macintosh computer.

1 Be sure you are connected to a Gopher server that can access an anonymous FTP server (try the Gopher at gopher.micro.umn.edu if your local Gopher doesn't offer this feature)

At the end of the previous lesson, Dennis successfully accessed the University of Minnesota opening menu, the first menu in Figure 6-10. He now looks for a menu item that gives him access to FTP sites. Item 5, "Internet file server (ftp) sites/", looks promising.

2 Select the menu item that offers access to an anonymous FTP server

Dennis selects item 5; the second menu in Figure 6-10 appears, displaying a short list of options regarding FTP server sites. Item 3, "Popular FTP Sites via Gopher/", looks like it will lead to FTP server sites.

3 Continue navigating through gopherspace until you find an FTP server that offers files you might want to access

Dennis selects item 3, which opens the third menu shown in Figure 6-10, "Popular FTP Sites via Gopher," and lists several popular anonymous FTP server sites.

4 Select the menu item that offers access to an FTP server site

Noticing that item 17 in the third menu (as shown in Figure 6-10) offers software archives, Dennis chooses this item to access the FTP server site at the University of Michigan.

FIGURE 6-10: Navigating through the University of Minnesota Gopher server to find software archives

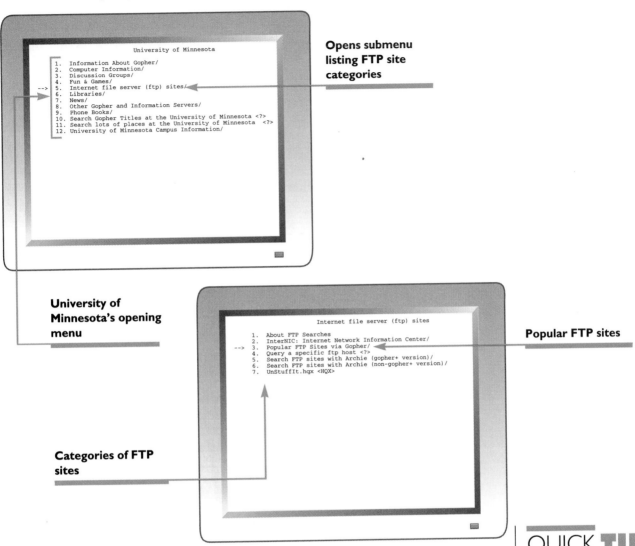

Opens submenu
listing FTP site
categories

University of
Minnesota's opening
menu

Popular FTP sites

Categories of FTP
sites

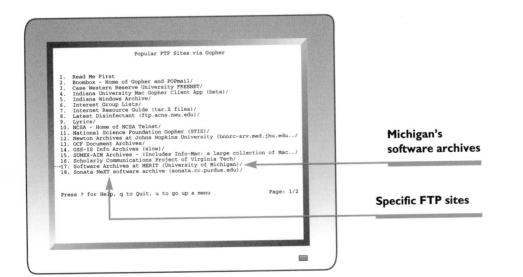

Michigan's
software archives

Specific FTP sites

QUICK TIP

To return quickly to
the opening menu of
your Gopher server,
press [m].■

NETIQUETTE

Anonymous FTP
servers are provided
free of charge, so try
to limit your access
to the server's low-use
hours (usually after
7 p.m., depending
on the time zone).■

Using Gopher to download a binary file

In the previous unit you learned how to download a binary file using FTP. With Gopher the process is much easier, because Gopher sends all the required FTP commands for you. You can treat a binary file as an item, the same way you treat a text file or submenu. See the related topic "Menu item types" for more information on other types of items. ▶ Now that Dennis has accessed the University of Michigan's anonymous FTP server, which he knows offers a variety of software files, he starts his search for the software that will help him set up a Gopher client on his Macintosh. As you follow Dennis through the steps at the University of Michigan FTP server, navigate an FTP server of your own, looking for a program that interests you.

1 Be sure you are connected to an anonymous FTP server via Gopher
2 Move through the FTP server in the same way you move through Gopher's menu structure until you find the file you want
   The opening menu for the software archives at the University of Michigan's FTP server, shown in Figure 6-11, offers both an item for Macintosh software (item 6) and for Internet tools (item 8). Dennis decides to try item 8. The Internet Tools Archive submenu opens, and Dennis first selects item 1, "mac." In the mac submenu, Dennis chooses item 3, "gopher," which opens the gopher submenu. The gopher submenu, shown in Figure 6-12, lists six Macintosh files that might be useful; the third, macgopher, looks the most promising. As he's been moving down the Gopher menu tree, he's also been moving through the directory of the anonymous FTP server. Gopher has been sending FTP commands to the server and relaying the results back to him.
3 Once you have found the file you're interested in, select the item
   Dennis presses [3] to retrieve the macgopher program, which is a binary file. He is prompted to enter a file name.
4 Enter the name you want to give the file on your local machine, then press **[Enter]**
   Dennis types "macgopher0.5b14.sit.hqx" after the Save in file prompt, and then presses [Enter], as shown in Figure 6-13. Gopher downloads this file to his account.
5 Press **[m]** to return to your site's opening menu

TABLE 6-5: Common gopher labels

TAG	MEANING	TAG	MEANING	TAG	MEANING
(none)	Text file	<BIN>	Binary file	<??>	ASK form
/	Submenu	<HQX>	BinHexed Macintosh file	<Picture>	Image file
<)	Sound file	<Movie>	Movie file	<TEL>	Telnet connection
<?>	Index search item	<PC BIN>	PC binary file		

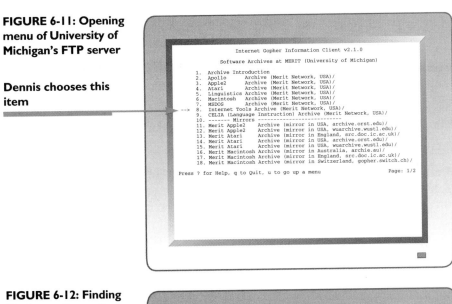

FIGURE 6-11: Opening menu of University of Michigan's FTP server

Dennis chooses this item

```
                    Internet Gopher Information Client v2.1.0

                  Software Archives at MERIT (University of Michigan)

      1.  Archive Introduction
      2.  Apollo    Archive (Merit Network, USA)/
      3.  Apple2    Archive (Merit Network, USA)/
      4.  Atari     Archive (Merit Network, USA)/
      5.  Linguistics Archive (Merit Network, USA)/
      6.  Macintosh  Archive (Merit Network, USA)/
      7.  MSDOS      Archive (Merit Network, USA)/
 -->  8.  Internet Tools Archive (Merit Network, USA)/
      9.  CELIA (Language Instruction) Archive (Merit Network, USA)/
     10.  ------- Mirrors -------------------------
     11.  Merit Apple2    Archive (mirror in USA, archive.orst.edu)/
     12.  Merit Apple2    Archive (mirror in USA, wuarchive.wustl.edu)/
     13.  Merit Atari     Archive (mirror in England, src.doc.ic.ac.uk)/
     14.  Merit Atari     Archive (mirror in USA, archive.orst.edu)/
     15.  Merit Atari     Archive (mirror in USA, wuarchive.wustl.edu)/
     16.  Merit Macintosh Archive (mirror in Australia, archie.au)/
     17.  Merit Macintosh Archive (mirror in England, src.doc.ic.ac.uk)/
     18.  Merit Macintosh Archive (mirror in Switzerland, gopher.switch.ch)/

Press ? for Help, q to Quit, u to go up a menu                  Page: 1/2
```

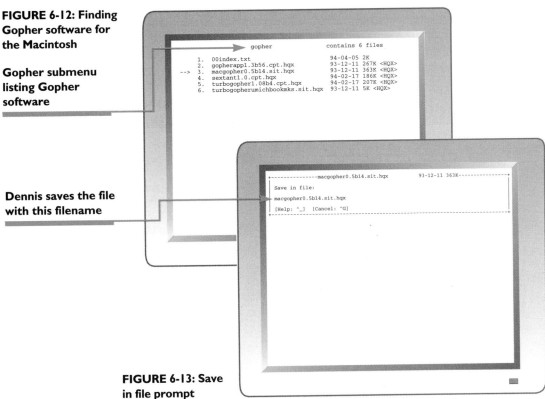

FIGURE 6-12: Finding Gopher software for the Macintosh

Gopher submenu listing Gopher software

```
            gopher              contains 6 files

      1.  00index.txt                      94-04-05 2K
      2.  gopherapp1.3b56.cpt.hqx          93-12-11 267K <HQX>
 -->  3.  macgopher0.5b14.sit.hqx          93-12-11 363K <HQX>
      4.  sextant1.0.cpt.hqx               94-02-17 186K <HQX>
      5.  turbogopher1.08b4.cpt.hqx        94-02-17 207K <HQX>
      6.  turbogopherumichbookmks.sit.hqx  93-12-11 5K <HQX>
```

Dennis saves the file with this filename

```
+------------macgopher0.5b14.sit.hqx          93-12-11 363K------------+
|                                                                     |
|  Save in file:                                                      |
|                                                                     |
|  macgopher0.5b14.sit.hqx                                            |
|                                                                     |
|  [Help: ^_]  [Cancel: ^G]                                           |
+---------------------------------------------------------------------+
```

FIGURE 6-13: Save in file prompt

Menu item types

Each item in a Gopher menu is classified as a specific type. So far, you've seen two menu item types: text files and submenus. An item is identified as a submenu by the front slash (/) tagged to the item name. Text files have no special labels. Gopher identifies other types of items with tags. For example, if you're connected to an anonymous FTP server through Gopher, binary files are usually identified by a <BIN>, <PC BIN>, or <HQX> label. The file Dennis Wu downloaded in this lesson had a <HQX> label. Table 6-5 shows a list of common Gopher labels and their meanings.

Using Gopher to access Telnet sites

Just as Gopher helped you access anonymous FTP servers, it can also help you find lists of public Telnet sites, offering convenient Gopher menus for easy access. The most popular Telnet sites are campus library computers that provide information on library holdings. ▶ Dennis Wu, having downloaded the file he wanted from the University of Michigan's FTP server, now decides to explore the on-line capabilities of MidWest University's campus library to see how easily he'll be able to conduct research for his classes. He can do this through Telnet, or he can let Gopher make the Telnet connection for him.

1 Be sure you are at your Gopher site's opening menu

2 Use Gopher to access a Telnet item (identified by the characters <TEL> appended to the item name)
Dennis is back at the same opening menu shown in Figure 6-8. He then selects item 10, "Library Catalogs and Services (The Electronic Library)/", to display the menu he wants shown in Figure 6-14. Item 3 is a Telnet item connecting to the MWU library card catalog.

3 Select the Telnet resource by either typing the resource number or moving the pointer to the resource and pressing **[Enter]**
Dennis presses [3] to create a Telnet session with the MidWest University Library Catalog computer. A prompt appears notifying Dennis that he is about to connect to the site, shown in Figure 6-15.

4 When prompted with this notice about connecting to the Telnet site, press **[Enter]**
The library computer responds with the Welcome screen shown in Figure 6-16. Dennis explores the catalog resources and begins learning about how to use it for his research. When he is finished with the library computer, he logs out (you can do the same at your site, using whatever command that computer requires) and is returned to the Gopher menu right where he left it.

FIGURE 6-14: Library Catalogs and Services menu with Telnet site

Telnet item

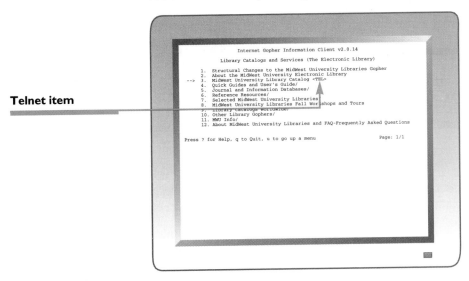

FIGURE 6-15: Telnet prompt

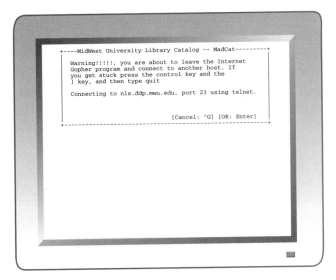

FIGURE 6-16: Opening screen of MWU's library computer catalog

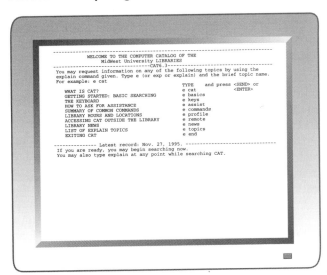

TROUBLE?

To disconnect from a Telnet session press [Ctrl][right bracket] to access a Telnet command prompt and then type "quit"; this terminates the Telnet session and returns you to the Gopher menu.■

QUICK TIP

If you want to keep up with the changes in Gopher and Gopher servers, consider subscribing to the comp.infosystems. gopher and alt.gopher newsgroups.■

Creating bookmarks

As you've seen, a Gopher server's menu structure can do a good job of organizing a wealth of diverse information. Sometimes you may feel it is a little *too* organized. After all, do you really have to go through five menu levels to get to that one service you're interested in? The answer is, not always. If you use an Internet resource regularly, you can create a **bookmark** that directly connects you to the resource and bypasses all the other menus. Gopher organizes your bookmarks into a customized Gopher menu that lists the resources that interest you. Table 6-6 shows the Gopher commands you use to create and maintain bookmarks, as well as a selection of additional useful Gopher commands. See the related topic "Suspending Gopher" in this lesson for another useful trick you can use during a Gopher session. ▶ Dennis Wu decides to add a bookmark for the anonymous FTP server he contacted to download the macgopher software in lesson 5.

1 Be sure you are at your Gopher site's opening menu

2 Navigate the Gopher menu tree to point to the item you want to tag as a bookmark
   Using the Gopher menus from the MidWest University Gopher server, Dennis returns to the list of popular anonymous FTP servers he accessed earlier and moves the pointer to item 17, the "Software Archives at MERIT (University of Michigan)", shown earlier in Figure 6-10.

3 Press **[a]** to add the item you want to your bookmark list, then enter a bookmark name when prompted
   Dennis presses [a] to add the University of Michigan software archive to his list of bookmarks. Gopher prompts him for the name of the resource, and he accepts the default name by pressing [Enter]. See Figure 6-17. Now that he's created the bookmark, he wants to see how his bookmark menu looks.

4 Press **[v]** to view your menu of bookmarks
   Dennis presses [v] to view his bookmark list, which appears as shown in Figure 6-18. He has added only one bookmark to his list so far. Any time he wants to access the University of Michigan software archives, he can press [v] to activate his bookmark menu and then press [1].

5 Press **[q]** to quit Gopher, then press **[y]** to return to the UNIX command prompt
   Dennis is now finished with his Gopher session. He has accessed four Internet hosts and several different Internet resources in one sitting.

FIGURE 6-17:
Bookmark prompt

Default bookmark name for software archives site

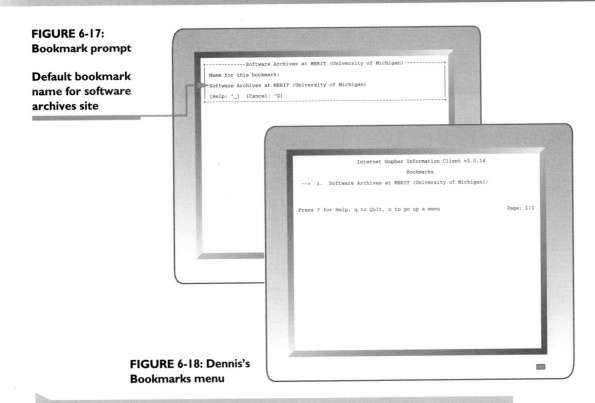

FIGURE 6-18: Dennis's Bookmarks menu

Suspending Gopher

If you need to use your local host but keep your Gopher session active, press [!] to suspend Gopher. You can then send e-mail to a colleague, view some of the files you accessed, or start another software program. To return to your Gopher session type "exit" at the UNIX command prompt. This command may not work for all clients, so you should talk with your instructor about ways of suspending Gopher on your system.

TABLE 6-6: Miscellaneous Gopher commands

COMMAND	DESCRIPTION
a	Adds current item to bookmark list
A	Adds current menu to bookmark list
v	Views bookmark list
d	Deletes bookmark/menu entry
q	Quits Gopher with a prompt
Q	Quits Gopher without a prompt
o *gopher name*	Opens the Gopher server *gopher name*
!	Escapes to the UNIX command prompt

QUICK **TIP**

To start Gopher with your bookmark list displayed rather than with the opening menu of the local Gopher server displayed, type "gopher -b" at the UNIX command prompt.■

CONCEPTSREVIEW

Label each of the elements shown in this figure.

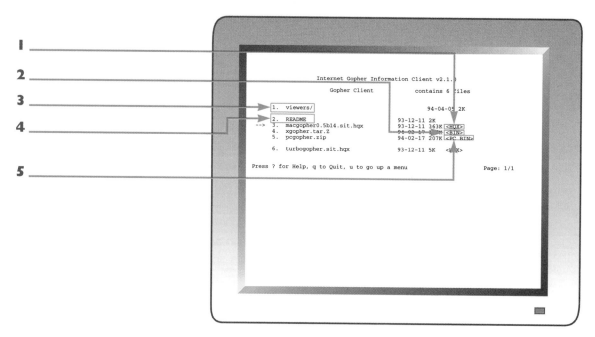

I

2

3

4

5

```
                    Internet Gopher Information Client v2.1.0

                    Gopher Client              contains 6 files

                                                    94-04-05 2K
            1.  viewers/
            2.  README                       93-12-11 2K
       -->  3.  macgopher0.5b14.sit.hqx      93-12-11 363K <HQX>
            4.  xgopher.tar.Z                94-00-19 1.7M <BIN>
            5.  pcgopher.zip                 94-02-17 207K <PC BIN>

            6.  turbogopher.sit.hqx          93-12-11 5K   <HQX>


     Press ? for Help, q to Quit, u to go up a menu           Page: 1/1
```

FIGURE 6-19

Match each of the statements with the term it describes.

6 A single full screen of information; either part of a Gopher menu or text file

7 The Internet host that organizes various Internet resources into Gopher menus

8 A user-defined item that connects you directly to a resource, bypassing the need to navigate through Gopher menus

9 The software program that receives and displays Gopher menus

10 The network of Gopher servers and their connections to other Internet resources

11 The arrow to select specific items within a Gopher menu

a. Gopher client program

b. pointer

c. Gopher server

d. gopherspace

e. bookmark

f. page

Select the best answer from the list of choices.

12 While viewing a text file, to save the contents to a file

 a. Press [s] and type the text filename when prompted.

 b. Type "get *filename.*"

 c. Type "save" and the text filename when prompted.

 d. Press [S] and the text filename when prompted.

 e. All of the above are correct.

13 To view the next page of a menu that covers several pages, press

 a. [Spacebar]

 b. [+]

 c. [>]

 d. All of the above are correct.

14 To view the menu one level up from the current menu, press

 a. [b]

 b. [-]

 c. [u]

 d. [<]

 e. All of the above are correct.

15 To connect to the Gopher server located at gopher.micro.umn.edu

    a. Type "gopher gopher.micro.umn.edu" at the UNIX command prompt.

    b. With Gopher running, press [o] and then "gopher.micro.umn.edu" when prompted.

    c. Navigate gopherspace to access the University of Minnesota Gopher server.

    d. All of the above are correct.

16 To save a binary file from an anonymous FTP server using Gopher

    a. Press [Enter] when the pointer is pointing to the binary file and give the file a name when prompted.

    b. Type the item number for the file, press [Enter], then give the file a name when prompted.

    c. Set the Gopher file option to binary and type "get *filename.*"

    d. Answers a & b are correct.

    e. Answers b & c are correct.

APPLICATIONS
REVIEW

Note that the Gopher servers in this review are currently active, but this may not always be the case. The menus also may change between the publication date of this book and time that it gets to you. If you have problems with this review, see your professor about other Gopher resources to practice with.

1 Use Gopher to access the House of Representatives Gopher server.

    a. Connect to the House of Representatives Gopher server by typing "gopher gopher.house.gov" at the UNIX command prompt.

    b. Select the first item on the opening menu, "About the US House Gopher/."

    c. Select the first item on the "About the US House Gopher" submenu titled "Welcome to the US House Gopher."

    d. Read the text file. Who should you send e-mail to if you have trouble using the House Gopher?

    e. Press [u] to return to the Gopher menus.

    f. Press [q] to quit Gopher.

2 You are planning a trip to Washington, D.C., and would like to know when public tours are given at the National Archives. Use Gopher to find this information.

    a. Connect to the National Archives Gopher server by typing "gopher gopher.nara.gov" at the UNIX command prompt.

    b. Choose "Exhibits, Events and Training Courses/" from the opening menu of the NARA Gopher server.

    c. Choose "Tours/" from the Exhibits submenu.

    d. View the text file "Public Tours Offered at the New National Archives in College Park." Save the text file to your account. What are the hours and days that tours are offered?

    e. Press [u] to return to the Gopher menus.

    f. Press [q] to quit Gopher.

3 Connect to your local Gopher server. By navigating gopherspace, try to reach the U.S. Bureau of the Census Gopher server and report on the present population of the United States.

    a. Connect to your local Gopher server by typing "gopher" at the UNIX command prompt.

    b. Select a menu item titled "Other Information Sources and Gopher Servers/" (or a variation of this title).

    c. Select a menu item titled "World-Wide Gopher Servers/."

    d. Continue to refine your selections until you reach a menu of Gopher servers organized by states. Choose "Gopher servers located in Washington DC." Within that menu choose the server for the U.S. Bureau of the Census.

    e. Within the U.S. Bureau of the Census Gopher choose "Enter the Main Data Bank/" from the opening menu and then "Population Data/."

    f. Choose the item "POPClock Projection" and report on the population of the United States. Be sure to record the exact date and time of POPClock's estimate.

    g. Using the u command, work your way up through the menu tree back to your local Gopher server.

4 Practice connecting to an anonymous FTP server with Gopher.

    a. Connect to the University of Minnesota Gopher by typing "gopher gopher.micro.umn.edu" at the UNIX command prompt, or navigate through gopherspace until you reach this server.

    b. Select the "Internet file server (ftp) sites/" menu item and then the "Query a specific ftp host <?>" item within that menu.

    c. When prompted for the domain name of the anonymous FTP server, enter one of the servers listed in Table 5-3 (or ask your instructor for an anonymous FTP server that you should use).

    d. Navigate through the directories of the server and download a binary file to your account.

    e. Using the u command, work your way up through the menu tree and back to your local Gopher server.

5 Practice connecting to a Telnet site with Gopher.

   a. Connect to the Library of Congress Gopher by typing "gopher marvel.loc.gov" at the UNIX command prompt or by navigating through gopherspace from your local gopher server

   b. Select the "Library of Congress Online Systems/" item from the opening menu.

   c. Select the public access LOCIS Telnet site.

   d. While connected to the Library of Congress Information System, access the Library of Congress Catalog and search for books written by Philip Gillett. How many books are recorded by the Library of Congress?

   e. Using instructions supplied by the LOCIS telnet site, exit the system, return to the Library of Congress Gopher, and quit Gopher.

INDEPENDENT
CHALLENGE 1

A popular activity on the Internet is called the "Internet Hunt," in which users compete in trying to track down obscure information. You can read the activities of the Internet Hunt by accessing the Gopher server at gopher.cic.net. Look in the submenu titled "The Internet Hunt." Here are a few examples of the questions posed for the hunt (the questions change once a month):

- I'm leaving for Japan tomorrow. Approximately how many yen can I get for my dollar, give or take a few yen?

- A hurricane just blew in! Where can I find satellite photos of its progress?

- How many copies of "Fear and Loathing in Las Vegas" does the University of Nevada at Las Vegas hold?

- What is the ISBN number for J.D. Salinger's *Nine Stories*?

To complete this independent challenge:

1 Access your local Gopher server or telnet to a public-access Gopher server.

2 Navigate through gopherspace, trying to locate Gopher servers and other Internet resources that deal with some of these questions.

3 Report your answers to the instructor, including where you discovered them. How many answers did you find?

You'll find the Internet Hunt an excellent way of testing and improving your skills. While you are searching for one piece of information you may discover something else that you weren't originally looking for that is also interesting. This is called "serendipity" and is a common occurrence while navigating gopherspace. In the next unit, you learn some ways to improve your ability to search for information on the network.

INDEPENDENT
CHALLENGE 2

If you want to locate the e-mail address of a colleague, the Internet Phone Book might be able to help. Phone books are available at several universities, and using Gopher you can access them easily. Try to use an Internet Phone Book to locate the e-mail address of Patrick M. Carey.

To complete this independent challenge:

1 Connect to the Gopher server at gopher.micro.umn.edu.

2 Select the item titled "Phone Books/".

3 Select the item titled "Phone books at other institutions/" and then work your way through the Gopher menus until you reach the Phone Book for the University of Wisconsin (titled "University of Wisconsin - Madison"). Select this item.

4 The UW-Madison Phone Book opens to reveal several fields that you can search by. Type "Patrick M Carey" in the name field and press [Enter].

5 What e-mail address is reported by the Phone Book?

Once you get experienced using the Phone Book, you can find e-mail addresses for friends and colleagues throughout the Internet.

UNIT 7

OBJECTIVES

▶ Use Archie to find a file

▶ Control output

▶ Establish search criteria

▶ Use an Archie client

▶ Use Veronica

▶ Conduct advanced Veronica searches

▶ Connect to a WAIS client

▶ Select a source

▶ Conduct a search

Finding
DATA ON THE INTERNET

A number of search tools have been developed recently that give users the ability to track down specific files or resources. Three of the most common are Archie , Veronica, and WAIS. With **Archie**, you search the contents of anonymous FTP sites without connecting to them. Similarly, with **Veronica**, you search the contents of Gopher menus without having to navigate gopherspace. With **WAIS**, you search the contents of Internet databases for files and articles on specific topics; finding the item that best matches your search criteria. ▶ Tony Donahue, an astronomy student at MidWest University, is a project assistant for astronomy professor Teresa Chou. Professor Chou is trying to keep up with scientific developments regarding the comet Shoemaker Levy-9, which collided with Jupiter in the summer of 1994. Dr. Chou asks Tony to keep her informed about the files passing through the Internet relating to the comet collision. ▶

Using Archie to find a file

Archie is an application that searches through the directories of anonymous FTP servers. There are two ways to access Archie. You can use Telnet to connect to an **Archie server**, a computer that maintains a list of the contents of anonymous FTP sites. Table 7-1 lists some popular Archie servers. Alternatively you can use an **Archie client**, which queries an Archie server for you and reports the results. You perform queries by specifying **search criteria**, a string of letters or words called **keywords** that describe the subject you are interested in. Archie responds by finding all file or directory names that match your criteria. ▶ Professor Chou has asked Tony to locate graphics on the collision of the comet. Tony uses Telnet to connect to an Archie server and search for files that might relate to the comet. Follow along with Tony using your own search subject, or one suggested by your instructor.

1 Type **telnet** *archieserver* at the UNIX command prompt, where *archieserver* is the domain name of the Archie server you want to connect to, then press **[Enter]**

Tony types "telnet archie.sura.net" to connect to the Archie server located at archie.sura.net in New Jersey. When you have successfully telnetted to the remote server, a login prompt appears.

2 Type **archie** at the login prompt, then press **[Enter]**

The Archie server displays an informational screen, as shown in Figure 7-1. Yours might look different. The archie command prompt tells Tony that he can now send commands to the server.

3 Type **find text** where *text* is the text you want Archie to search for, then press **[Enter]**

Tony types "find JupiterComet" to tell Archie to search for files or directories containing the letters "jupitercomet" (the search is not case-specific). The Archie server indicates that Tony is first in the search queue, and the estimated time for his search is about 5 seconds. Depending on the server and the time of day, you may find many users ahead of you in the queue and your searches may take much longer than 5 seconds. After the search is completed, the server displays the domain names of the anonymous FTP sites and filenames that match the search criteria, some of which are shown in Figure 7-2. Tony notices the file called JupiterComet.jpg located in the /pub/astro/SL9/images directory of the seds.lpl.arizona.edu anonymous FTP server. He knows the "jpg" extension means this is a graphics file, which might be just what Professor Chou needs. Tony records this information and quits Archie; you should record information on a file you found that looks interesting.

4 Type **quit** and then press **[Enter]** to exit the Archie server

5 Retrieve the file you found in your search using the anonymous FTP commands you learned in Unit 5

Tony connects to the FTP site at seds.lpl.arizona.edu and moves to the /pub/astro/SL9/images directory; you should connect to the site and move to the directory containing the file you found. Once Tony has the .jpg file, he starts his graphics software and views the file, which is a picture of the track of the comet as it approached Jupiter, as shown in Figure 7-3. If you retrieve a graphics file and aren't sure how to view it, talk to your instructor about which graphics software you might use.

FIGURE 7-1:
Telnetting to an
Archie server

Logging on

Information about
Archie server

Archie command
prompt

Telnet command to
connect to Archie
server

Find command to find
files matching search
criteria

Search time
information

Graphics file Tony
is interested in

Selection of files
matching Tony's
search criteria

Leaving Archie

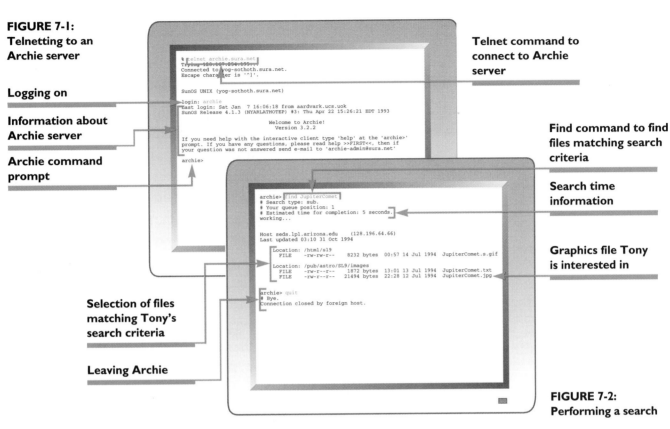

FIGURE 7-2:
Performing a search

FIGURE 7-3: The
JupiterComet.jpg file

TABLE 7-1: Popular Archie servers

DOMAIN NAME	LOCATION
archie.uqam.ca	Canada
archie.doc.ic.ac.uk	United Kingdom
archie.sura.net	USA: Maryland
archie.unl.edu	USA: Nebraska
archie.rutgers.edu	USA: New Jersey
archie.internic.net	USA: New Jersey

QUICK **TIP**

Popular Archie
servers can be very
busy at peak hours, so
you might want to get
a list of other Archie
servers you could use
by typing "server" at
the archie command
prompt.■

TROUBLE?

If an Archie search is
taking too long, you
can press [Ctrl][c]
to cancel the search.■

Controlling output

In the previous lesson you used Archie to locate a file on the Internet by entering search criteria and having the server locate all files matching those criteria. In this lesson you look at ways of controlling how Archie works by using the **set** command to set **search parameters**, additional information in the command line that limits the search. For example, the command "set search exact" tells Archie to look for files in subsequent searches that match your text string exactly, including upper and lower cases. The search Tony performed in the previous lesson was not an exact search because it was not case-sensitive. See the related topic "Types of searches" in this lesson for more information on using different search parameters to alter your searches. In this lesson you'll use a set command that tells Archie where to mail a copy of your search results. ▶ Tony continues looking for files dealing with the Shoemaker Levy-9 comet, this time using the search criteria "shoemaker." Tony decides to take advantage of Archie's mail capabilities to mail the results to himself. He can then save the resulting e-mail message and edit it before forwarding it to Professor Chou. You can try these steps using an Archie server on a topic that interests you.

1   Connect to an Archie server
As in the previous lesson, Tony types "telnet archie.sura.net" to connect to the Archie server at archie.sura.net. He logs on with the user name "archie." Tony now tells Archie to mail all subsequent search results to his e-mail address.

2   Type **set mailto** *address* at the Archie command prompt, where *address* is the e-mail address you want results sent to, then press **[Enter]**
Tony types "set mailto donahue@students.mwu.edu" so that Archie will send future search results to his e-mail address, as shown in the first part of Figure 7-4.

3   Type **find** *text* at the archie command prompt, where *text* represents the topic you're interested in, then press **[Enter]**
Tony types "find shoemaker" at the archie command prompt to find any files or directories containing the word "shoemaker." After a few minutes Archie displays the results on the screen. Figure 7-4 shows a selection of the results. Tony now uses the mail command to tell Archie to mail the search results to the e-mail address he specified in the set mailto command.

4   Type **mail** at the archie command prompt, then press **[Enter]**
The Archie server mails the results to Tony's e-mail account.

5   Type **quit** and press **[Enter]** to exit the Archie server

FIGURE 7-4: Mailing search results to an e-mail address

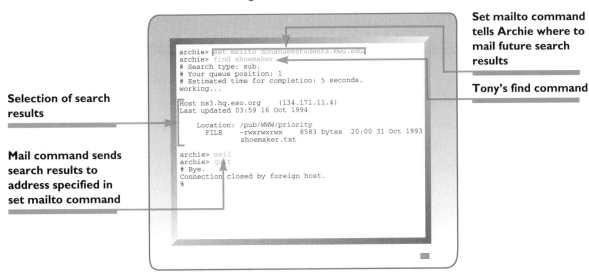

Set mailto command tells Archie where to mail future search results

Tony's find command

Selection of search results

Mail command sends search results to address specified in set mailto command

```
archie> set mailto donahue@students.mwu.edu
archie> find shoemaker
# Search type: sub.
# Your queue position: 1
# Estimated time for completion: 5 seconds.
working...

Host ns3.hq.eso.org    (134.171.11.4)
Last updated 03:59 16 Oct 1994

    Location: /pub/WWW/priority
       FILE     -rwxrwxrwx    8583 bytes  20:00 31 Oct 1993
                shoemaker.txt

archie> mail
archie> quit
# Bye.
Connection closed by foreign host.
%
```

Types of searches

There are three basic searches you can use with Archie. The default method is the **sub search**, which searches for filenames that contain the text string you specify, regardless of case or position in the file text string. This is the kind of search Tony performed in the previous lesson. To use a different search method, you specify the search parameter with the set command, as Tony did in this lesson. A second search method is the **subcase search**, which searches for filenames that contain your search criteria with the proper case. If Tony had performed a subcase search on "shoemaker," for example, Archie would have returned shoemaker levy-9.mpg but not SHOEMAKER.TXT. A final search method is the **exact search**, which returns only filenames that match the text string exactly, with the proper case and without any extraneous letters. Using the exact search for the text string "shoemaker" would return a file named shoemaker, but not SHOEMAKER.TXT or shoemaker levy-9.mpg. You use an exact search when you know the exact name of the file you want and do not want to receive a lot of extra output.

TROUBLE?

If your search returns no files, check the search parameter by typing "show search" at the Archie prompt to verify that the search is not set to exact.■

QUICK TIP

To limit the number of files that Archie returns, type "set maxhits *number*" at the archie command prompt, where *number* is the largest number of files matching the query you want reported.■

Establishing search criteria

In Tony's searches so far, he has entered search criteria that he thinks will find good matches. He can, however, get help on selecting which criteria to enter by performing a **whatis search**, a search that identifies files according to sets of keywords by using the **Software Description Database**, a database created by system administrators containing thousands of entries that describe the files loaded on their servers. For example, a system administrator who receives a graphic file of Jupiter pinpointing the location of Shoemaker Levy-9's impact might assign the following keywords: "Jupiter," "comet," and "Shoemaker-Levy." Whatis searches are limited since a keyword list does not exist for all FTP servers, nor is the list always up-to-date at those sites where the list is used. For example, searches with the keyword "impact" would not locate this file. Still, whatis searches can be useful when you know general information about the topic but don't have an exact file-name. Table 7-2 shows other useful Archie commands. ▶ For an astronomy project, Tony Donahue is searching for a software program that calculates the time that the moon sets on any given day. To find such a program, Tony could search for files containing the word "moon," but the search results would probably include many irrelevant files. He decides to use a whatis search to see whether such a program has been entered in the Software Description Database. Follow along with Tony using a search word of your own.

I Connect to an Archie server
Tony types "telnet archie.sura.net" to connect to the Archie server at archie.sura.net and logs on with the username "archie."

2 Type **whatis text** at the archie command prompt where *text* is a keyword describing the general information you are interested in, then press **[Enter]**
Tony types "whatis moon" at the archie command prompt to list files related to the moon. The Archie server searches the Software Description Database and returns two columns of information. The left column shows keywords for various anonymous FTP files, while the right column describes what the keyword refers to. Tony sees immediately that the keyword "rise_set" refers to a program that calculates rising and setting information for the sun and moon. See the first part of Figure 7-5.

3 Type **find text** at the Archie command prompt, where *text* is one of the keywords returned by the whatis command, then press **[Enter]**
Tony types "find rise_set" at the Archie command prompt to find the location of the rise_set program. Archie responds with the locations of files that include "rise_set" in their filenames. Figure 7-5 shows a portion of the results of Tony's search. He decides to retrieve the file rise_set.Z.

4 Type **quit** to exit the Archie server, then press **[Enter]**

5 Retrieve the file you found using the FTP commands from Unit 5
Tony retrieves the file rise_set.Z from the anonymous FTP site located at wuarchive.wustl.edu in the /usenet/comp.sources.unix/volume05 directory.

FIGURE 7-5: Performing a whatis search

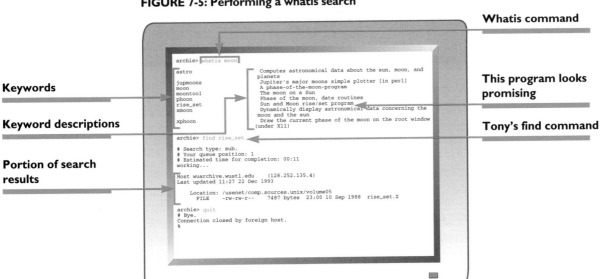

Whatis command

Keywords

Keyword descriptions

Portion of search results

This program looks promising

Tony's find command

TABLE 7-2: Commonly used Archie server commands

COMMAND	DESCRIPTION	COMMAND	DESCRIPTION
find *text*	Searches anonymous FTP sites for files or directories with the word *text*	set search exact	Searches for an exact pattern that discerns case and finds files containing only the text string you enter
help	Displays a list of Archie server commands	set search exact_sub	Tries an exact search first and then uses a sub search
mail	Mails the results of a search to an e-mail address set using the set mailto command	set search sub	Searches for anything that contains the pattern, regardless of case
manpage	Displays the Archie server manual (use set pager first to display the manual one page at a time)	set search subcase	Searches for anything that contains the pattern, but distinguishes by case
quit	Exits the Archie server	set sortby filename	Sorts search results by filename
server	Displays a list of Archie servers	set sortby hostname	Sorts search results by hostname
set maxhits *number*	Sets the maximum number of items matching the search criteria to *number*	set sortby time	Sorts search results by time and date, youngest to oldest
set pager	Shows results one full screen at a time	show	Shows the status of all Archie server variables

Using an Archie client

In the last several lessons Tony telnetted to an Archie server to perform his searches, but you may have found that telnetting is more trouble than it's worth because the servers are too busy to let you in. A common solution is to use an **Archie client**, a program that contacts the Archie server for you, making the queries that you have defined and returning the information back to your local computer. Your Internet host may include an Archie client in its software library. The client program, since it is local to your computer, is always available and is much faster than telnetting to the Archie server. You can send special commands to the Archie server by including parameters or switches (as discussed in Unit 1) with the Archie client. Table 7-3 shows a list of these parameters. ▶ Because of increased use of anonymous FTP sites, MidWest University computer system administrators have decided to install an Archie client program on their machine. Tony Donahue uses the new Archie client software to look for additional graphics files containing pictures from the Voyager space probe for Professor Chou. He uses a single command to set two search parameters and to specify his search criteria.

1   Type **archie *parameters text*** at the UNIX command prompt, where *parameters* are any special parameters you want to include and *text* is the text you want to search for, then press **[Enter]**
    Tony types "archie -m10 -t voyager" at the UNIX command prompt. The -m10 parameter tells Archie to return a maximum of 10 files, while the -t parameter sorts the files by date and time. After a moment, the Archie client reports the results from the Archie server, shown in Figure 7-6. Because Tony's keyword was so general, he receives some irrelevant information, like a file on the Star Trek Voyager television series. Note that some of the matches are directories, not files, such as the /pub/spacegifs/voyager directory located at the ftp.vmars.tuwien.ac.at anonymous FTP site.

2   Use FTP to locate and retrieve the file that interests you using the commands you learned in Unit 5
    Tony searches through the directories returned by Archie and finds a file containing a picture taken by Voyager of the rings of Saturn, as shown in Figure 7-7. He knows Professor Chou will be interested in this file, so he retrieves it.

3   View the file using the appropriate software
    Tony uses a graphics package to open the file, which Professor Chou later converts to a slide and uses in her lecture.

FIGURE 7-6:
Performing a search using an Archie client

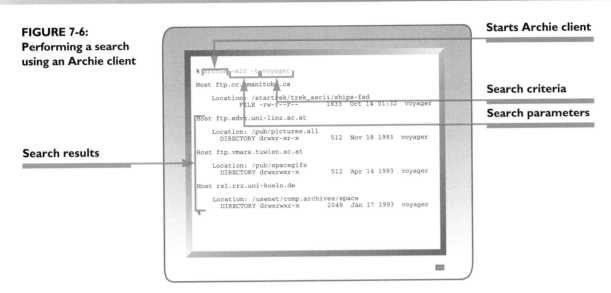

Starts Archie client

Search criteria

Search parameters

Search results

```
% archie -m10 -t voyager
Host ftp.cc.manitoba.ca

      Location: /startrek/trek_ascii/ships-fed
               FILE -rw-r--r--      1833  Oct 14 01:32  voyager
Host ftp.edvz.uni-linz.ac.at

      Location: /pub/pictures.all
         DIRECTORY drwxr-xr-x        512  Nov 18 1993  voyager
Host ftp.vmars.tuwien.ac.at

      Location: /pub/spacegifs
         DIRECTORY drwxrwxr-x        512  Apr 14 1993  voyager
Host rs1.rrz.uni-koeln.de

      Location: /usenet/comp.archives/space
         DIRECTORY drwxrwxr-x       2048  Jan 17 1993  voyager
%
```

FIGURE 7-7:
Graphics file showing rings of Saturn

TROUBLE?

The default search setting for the Archie client is "-e" (the exact setting), so if you want to allow searches that include both upper and lower cases, be sure to enter the -s parameter in your Archie command.■

TABLE 7-3: Parameters used with the Archie client

PARAMETER	DESCRIPTION
-c	Searches for patterns containing the text string, case sensitive (equivalent to "set search subcase")
-e	Searches for an exact match to the text string (equivalent to "set search exact")
-s	Searches for patterns contain the text string, regardless of case (equivalent to "set search sub")
-o *filename*	Sends output to a file named *filename*
-t	Sorts output by date and time
-m*number*	Sets the maximum number of files returned by the server to *number*
-h *domain*	Specifies the Archie server with the domain name *domain* to tell your client which Archie server to connect to
-L	Shows a list of Archie servers
-V	Makes comments during a long search

Using Veronica

Veronica is a search tool like Archie, except that Veronica searches gopherspace rather than anonymous FTP servers. Veronica has several advantages over Archie. Veronica performs more complicated searches and looks for types of files as well as filenames. Once you find the file, you can instantly retrieve it, while with Archie you have to leave the Archie server and then start an anonymous FTP session. Finally, since anonymous FTP servers are a part of gopherspace, you can use Veronica to duplicate many Archie searches. There is one drawback, though. Since there are no Veronica clients, you can only run Veronica within Gopher, and you must navigate through gopherspace to find the Veronica program. Often it is located within a menu that directs you to other gopher servers, such as "Other Information Sources and Gopher Servers/." ▶ Tony Donahue continues his research into the Voyager probe by using Veronica to search for the keyword "voyager" in gopherspace. Follow along with Tony by navigating gopherspace from your site; your instructor can help you find which Gopher menus you should navigate to find the Veronica program.

1   Type **gopher** at the UNIX command prompt then press **[Enter]**
2   Search gopherspace, selecting a menu item similar to **Other Information Sources and Gopher Servers/**
    Tony selects item 15 on the opening Gopher menu at MidWest University, which points to other information sources; you can refer back to Figure 6-1 in the previous unit if you want to see this menu.
3   Look for a menu item similar to **Search Gopherspace using Veronica/** and select it
    Tony selects a menu item titled "Search Gopherspace using Veronica/." Gopher then gives him a wide choice of servers and searches. Item 6 on Tony's menu lets him search gopherspace for menu items only (as opposed to menus and files). Your menu might have any combination of these items; choose whichever seems likeliest to accommodate a search of just menu items. Your instructor can help you navigate gopherspace from your site to find an appropriate Veronica server.
4   Type the menu item corresponding to the Veronica server and the type of search you want, then press **[Enter]**
    If you have successfully started Veronica, you are prompted to enter your search criteria.
5   Type your search criteria, then press **[Enter]**
    As shown in Figure 7-8, Tony types "voyager" at the prompt. After a few seconds (or minutes, depending on how busy the Veronica server is), a list of Gopher items containing the word "voyager" (not case sensitive) is returned on a menu all its own, as shown in Figure 7-9. The menu title specifies which Veronica item you chose in step 4 and which search criteria you entered in step 5.
6   Navigate the Gopher menus that resulted from your search until you find the item you want
    Tony selects item 2 in Figure 7-9 to look at the contents of the first VOYAGER directory. He eventually discovers a file containing the daily Voyager mission logs. Figure 7-10 shows the Voyager mission log Tony finds for January 4, 1991.

Simplified veronica: Find Gopher MENUS only
Words to search for
voyager
[Help: ^_] [Cancel: ^G]
Tony's search criteria

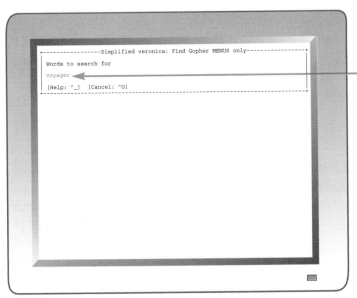

FIGURE 7-8: Veronica search prompt

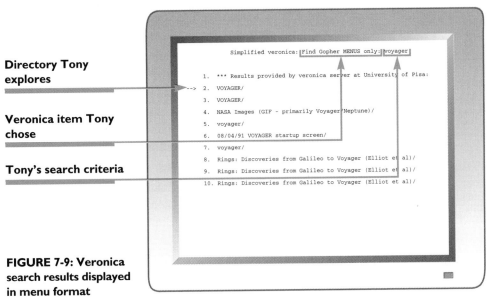

Directory Tony explores
Veronica item Tony chose
Tony's search criteria
Simplified veronica: Find Gopher MENUS only: voyager
1. *** Results provided by veronica server at University of Pisa:
--> 2. VOYAGER/
3. VOYAGER/
4. NASA Images (GIF - primarily Voyager/Neptune)/
5. voyager/
6. 08/04/91 VOYAGER startup screen/
7. voyager/
8. Rings: Discoveries from Galileo to Voyager (Elliot et al)/
9. Rings: Discoveries from Galileo to Voyager (Elliot et al)/
10. Rings: Discoveries from Galileo to Voyager (Elliot et al)/

FIGURE 7-9: Veronica search results displayed in menu format

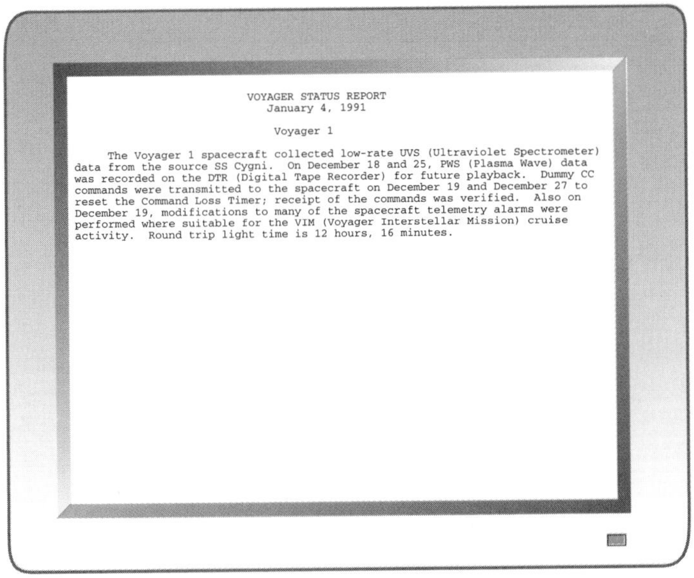

VOYAGER STATUS REPORT
January 4, 1991
Voyager 1
The Voyager 1 spacecraft collected low-rate UVS (Ultraviolet Spectrometer) data from the source SS Cygni. On December 18 and 25, PWS (Plasma Wave) data was recorded on the DTR (Digital Tape Recorder) for future playback. Dummy CC commands were transmitted to the spacecraft on December 19 and December 27 to reset the Command Loss Timer; receipt of the commands was verified. Also on December 19, modifications to many of the spacecraft telemetry alarms were performed where suitable for the VIM (Voyager Interstellar Mission) cruise activity. Round trip light time is 12 hours, 16 minutes.

FIGURE 7-10: Voyager mission log text file

QUICK TIP

When you discover the location of the Veronica server, create a bookmark for it (as discussed in Unit 5) so you can access it quickly the next time you need it.

Conducting advanced Veronica searches

Like Archie, Veronica offers many options for performing more advanced searches. The related topic "Search parameters" in this lesson gives more information on Veronica search parameters, while Table 7-4 gives you the specific switch names to include. In addition, Veronica allows the use of qualifiers such as and, or, and not. For example, to search gopherspace for items containing the words "Jupiter" or "comet," you enter "Jupiter or comet" as your search criteria. You can also use parentheses to combine different search criteria. To search for items that contain the words "images" and either "Jupiter" or "comet," you enter "(Jupiter or comet) and images" as your search criteria. ▶ Tony uses Veronica to search specifically for graphics files of the comet Shoemaker Levy-9 for Professor Chou.

1 **Navigate the menu tree to search for both menu items and files**
   Tony returns to the menu that lists Veronica servers and selects item 7, which lets him search for all files as well as menus. He is again prompted for his search criteria.

2 **Enter your search criteria, using appropriate qualifiers, then press [Enter]**
   Tony types "(jupiter and comet) or shoemaker -tI -m50," as shown in Figure 7-11. This instructs Veronica to search for gopher items containing the words "jupiter" and "comet" or the word "shoemaker." The "-tI -m50" switches tell Veronica to search for image (graphics) files and to return no more than 50 such files. Figure 7-12 shows the results of Tony's search. Note that the results of this search are provided by a different Veronica server than the one that performed Tony's previous search. When one server is busy, a second or third server will be queried automatically.

3 **Navigate through the Gopher menu returned by Veronica until you find an item that interests you**
   Tony retrieves another one of the image files and forwards it to Professor Chou using FTP.

4 **Press [q] to quit Gopher**

TABLE 7-4: Veronica Switch names to use in Search Parameters

PARAMETER	DESCRIPTION
-t0	Retrieves text files
-t1	Retrieves directories
-t4	Retrieves Macintosh HQX files
-t5	Retrieves PC binary files
-t8	Retrieves Telnet sessions
-ts	Retrieves sound files
-tI	Retrieves images files
-tg	Retrieves gif graphics files
-m*number*	Retrieves no more than a total of *number* files

FIGURE 7-11:
Performing an
advanced search

Qualifiers

Search parameters

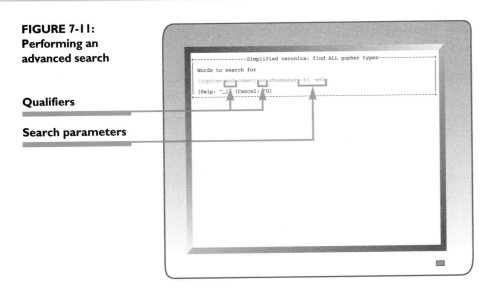

FIGURE 7-12:
Veronica search results

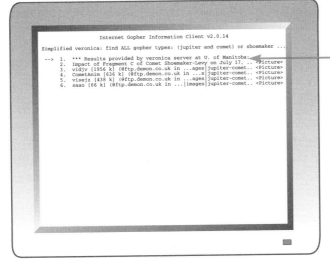

Results provided by
a different server

Search parameters

You can add the parameters or switches shown in Table 7-4 to better define your search. For example, including the parameter "–m100" in your search limits the results to 100 items. Adding the parameter "–t0" returns only text files. If Tony wanted only text files that included the word "shoemaker" in their titles, he would enter as his search criteria "shoemaker –t0." You can enter parameters in any order, and can place them either before the text string or after.

QUICK **TIP**

You can combine search parameters; for example, using the parameter "–ts0" searches for both sound files and text files.■

Connecting to a WAIS client

Another popular Internet search tools is **WAIS**, Wide Area Information Service, which searches the contents of indexed databases called **sources** for information. To use WAIS (pronounced *"wayz"*) you supply several keywords describing the topic you're interested in and the sources in which you want WAIS to look. Your search results can include Usenet news articles, text files, or just about any resource that can be referenced in a database's index. WAIS determines which items match the search criteria best by looking into the index and counting how many times each item contains the search keywords. The item with the most hits is given a score of 1000, and the strength of other matches is reported relative to that score. For example, you could specify the keywords "hubble," "shuttle," and "repair." The documents that feature these three words most prominently would receive the highest WAIS score. Unlike Archie and Veronica, WAIS searches not only filenames, but also the contents of the files themselves. To use WAIS, you either run a WAIS client program on your host, which connects you with the server containing the database index, or you telnet to a public-access WAIS client program (Table 7-5 shows some public WAIS sites). See the related topic "WAIS clients" in this lesson for a further discussion of WAIS client programs. ▶ Tony uses WAIS to expand his search for documents that pertain to Shoemaker Levy-9 comet.

1   Connect to a public-access WAIS client by typing **telnet** *host* at the UNIX command prompt, where *host* is the domain name of the Internet host running the WAIS client, then press **[Enter]**

Since the MidWest University doesn't have a WAIS client, Tony telnets to the public-access WAIS client located at quake.think.com. If your site has a local WAIS client, ask your instructor how to access it.

2   Type the login name (often **wais** or **swais**), then press **[Enter]**

Tony types "wais" as the login name for quake.think.com, the login name specified in Table 7-5.

3   If prompted, enter your e-mail address and terminal type

Tony enters "donahue@students.mwu.edu" as his user identification and types "vt100" as the terminal type (the most common; your instructor can tell you if yours is different). The host at quake.think.com initiates the WAIS client program, in this case the SWAIS program, after a few seconds. Once the opening SWAIS screen shows the list of sources, as in Figure 7-13, you are successfully connected to the WAIS client and can begin your search. You'll learn more about this in the next lesson. (If you telnetted to a different site, your sources will be different.)

TABLE 7-5: Public-Access WAIS clients

DOMAIN NAME	LOGIN NAME
quake.think.com	wais
sunsite.unc.edu	swais
swais.cwis.uci.edu	swais

FIGURE 7-13: Opening WAIS screen at quake.think.com

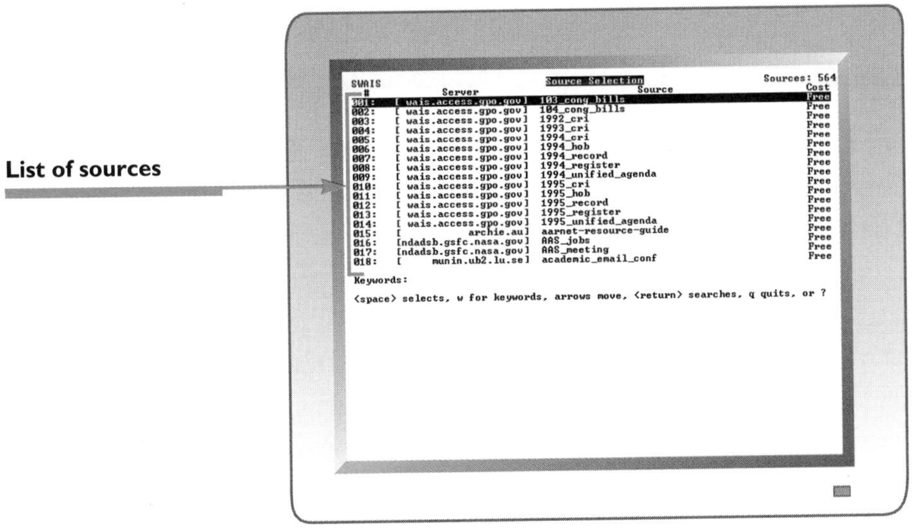

List of sources

WAIS clients

WAIS uses a client/server structure in which a client program sends a query to the WAIS server, which in turn performs the query and returns the results back to the client. There are several different WAIS clients that you can use. The most popular UNIX clients are **SWAIS** and **WAISSearch**. Other clients commonly used are **XWAIS** for the X-Windows system, **WinWais** for Windows, and **MacWais** for the Macintosh. Table 7-6 lists these clients and where you can find them.

TABLE 7-6: WAIS client software

PROGRAM	OPERATING SYSTEM	ANONYMOUS FTP LOCATION
SWAIS	UNIX	ftp.tau.ac.il in: /pub/sources/network/wais/freeWAIS-0.3/bin
WAISSearch	UNIX	julian.uwo.ca in: /pub/unix/network/freeWAIS-0.3/bin
XWAIS	X-Windows	ftp.tau.ac.il in: /pub/sources/network/wais/freeWAIS-0.3/bin
WinWais	Windows	ftp.univ-rennes1.fr in: pub/pc/general/wais/winwais
MacWais	Macintosh	wais.com in: /pub/freeware/mac

Selecting a Source

Once you have connected to WAIS, you select a source or sources from which to conduct your search. With about 500 WAIS sources available and more being added all the time, this is not a trivial task. Fortunately, you can use WAIS to search a source called the **directory of servers** that lists available WAIS sources. In searching for a relevant source you should enter general keywords. For example, when Tony searches for information on the Shoemaker Levy-9 comet, he should look for sources that deal with astronomy and related topics, as it is unlikely that he will find a source dedicated exclusively to the Shoemaker Levy-9 comet. Tony is using the WAIS software at quake.think.com, SWAIS, to perform his search. If you are using a different WAIS client, ask your instructor for information on differences in the search procedures. ▶ Tony continues his search for Professor Chou on the Shoemaker Levy-9 comet by first trying to identify an appropriate information source.

1   **Connect to a WAIS client, as described in the previous lesson, and be sure you are viewing the source list**
Tony has connected to the WAIS client at quake.think.com. He now requests the directory of servers so that he can search for an appropriate source for astronomy.

2   **Press [/] to display the search prompt, type the name of the source you want to find in the list of sources, then press [Enter]**
Tony types "directory-of-servers" (including the hyphens) at the Source Name prompt that appears. SWAIS highlights the source called "directory-of-servers" in the source list.

3   **Press [Spacebar] to select the highlighted source**
An asterisk appears next to the directory-of-servers source, indicating that it is selected for future searches. See Figure 7-14. Tony is ready to enter his search keywords.

4   **Press [w] to display the Keywords prompt, type the list of keywords for your search, then press [Enter]**
Tony enters a string of keywords, "astronomy planets jupiter comet hubble images," as shown in Figure 7-15. SWAIS responds with the WAIS sources that best cover the keywords listed, shown in Figure 7-15. The best match receives a score of 1000, and all other sources are scored relative to the best match. In Tony's case, the best match comes from sci.astro.hubble (another item containing information on the directory-of-servers database also receives a score of 1000 but is not relevant to Tony's search). Other matches are less successful. Some of the sources on the list may have little or nothing to do with your topic.

5   **Use the arrow keys to highlight the source in which you're interested, then press [Enter]**
Tony presses the down arrow key until he has highlighted the sci.astro.hubble source. Figure 7-16 shows a description of the hubble source, which is an archive of materials posted to the sci.astro.hubble newsgroup. After viewing the source information, Tony presses [Enter] to return to the search results shown in Figure 7-16. Tony decides to use the sci.astro.hubble source for further searches on the Shoemaker Levy-9 comet.

FIGURE 7-14: Source list with directory-of-servers selected

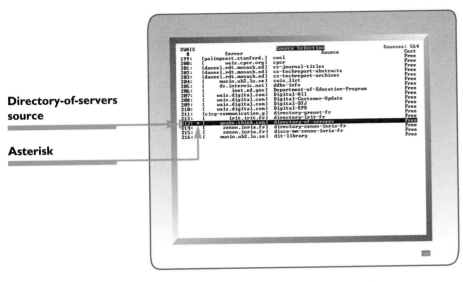

Directory-of-servers source

Asterisk

FIGURE 7-15: Sources found by the search

Score of 1000

Useful sources for Tony's keywords

Most promising source

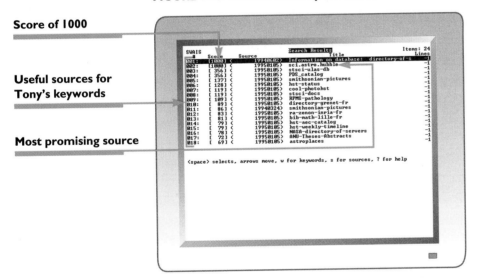

FIGURE 7-16: Information on the sci.astro.hubble source

Information on a promising source

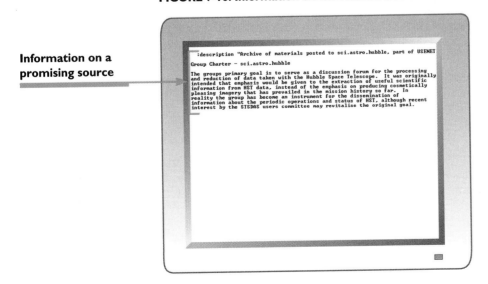

QUICK TIP

SWAIS commands are case sensitive. Pressing [W] is not the same thing as pressing [w].■

TROUBLE?

Not all WAIS clients use the same source list, but if you're working on a client installed on your host, you can usually add new sources as you discover them.■

Conducting a Search

Once you've decided on which source or sources you want to query, you are ready to perform a WAIS search. The methods and commands are identical to the process you used to find and select a source, except that now you are trying to find a specific article or document. Table 7-7 summarizes common SWAIS commands; remember the commands for using a different WAIS client might be slightly different. ▶ Having used WAIS to discover the sci.astro.hubble archives, Tony conducts a more detailed search focusing on information pertaining to the Shoemaker Levy-9 comet.

1 Be sure you have found a promising source to search, as described in the previous lesson, press **[s]** to display the list of sources, then press **[Spacebar]** to de-select the directory-of-servers source

2 Press **[/]** to display the Source Name prompt, enter the name of the source you want to search, then press **[Spacebar]** to select the source
Tony types "sci.astro.hubble," the most promising source from his search for sources in the previous lesson. SWAIS highlights the source, and Tony presses [Spacebar] to select it.

3 Press **[w]** to display the Keywords prompt, delete prior keywords if necessary, enter your search keywords, then press **[Enter]**
The keywords from Tony's previous search appear at the Keywords prompt, so Tony presses [Backspace] to delete the previous keywords. He then types "Shoemaker Levy Shoemaker Levy-9" for the new keyword list, as shown in Figure 7-17. If the search is successful, WAIS displays a list of articles. See your instructor if you are having trouble initiating a successful search.

4 Highlight an article that interests you, then press **[Enter]** to view its contents
A total of 40 articles match Tony's search, as shown in Figure 7-18. He selects the one receiving the highest score, and WAIS displays an article from the sci.astro.hubble archives describing images of the comet's impact, shown in Figure 7-19. The images are available on an Internet resource called the World Wide Web, which is a topic you'll be learning about in the next unit.

5 Press **[Enter]** to return to the list of sources, then repeat step 4 as necessary to view all the articles that interest you
Record the source information, and when you've searched all the articles, quit WAIS.

6 Press **[q]** to quit WAIS
Tony returns to the UNIX command prompt.

TABLE 7-7: SWAIS commands

COMMAND	DESCRIPTION	COMMAND	DESCRIPTION
=	Unselects all selected sources	k	Moves up 1 line
[Spacebar]	Selects or unselects a source	K	Moves up 1 page
h	Displays list of commands	q	Quits SWAIS
j	Moves down 1 line	s	Redisplays the list of sources
J	Moves down 1 page	w	Enters keywords for a search

FIGURE 7-17: Keywords for new search

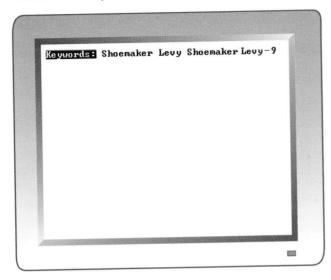

FIGURE 7-18: Articles selected by the Shoemaker Levy-9 search

Best score

Articles that match
Tony's keywords

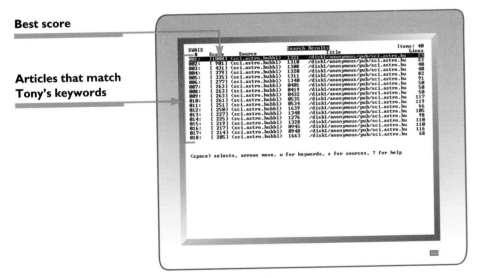

**FIGURE 7-19: Article describing location of Shoemaker Levy-9
images**

A World Wide Web
source for impact
images

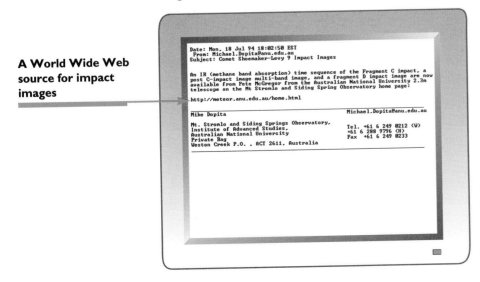

TROUBLE?

The availability of
WAIS and WAIS
sources is unpre-
dictable. If a WAIS
client or source is
not available, try your
search later. It may be
available then.■

QUICK TIP

To remove all the
previous search
keywords, press
[Ctrl][u] at the
Keyword prompt.■

CONCEPTSREVIEW

Label each of the elements shown in this figure.

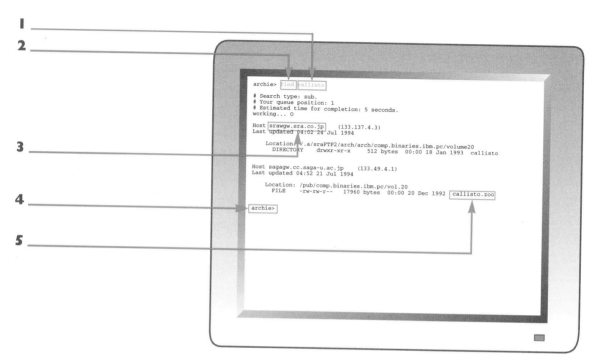

FIGURE 7-20

Match each of the statements with the term it describes.

6 A list of keywords that describes the contents of a file in some anonymous FTP sites

7 A machine that maintains a listing of the contents of anonymous FTP sites

8 A machine that maintains a listing of the contents of Gopher menus

9 A machine that communicates with an Archie server

10 An indexed database searched by WAIS

a. Veronica server

b. Source

c. Archie server

d. Software Description Database

e. Archie client

Select the best answer from the list of choices.

11 To search for files stored on anonymous FTP sites you can:

  a. Telnet to an Archie server.

  b. Run an Archie client off your local machine.

  c. Access a Veronica server using Gopher.

  d. (All of the above)

12 If you set an Archie search to "sub," which file will be returned by typing "find voyager" at the Archie command prompt?

  a. Voyager.txt

  b. voyager-photos

  c. voyager

  d. (All of the above)

13 With the search set to "exact," which file will be returned by typing "find voyager" at the Archie command prompt?

  a. Voyager.txt

  b. voyager-photos

  c. voyager

  d. (All of the above)

14 To find Gopher text items only that contain the words "Jupiter" and "Comet" in the filename, type the following for the Veronica search:

a. Jupiter and Comet -t0

b. Jupiter Comet -t0

c. -t0 Jupiter and Comet

d. (Any of the above)

15 To find 25 examples of Gopher text items that contain the words "Jupiter" and "Comet" or the word "Shoemaker" in their titles, type the following for the Veronica search:

a. (Jupiter and Comet) or Shoemaker and 25

b. Jupiter and Comet or Shoemaker -m25

c. (Jupiter and Comet) or Shoemaker -m25

d. (Jupiter and Comet) or Shoemaker -maxhits25

16 When using SWAIS, which of the following should you do to find a source in the directory of servers with the word "biology" in its title?

a. Press [s], then type the word "biology" when prompted by SWAIS.

b. Press [w], then type the word "biology" when prompted by SWAIS.

c. Press [/], then type the word "biology" when prompted by SWAIS.

d. Press [S], then type the word "biology" when prompted by SWAIS.

17 A WAIS search returns an item with a score of 1000. This tells you:

a. The document has 1000 keyword matches.

b. The document has 1000 lines of text.

c. The document is a perfect match to your search keywords.

d. The document is the best match to your search of all items in the source database.

APPLICATIONS
REVIEW

Note that anonymous FTP sites, Gopher menus, and WAIS servers are in a constant state of change. Some of the search results you receive here may be different. Your instructor might give you different instructions.

1 Use Archie to find a copy of the U.S. Constitution.

a. Telnet to an Archie server (archie.sura.net or archie.rutgers.edu).

b. Once connected, type "archie" as the login.

c. Type "find constitution" at the archie command prompt.

d. What filenames does Archie return?

2 Use the Archie server commands to mail a copy of the search from the previous question to your e-mail account.

a. Type "mailto *address*" at the archie command prompt, where *address* is your e-mail address, then press [Enter].

b. Type "find constitution" again at the archie command prompt.

c. After the search is completed, type "mail" and then press [Enter] to mail the results to yourself.

d. Type "quit" to quit the Archie server.

3 Use Archie to find an on-line dictionary program.

a. Telnet to an Archie server (archie.sura.net or archie.rutgers.edu).

b. Once connected, type "archie" as the login.

c. Type "whatis dictionary" at the archie command prompt.

d. Based on the keywords that the "whatis" command returns, search for an on-line dictionary that is ASCII-based (that is, it uses text characters). What program and locations did you find?

e. Type quit to quit Archie.

4 Many files for the PC are compressed into a format called a .zip format. To "unzip" these files you need a software program such as pkunzip. Use Veronica to locate the pkunzip program and save it to your account.

a. Connect to your local Gopher client.

b. Connect to a Veronica server that finds all Gopher item types.

c. Type "pkunzip -t5" to tell Veronica to look for PC binary files that contain the word "pkunzip" in their filenames.

d. When the list of files appears, select one of the Gopher items and press [s] to save the file to your account.

5 Use WAIS to search for documents dealing with the ozone hole.

a. Connect to a WAIS client (either by running a client on your local system or by telnetting to one of the public-access WAIS clients shown in Table 7-5).

b. Select the directory of servers as your source.

c. Start a general search. Use the word "environment" as your keyword.

d. Based on the results of your search, which source has the highest score?

e. Return to the list of sources. Deselect the directory-of-servers source, and find and select the source that had the highest score in part d above.

f. Start a more specific search with this source. Use the keywords "ozone hole."

g. Which document has the highest score in matching to your keyword's search? Is this document particularly useful? Are there other documents with lower scores that seem more valuable? Can you think of ways to improve your search?

h. Exit the WAIS client and return to your account.

INDEPENDENT
CHALLENGE 1

Sometimes you might not need the results of an Archie search immediately. Consider sending your search criteria to an Archie server through e-mail. This is especially useful when you are having trouble connecting to a server, because your e-mail messages are always accepted (though it may take awhile). To use an Archie server in this fashion you have to include the Archie server commands in the text of the message. Be sure to tell Archie to mail the results back to you. Try sending the necessary commands in an e-mail message to the server at archie.sura.net (the e-mail address is archie@archie.sura.net) in order to search for filenames that include the word "voyager."

To complete this independent challenge:

1 Address an e-mail message to archie@archie.sura.net.

2 In the message body, type the following commands (be sure you don't include any other text):

    set mailto *address* (where *address* is your e-mail address)
    set sortby time
    set maxhits 10
    find voyager
    mail
    quit

3 Be sure you don't include a signature or Archie might try to interpret your signature as a command.

4 Send the message.

5 Check your e-mail after a reasonable amount of time, and review the search results.

INDEPENDENT
CHALLENGE 2

Now that you have had a little more experience with searching on the Internet, try some of the following Internet Hunt questions (the Internet Hunt was introduced in Unit 6). Use Telnet or Usenet mailing lists, in addition to the search techniques you practiced in this unit, if you think they will help you.

To complete this independent challenge, answer the following questions:

1 Where can I find the text of Bill Clinton's speech on the 50th anniversary of the Normady Invasion?

2 A useful Windows graphics package for viewing images like the Jupiter graphics from this unit is called "Wingif." Where can I find this software?

3 What does the U.S. Food and Drug Administration mean when it labels foods as being "light" or "lite"?

4 How can I find out what the requirements are for U.S. citizens traveling to Kuwait?

5 Who is the California state senator for Gridley?

6 Where can I find archives of Internet Hunt questions from years past?

UNIT 8

OBJECTIVES

▶ Understand the World Wide Web

▶ Use browsers

▶ Start Mosaic

▶ Navigate the Web

▶ Connect to Gopher

▶ Search the Web

▶ Use Multimedia

▶ Visit interesting URLs

Introducing THE WORLD WIDE WEB

As you've progressed through this book, you've experimented with a number of widely used Internet tools. This unit introduces you to an Internet device that is in some ways the culmination of all you have worked with so far: the World Wide Web, or, as it is more commonly known, the Web. The Web offers a different way of accessing information on the Internet than the tools you've explored in previous units. The Web organizes Internet resources into documents linked by topic that are stored on Internet hosts across the world. Using the links, you move effortlessly from document to document until you find the information you need. Because Web document creators try to outdo each other in designing interesting and beautiful documents, the simple aesthetic pleasure to be gained by admiring document layouts makes the Web a particularly delightful tool. ▶ Mary Kemper, a computer science student soon to graduate from MidWest University, uses the World Wide Web to look for a job. ▶

Understanding the World Wide Web

The **World Wide Web** has the same mission as Gopher; namely, to organize the vast resources of the Internet in order to give you easy access to information. However, whereas Gopher uses a menu system to organize Internet resources, the Web uses hypertext documents. A **hypertext document** contains elements that you can select, usually by clicking a mouse, to call up another document. The act of moving from one page to another is called a **jump**. The part of the document that activates the jump is called a **link**. Links can be either textual or graphical. For example, Figure 8-1 illustrates how three Web hypertext documents, commonly called **pages**, are linked on the Internet. Mary Kemper, the MidWest University student who wants to use the Web to begin her career search, might start with the top page, which displays five different aspects of career searching, each represented by a small graphic or **icon**. For example, Mary could click the COMPANIES link (an icon link) to find information on employer profiles. The Web responds by displaying the Companies page, the middle page in Figure 8-1. From the Companies page, Mary can jump to specific information about each employer. To see a profile for Computer Express, for example, she could click the "Computer Express" link (a text link) to jump to the bottom page in Figure 8-1, which displays the information she needs. The related topic "Jump destinations" in this lesson describes the flexibility of hypertext jumps on the Internet. ▶ Given that Gopher also lets you move from one Internet resource to another, you might wonder whether the Web is really all that new. Consider, however, these important differences:

■ The Web page is more informative than the Gopher menu because it provides not only links to Internet resources but also text and graphics describing the contents of those links. For more information on how to learn more about newsgroups, see the related topic "Usenet newsgroups related to the Web."

■ Hypertext links can send you to an article or specific point *within* the article, while Gopher can access only the article as a whole document.

■ The Web is easier to understand. In a properly designed Web page, the links appear naturally within the structure of a document (as in Figure 8-1). In order to understand a Gopher menu, you might have to retrieve a Readme file and a few other documents first.

■ You can easily create a Web page, if your site allows it. Part of the explosion of the Web is the ability for Internet users to create their own Web page and make it available to the global Internet community.

FIGURE 8-1: Hypertext links

Page with graphical links

Mary clicks COMPANIES link to jump to Companies page

Page with textual links

List of companies

Mary clicks Computer Express link to jump to Computer Express Inc. page

Profile of Computer Express Inc.

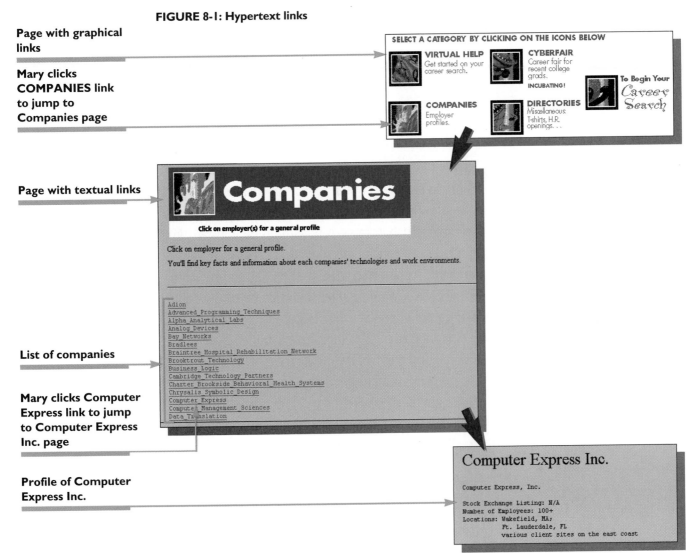

Jump destinations

If you have ever worked with a Windows Help file or the Macintosh Hypercard program, you have a pretty good idea of what hypertext can do. Part of the Web's appeal, however, is that its links can lead you almost anywhere, not just to other documents. A Web link can point you to Internet resources, including Usenet newsgroups, Telnet sites, anonymous FTP servers, and Gopher menus. Beyond this, the Web offers not only hypertext but also **hypermedia**, in which jumps point to multimedia elements like video or sound. Mary, for example, might use the hypermedia capabilities of the Web to play a video clip describing a company's benefits package.

Usenet newsgroups related to the Web

For information about the Web, consider subscribing to the following Usenet newsgroups: comp.infosystems.www.announce, comp.infosystems.www.misc, comp.infosystems.www.providers, and comp.infosystems.www.users.

Using browsers

To access Web pages you need a Web client program called a **browser**. Browsers access the contents of a Web page stored on a server and present the page in a hypertext format. Browsers can be either text-based, as shown in Figure 8-2, or graphical, as shown in Figure 8-3. Text-based browsers allow only the display of text, while graphical browsers allow graphics (called **inline images**) within the document. Table 8-1 lists a variety of anonymous FTP servers from which your system administrator can obtain a browser. You can also connect to a public-use text-only browser called Lynx by telnetting to kufacts.cc.ukans.edu (log on as "kufacts"). It is strongly recommended that your system administrator install the client software on your host so as not to overwhelm this site with too many telnetters. ▶ MidWest University runs the client program **Mosaic**, the first Web graphical browser. Mosaic was developed for the UNIX X-Windows interface by Marc Andreessen, an undergraduate at the University of Illinois at Urbana-Champaign. Mosaic is still one of the most popular browsers, though many others have appeared as more people have discovered the advantages of the Web. If your site uses a different browser, follow the lessons in this unit to get a general flavor of what is possible with the Web and talk to your instructor to learn the specifics of how your own browser handles these tasks. You'll probably find that your browser works identically to Mosaic for most tasks. Some of Mosaic's most useful features, which your browser may or may not share, include:

■ **A graphical user interface (GUI)**
You navigate the Web by clicking a link that jumps you to another Web page. Text links are usually underlined and in a different color, though links can also be icons, as in Figure 8-3. Another GUI feature is the **toolbar**, which contains buttons that give you single-click access to a variety of tasks, including moving forward and backward through a series of Web pages. The toolbar also includes a Home button to return you to the first Web page you visited.

■ **History list**
A history list keeps track of all the Web pages you've visited in a given session, and lets you return to an earlier page no matter where you are on the Web.

■ **Bookmarks**
You can add pages that you intend to visit frequently to a bookmark list, similar to the bookmarks you created using Gopher. Accessing the bookmark takes you directly to the page.

■ **Annotations**
You can add personal notes to Web pages, including comments you have on the Web page, or your own hypertext jumps to other Web resources. The annotation appears only on your browser, and not on anyone else's.

■ **Viewers**
By properly configuring your browser, you can have it access a file viewer whenever it encounters a specific file type. For example, you can configure Mosaic so that it launches a movie viewer whenever you try to access a video clip from a Web page.

FIGURE 8-2:
Text-based browser

Links are boldface text

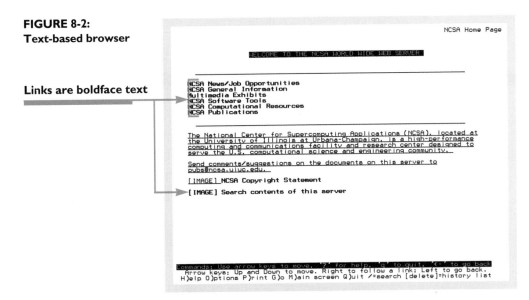

FIGURE 8-3:
Graphical browser

Toolbar

Icon links

Links can be icons or underlined text

Text links

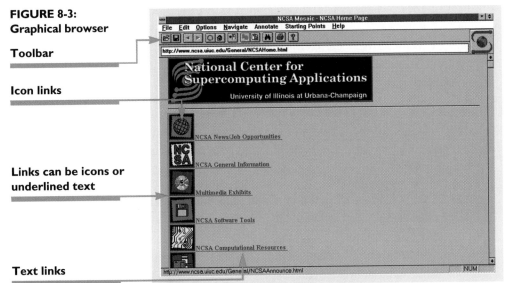

TABLE 8-1: World Wide Web browsers

BROWSER	AVAILABLE FROM	BROWSER TYPE	OPERATING SYSTEM
Albert	gopher.ufl.edu	Textual	VMS
Cello	ftp.law.cornell.edu	Graphical	Windows
Lynx	ftp2.cc.ukans.edu	Textual	DOS, UNIX
MacWeb	ftp.einet.net	Graphical	Macintosh
Mosaic	ftp.ncsa.uiuc.edu	Graphical	Windows, Macintosh, X-Windows
Netscape	ftp.mcom.com	Graphical	Windows, Macintosh, X-Windows
WinWeb	ftp.einet.net	Graphical	Windows

Starting Mosaic

Once you have a Web browser like Mosaic, you can begin to explore the Web. When you start your browser, the first screen you usually see is a page created by your site, called the **home page**, that gives you access to the Web. Home pages at some sites include useful local information in addition to access to the universal Web. The home page for a university site, for example, might include links to university services such as the campus library or the staff directory. ▶ The MidWest University Web home page offers access to different departments and services within the university. MWU uses Mosaic as its browser. Mary Kemper decides to use the Web to assist her in her job search. The first page she encounters is MWU's home page.

1 **Log on to your account**
Until now you've been primarily using UNIX and running applications with a command-line interface. The rest of this unit assumes that you have access to a computer with a graphical user interface. If you don't have access to a graphical browser like Mosaic, talk to your system administrator about using Lynx, a text-based browser that runs under UNIX. Mary Kemper starts Microsoft Windows on one of MWU's PCs and connects the PC to the Internet. Your site will have its own login method.

2 **Locate the icon representing your site's Web browser**
At MWU, the Mosaic icon is located in a Microsoft Windows group window shown in Figure 8-4. Your site might use a different platform. If you don't know how to use a mouse or other pointing device to navigate a graphical user interface, see your instructor for available training opportunities.

3 **Start your browser using the method available at your site**
Mary double-clicks the Mosaic icon shown in Figure 8-4 to start the program. Mosaic opens, showing the MWU home page as displayed in Figure 8-5. Windows users will recognize standard Windows elements like the title bar, menu bar, toolbar, scroll bar, and status bar. Table 8-2 explains the basic features of the Mosaic screen. Depending on the browser and system you are using, some of these elements may be missing, and others may be included.

4 **Move your mouse pointer over an underlined entry or icon on your site's home page**
As Mary moves the pointer ⌖ over the Computer Science entry on the MWU home page, it changes from ⌖ to ⬆. Whenever the pointer appears as ⬆, you are pointing at a link. Clicking that link jumps you to a new Web page. In addition, the address of the document that the link points to appears in the status bar at the bottom on the screen. In the next lesson, you'll learn more about Web addresses and you'll see how to use Mosaic to jump to new Web pages.

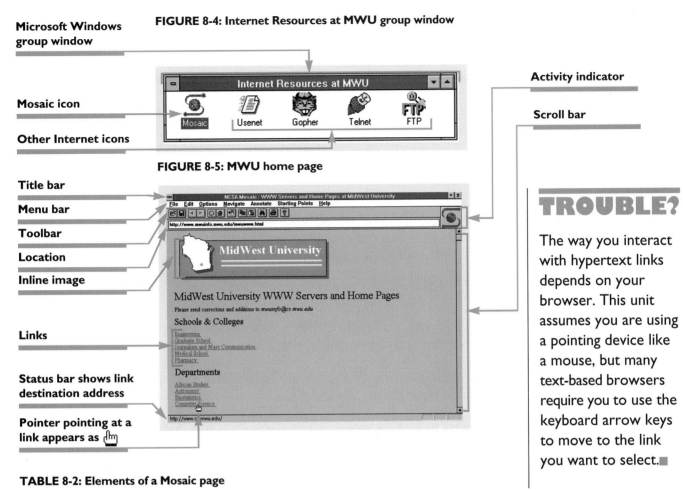

Microsoft Windows group window

FIGURE 8-4: Internet Resources at MWU group window

Mosaic icon

Other Internet icons

Activity indicator

Scroll bar

FIGURE 8-5: MWU home page

Title bar

Menu bar

Toolbar

Location

Inline image

Links

Status bar shows link destination address

Pointer pointing at a link appears as

TROUBLE?

The way you interact with hypertext links depends on your browser. This unit assumes you are using a pointing device like a mouse, but many text-based browsers require you to use the keyboard arrow keys to move to the link you want to select.

TABLE 8-2: Elements of a Mosaic page

PAGE ELEMENT	DESCRIPTION
Title bar	The area at the top of the window that displays the name of the browser and the current page
Menu bar	The area just below the title bar that provides access to Mosaic commands
Toolbar	The area just below the menu bar that contains buttons (small graphical icons) that give you immediate access to the most common commands
Scroll bar	The area at the right of the window (and sometimes the bottom) that lets you view more of the page by clicking the arrows at the top and bottom of the scroll bar to move to other parts of the page.
Location	Address of the current page
Inline Image	Graphics that enhance the appearance of the page and provide additional information to the user
Links	Text or icons that you can select to move to different pages. Text links are usually a different color and underlined.
Activity indicator	A globe-shaped icon that spins when Mosaic is accessing a Web page.
Status bar	The area at the bottom of the window that displays the address of the currently highlighted link and the progress of any commands that Mosaic is currently running

Navigating the Web

Once you finish exploring the contents of your home page, you can easily move to other documents by clicking the appropriate link (again, either underlined text or a graphic). Your browser responds by moving you to the Web page indicated by the link. How does the browser know where to go? The location of each Web document is indicated by its **URL**, short for Uniform Resource Locator, which you can think of as the document's address within the World Wide Web. For example, the URL for the MidWest University's home page is "http://www.mwuinfo.mwu.edu/mwuwww.html" (you can verify this by checking Figure 8-5 on the previous page). Remember that this is a fictional location, so you won't be able to find it on the Web. See the related topic "Understanding URLs and HTTP" in this lesson for more information about interpreting URLs. ▶ Mary begins her job search by navigating through the Web job-posting pages at her university. Follow along with her at your home site, but choose a topic of your own. Because this example is fictional, you won't find the pages Mary encounters, though you may be able to find similar ones.

1   Start your browser if it is not already started, then access your home page, as described in the previous lesson

2   Click a link on the home page to jump to a new document
In the previous lesson Mary moved her mouse pointer to the MWU Computer Science link (shown in Figure 8-5 on the previous page). Now she clicks the highlighted text, causing her browser to load the page for the MWU Computer Science department, which appears as shown in Figure 8-6.

3   View the contents of the new page, then click another link that interests you
One of the topics listed in the MWU Computer Science page is a link to a Job Postings page. Mary clicks the text link and Mosaic responds by loading the Job Postings page shown in Figure 8-7. Mary is glad to see that she meets many of the qualifications for the first job posted and decides to print the contents of the Job Postings page so that she can file it with her other job prospects. Try using the Print button to print your active page. Note that your browser might handle printing differently (perhaps through a menu and not a toolbar); see your instructor if you need help.

4   Click the **Print button** 🖨 on the Mosaic toolbar to print the active page
Printing a page gives you a hard-copy version of the entire page, not just the amount shown on the screen. Mary, for example, gets a hard copy of all the job postings listed on the Computer Science Department's Job Postings page. Now return to your home page (remember, your browser might have a different method of doing this).

5   Click the **Load Home Page button** 🏠 on the Mosaic toolbar to return to your home page
Mary is back at the MWU home page.

FIGURE 8-6: MWU Computer Science page

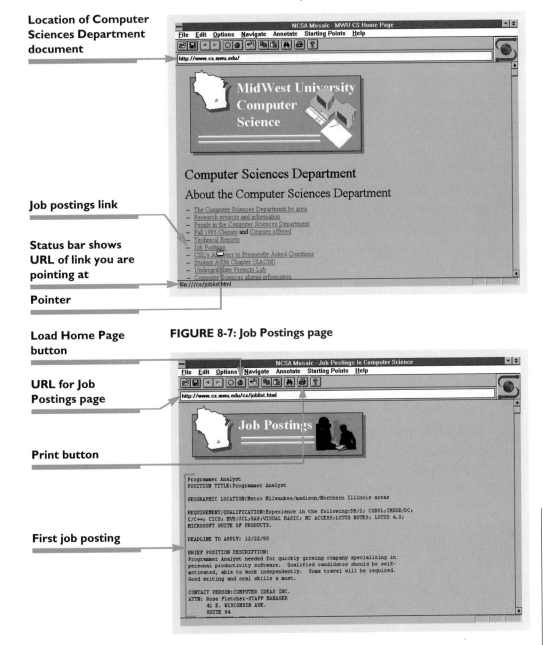

Location of Computer Sciences Department document

Job postings link

Status bar shows URL of link you are pointing at

Pointer

Load Home Page button

FIGURE 8-7: Job Postings page

URL for Job Postings page

Print button

First job posting

TROUBLE?

To print a page successfully, you must have scaleable versions of the fonts used to display the page's text (this is determined by your browser or your operating system).■

QUICK TIP

Use the Print Preview command on the File menu to view how your page will look when it is printed.■

Understanding URLs and HTTP

The location of each Web page within the World Wide Web is given by its URL, or Uniform Resource Locator. URLs appear in the following format: *method://host/path*. For example, the URL for MidWest University's Computer Science Department Job Posting page is "http://www.cs.mwu.edu/cs/joblist.html," as shown in Figure 8-7. This means that a browser connecting to this page accesses a file called "joblist.html" in a directory called "cs" that is located on the host "www.cs.mwu.edu," using the http method. **HTTP** stands for Hypertext Transfer Protocol and is the communication language used by Web servers and Web clients. HTML stands for Hypertext Markup Language the language in which Web pages are written.

Connecting to Gopher

The Web can access most of the Internet resources you've learned about in this book, such as Telnet sites, Gopher servers, WAIS sources, and anonymous FTP servers. The URL method portion (recall this is the first part of the URL address) shows the communication method. For example, the method for an anonymous FTP server is "ftp," so the URL for the FTP server located at terminator.rs.itd.umich.edu (used in Unit 5 to access Shakespeare's plays) is "ftp://terminator.rs.itd.umich.edu/". Not surprisingly, for a Gopher menu the method is "gopher;" for a Telnet site, the method is "telnet;" and for a WAIS server, the method is "wais." Some of the new browsers are even able to act as Usenet newsreaders by using an URL with the "news" method. ▶ Mary has heard that the MWU Gopher also offers access to employment possibilities, so she uses Mosaic to access the contents of the MWU Gopher. Try accessing the Gopher nearest your own site using your browser.

1 Start your browser if you have not already done so

2 Click the **Open URL button** 🖼 on the toolbar
The Open URL dialog box appears. Remember that your browser may require you to locate this dialog box some other way.

3 Type **gopher://host** in the URL box, where *host* is the domain name of the Gopher server you want to access
Mary types "gopher://gopher.mwu.edu" in the Open URL dialog box, as shown in Figure 8-8. The domain name that you should enter for your Gopher server will, of course, be different.

4 Click the **OK button**
The opening menu of the MWU Gopher server appears, as in Figure 8-9, with each of its menu items transformed into a hypertext link. Your menu will, of course, be different. Notice that each menu item is preceded by a small icon. Table 8-3 shows the meaning of these icons. For example, menus or directories appear as open folders 📂. Mary now uses Gopher to find additional employment resources.

5 Click the menu item you want to examine
Mary clicks the "Employment, Financial Aid, Scholarships and Grants" link, shown in Figure 8-9, to open the Employment menu, which appears as in Figure 8-10.

6 Continue to move through the menu structure of the Gopher server by clicking the appropriate links until you reach the Gopher item you want
Mary continues to move through the MWU Gopher menus, finally obtaining another job listing, shown in Figure 8-11, which she adds to her list of job prospects. Mary is pleased that she can so easily access Gopher without having to leave Mosaic.

TABLE 8-3:
Gopher menu icons

ICON	DESCRIPTION	ICON	DESCRIPTION
📂	Menu or directory	🗐	Search tool
📄	Text file	🖥	Telnet session

FIGURE 8-8:
Open URL dialog box

Method

Domain name

OK button

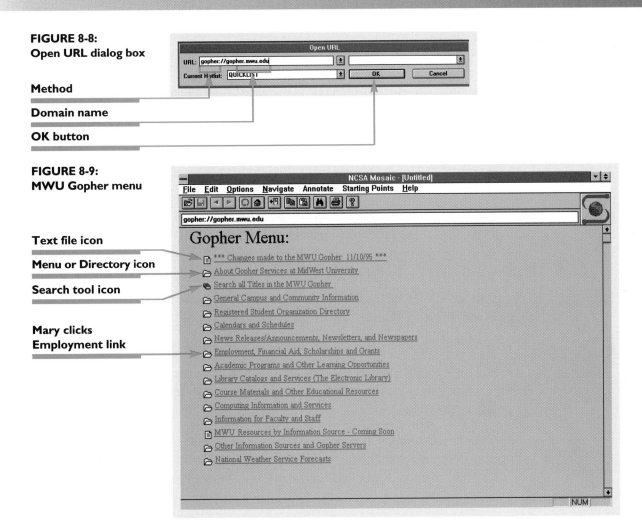

FIGURE 8-9:
MWU Gopher menu

Text file icon

Menu or Directory icon

Search tool icon

Mary clicks
Employment link

FIGURE 8-10:
Gopher Employment menu

Mary clicks
Employment link

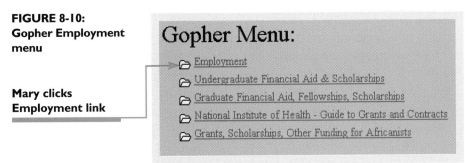

FIGURE 8-11:
Gopher job posting

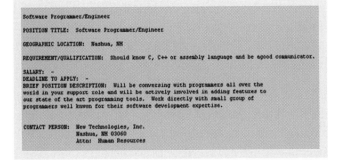

QUICK TIP

To move back up the Gopher menu tree, click the Back button ◄ on the toolbar.■

TROUBLE?

You can only access anonymous FTP servers with the Web, not servers that require logins other than "anonymous," because you won't be prompted for their passwords.■

Searching the Web

There are literally thousands of Web pages throughout the World Wide Web, and they cover a multitude of topics. The Web offers several search resources, called **engines** that can help you find a Web page that covers a specific topic. When you use these resources you are not really browsing through the Web as much as you are searching a database that contains information about Web pages and their URLs. Your ability to search the Web extends to what is included in these databases. Since the Web is growing constantly, most databases are out-of-date as soon as they're available. Trying to keep up is a full-time occupation! Databases get their information from programs called **robots** or **spiders** that explore the Web looking for documents to add to the database. Table 8-4 contains a lists of some popular Web search engines from which you can initiate a search. ▶ Mary decides to widen her job search to Web pages outside of MidWest University. Not knowing where to look, she decides to search the Web for any pages dealing with careers.

1 **Start the Web browser located at your site if you have not already done so**
In the last lesson, Mary was accessing information from the MWU Gopher. She is still using Mosaic as this lesson begins.

2 **Click the Open URL button 🖼 from the Mosaic toolbar, enter the URL of a Web search engine in the URL text box, then click OK**
Remember that your browser might handle this step differently. Mary types "http://cuiwww.unige.ch/meta-index.html," as shown in Figure 8-12. This is the URL for a Web search engine that points to several of the popular Web search tools. Mosaic retrieves a document listing these Web search engines for Mary.

3 **Following the directions on the Web page, enter a keyword or keywords describing your topic, then submit the query to the search engine**
The page that Mary has accessed contains several search engines, each of which appears as a link, with a box next to it into which she can type the keyword describing her topic. The search page you find might look very different from Mary's, and your browser might handle searching very differently. See your instructor for help if necessary. Mary scrolls through the document until she sees "CUI World Web Catalog" (one of the more popular search engines). She types the keyword "career" in the box, then clicks the submit button, as shown in Figure 8-13. If the search is successful, Mosaic will display the references to appropriate Web pages, which you will probably have to scroll to see. In Mary's case, several Web pages that contain the word "career" appear. Different search engines display search results in a variety of ways, so, again, your search results may be organized differently. Scrolling through the list, Mary notices one link entitled "CareerMosaic," shown in Figure 8-14. She decides to click this link.

4 **Click the link for the Web page you want to explore**
The CareerMosaic page displays a listing of job opportunities; in navigating through them, Mary finds an interesting one posted by the Read-Rite Corporation, shown in Figure 8-15. She has yet another posting to add to her growing collection of employment possibilities. Her next step might be to start sending out resumes!

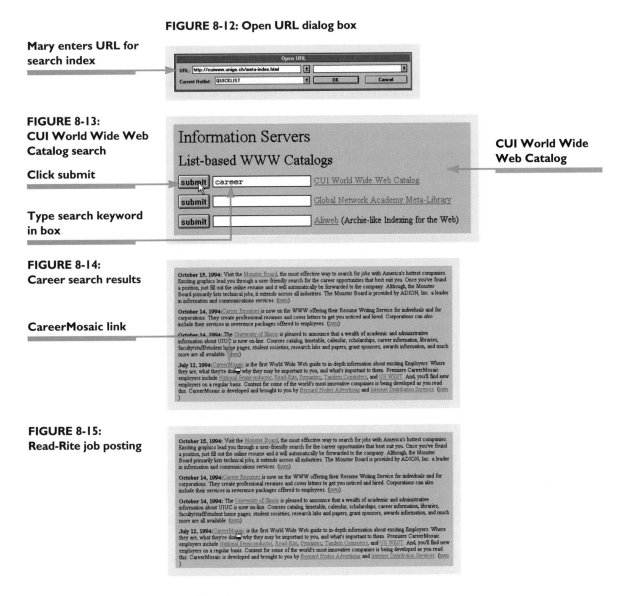

FIGURE 8-12: Open URL dialog box

Mary enters URL for search index

FIGURE 8-13:
CUI World Wide Web Catalog search

CUI World Wide Web Catalog

Click submit

Type search keyword in box

FIGURE 8-14:
Career search results

CareerMosaic link

FIGURE 8-15:
Read-Rite job posting

TABLE 8-4: Popular Web search engines

SEARCH ENGINES	URL
Aliweb	http://www.cs.indiana.edu/aliweb/search
CUI World Wide Web catalog	http://cuiwww.unige.ch/cgi-bin/w3catalog
Global Network Academy Meta-Library	http://uu-gna.mit.edu:8001/cgi-bin/meta
Index of Web search engines	http://cuiwww.unige.ch/meta-index.html
Lycos WWW search engine	http://lycos.cs.cmu.edu/
WebCrawler	http://webcrawler.cs.washington.edu/WebCrawler/WebQuery.html
World Wide Web Worm	http://www.cs.colorado.edu/home/mcbryan/WWW.html

Using Multimedia

One of the most exciting aspects of the Web is its use of multimedia. If your browser is configured correctly, you can view graphics, listen to sound clips, and even play movies. For the best Web multimedia experience, you should have a fast machine, a monitor capable of displaying 256 colors or more, a sound card, and speakers. To display the multimedia files, you'll also need special software programs called **viewers**. Many browsers do not come pre-installed with these viewers (Mosaic doesn't), so you or your system administrator will have to get them separately. Table 8-5 lists the locations of several popular viewers. ► In the previous lesson, Mary Kemper read a job notice from the Read-Rite Corporation appearing on the CareerMosaic page. Before she sends out a resume, she takes advantage of the CareerMosaic page's corporate information, which includes a video clip from the CEO of Read-Rite. If your browser is not configured to access multimedia, you might have to skip this lesson.

1 Go to a Web page with a multimedia link

2 Navigate through the Web to the page containing the multimedia file
Mary moves back a few pages to the CareerMosaic home page, shown in Figure 8-16. She clicks the Employers link to jump to the Employers page, shown in Figure 8-17. She jumps to the Read-Rite page. An icon link for a video clip appears at the bottom of the screen.

3 Click the link that accesses the multimedia file
Mary clicks the video clip icon as shown in Figure 8-18. Mosaic retrieves the file and starts the appropriate viewer. Notice that the status bar gives the URL for this resource: http://www.career-mosaic.com/cm/readrite/images/RRCyril.mov. The ".mov" indicates that this is a movie file. Once the movie file is downloaded (this takes awhile as it is 2.6 megabytes in size), the video clip plays, as shown in Figure 8-19. Be sure your site has an appropriate viewer before you try to download a file of this size. Viewing the movie introduces Mary to the CEO and the company.

TABLE 8-5: Locations of viewers for Windows and Macintoshes

PROGRAM	PURPOSE	URL ADDRESS FOR DOWNLOADING
Fast Player	Plays Quicktime movies (Mac)	ftp://ftp.ncsa.uiuc.edu/Web/Mosaic/Mac/Helpers
MpegPlay	Plays MPEG movies (Windows)	ftp://ftp.ncsa.uiuc.edu/Mosaic/Windows/viewers
Quick Time	Plays Quick Time movies (Windows)	http://www.ncsa.uiuc.edu/SDG/Software/WinMosaic/Viewers/qt.html
Sound Machine	Plays/records sound files (Mac)	ftp://ftp.ncsa.uiuc.edu/Web/Mosaic/Mac/Helpers
Sparkle	Plays MPEG movies (Mac)	ftp://ftp.ncsa.uiuc.edu/Web/Mosaic/Mac/Helpers
Wplany	Plays/records sound files (Windows)	ftp://ftp.ncsa.uiuc.edu/Mosaic/Windows/viewers

FIGURE 8-16:
CareerMosaic home
page

Employers link

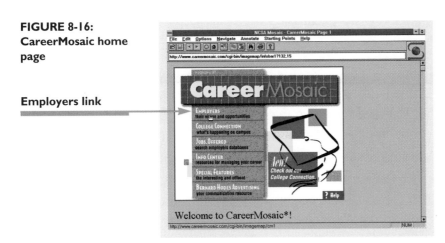

FIGURE 8-17:
CareerMosaic
Employers page

Read-Rite icon

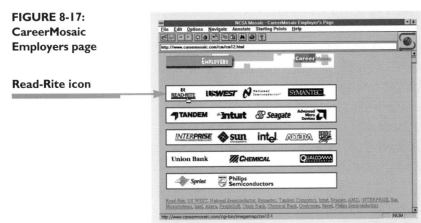

FIGURE 8-18:
Read-Rite Web Page

URL for video clip

Click the video clip icon

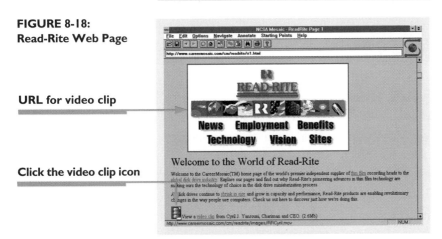

FIGURE 8-19:
Video viewer showing
Read-Rite's CEO

QUICK TIP

Before retrieving a large multimedia file that you know you'll want to keep, select the Load to Disk command from Mosaic's Options menu (or a similar command available with your browser). This command instructs Mosaic to save a copy of the file on your disk as well as to display it. After you have retrieved the file, select Load to Disk again to revert Mosaic back to a display mode.■

Visiting Interesting URLs

Because the World Wide Web is considered by many to be the most exciting part of the Internet, this book concludes with a look at a variety of Web pages. The Web is in a constant state of change, so some of these pages might no longer be available, or might look quite different tomorrow. That can be annoying, but it is also one of the Internet's greatest strengths: it is constantly growing, changing, and improving. In this book you've been introduced to some tools you can use to take advantage of Internet resources, but perhaps the greatest resource of all is the sense of adventure and curiosity that you can bring along as you explore the Internet.

- **Best of the Web 1994**, URL: http://wings.buffalo.edu/contest/awards/index.html
Award-winning Web pages of 1994
- **CERN Subject Catalog**,
URL:http://info.cern.ch/hypertext/DataSources/bySubject/Overview.html
A useful catalog of Web pages broken down by subject
- **Internet Business Directory**, URL: http://ibd.ar.com/
A directory of hundreds of businesses offering product information
- **Le WebLouvre**, URL: http://sunsite.unc.edu/louvre/
Tour Paris and the Louvre
- **NetFrog**, URL: http://curry.edschool.virginia.edu/~insttech/frog
Dissect a frog over the Internet
- **Nine Planets Tour**,
URL: http://seds.lpl.arizona.edu:80/nineplanets/nineplanets/
Tour the nine planets, courtesy of NASA
- **Remote Robot Arm**, URL: http://telerobot.mech.uwa.edu.au
Operate a robot arm over the Internet
- **Security APL Quote Server**, URL: http://www.secapl.com/cgi-bin/qs
Stock quotes and financial information available on the Internet
- **Star Trek Voyager**, URL: http://voyager.paramount.com/
For fans of the science fiction television series, *Star Trek: Voyager*, shown in Figure 8-20
- **The White House**, URL: http://www.whitehouse.gov
The White House home page, shown in Figure 8-21
- **The Whole Internet Catalog**, URL: http://www.digital.com/gnn/wic/index.html
A useful catalog of Web pages
- **Thomas**, URL: http://thomas.loc.gov/
Legislative Information on the Internet, shown in Figure 8-22
- **Vatican Exhibit**, URL: http://sunsite.unc.edu/expo/vatican.exhibit/Vatican.exhibit.html
Pictures from the Library of Congress Vatican Exhibit
- **World Map**, URL: http://pubweb.parc.xerox.com/map
Zoom in on any spot on the globe using an interactive map, shown in Figure 8-23
- **World Wide Web Servers**,
URL: http://info.cern.ch/hypertext/DataSources/WWW/Servers.html
A list of Web servers organized by location

FIGURE 8-20:
Star Trek Voyager

FIGURE 8-21:
White House

FIGURE 8-22:
Legislative Information
on the Internet

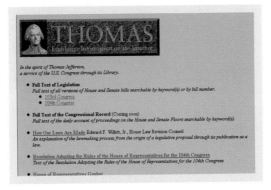

FIGURE 8-23:
World Map home page

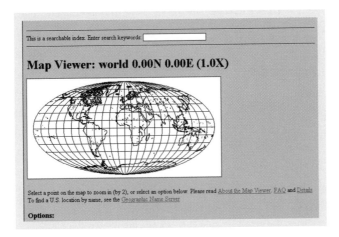

CONCEPTSREVIEW

Label each of the elements shown in this figure.

1 _____

2 _____

3 _____

4 _____

5 _____

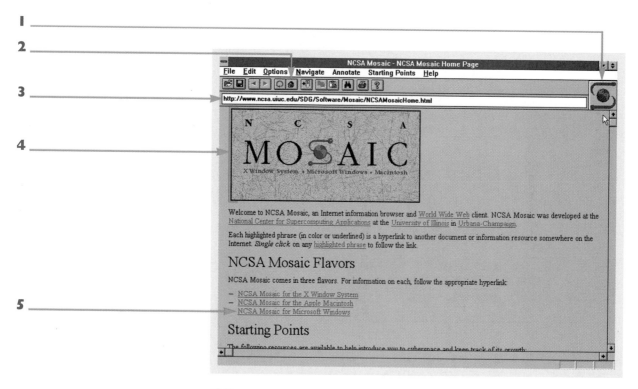

FIGURE 8-24

Match each of the statements with the term it describes.

6 The address of a Web document

7 The communication protocol used between a Web server and a Web client

8 A document containing links that when selected jump the user to another document

9 The part of a hypertext document that when selected jumps the user to another document

10 A Web client capable of displaying a Web page

11 A graphic embedded on a Web page

a. link

b. HTTP

c. hypertext document

d. web browser

e. URL

f. inline image

Select the best answer from the list of choices.

12 The Web differs from Gopher in that

   a. Web pages include text and graphics that increase the user's understanding of the information.

   b. The Web can connect users to points *within* an article whereas Gopher can only send the user the entire article.

   c. It's easier for Web users to create their own home pages than to create their own Gopher menus.

   d. (All of the above)

13 Two types of browsers are

   a. HTTP and URL

   b. Textual and graphical

   c. Serial and parallel

   d. Hypertext and hypermedia

14 The home page

   a. Is the first page the user sees when starting a Web browser

   b. Is the Web page devoted to the realty business

   c. Is set by the Web browser and cannot be changed

   d. (All of the above)

15 The activity indicator

   a. Shows whether your network host is working

   b. Shows whether the Web server is working

   c. Shows that the Web browser is in the process of transferring data

   d. Shows whether you have e-mail waiting for you

16 To connect to an anonymous FTP server located at wuarchive.wustl.edu, the URL is

   a. http://wuarchive.wustl.edu

   b. ftp://wuarchive.wustl.edu

   c. ftp.wuarchive.wustl.edu

   d. http://ftp/wuarchive.wustl.edu

17 The URL for connecting to a Gopher server located at gopher.micro.umn.edu is

   a. gopher.micro.umn.edu

   b. gopher://micro.umn.edu

   c. gopher://gopher.micro.umn.edu

   d. http://gopher.micro.umn.edu

18 URL stands for

   a. Universal Resource List

   b. Uniform Resource List

   c. Uniform Resource Locator

   d. Uniform Revised Listings

19 Robots are

   a. Fully automated home pages

   b. Not discussed on the World Wide Web

   c. Programs that explore the Web looking for new pages

   d. Programs that allow the Web browser to display multi-media applications

20 HTTP stands for

   a. Hypertext transfer page

   b. Hypermedia, Telnet, Text all in one Page

   c. Hypertext transfer protocol

   d. Hypermedia text placement

APPLICATIONSREVIEW

1 Start your browser.

   a. Log on to your account.

   b. Locate the appropriate icon or command to start your browser (for Mosaic, you locate the Mosaic icon, then double-click it). You should be at your site's home page.

2 Select a topic you want to explore from the options available on your site's home page, then print a page that interests you. Your instructor may have some suggestions for topics.

   a. Click the appropriate links to move to new pages.

   b. When you arrive at a page you'd like to print, click the Print button.

   c. Click the Load Home Page button to return to your site's home page.

3 Connect to your site's main Gopher menu.

   a. Click the Open URL button, or choose an appropriate command for your browser.

   b. Type "gopher://*host*" where *host* is the domain name of your site's Gopher server, then click OK. The Gopher menu should appear on a Web page.

   c. Navigate the Gopher menu to search an item of interest. Your instructor may have some ideas of good topics.

4 Select a keyword (your instructor might suggest one), then search for the Web pages containing that search keyword.

   a. Click the Open URL button, then enter the URL of a Web search engine. Your browser may handle this differently.

   b. Enter the keyword for the topic you are searching, then click the submit button. A list of applicable pages should appear.

   c. Click the link for the Web page you want to view.

5 Locate and view a multimedia clip. Your instructor may be able to suggest a page containing an interesting one. Be sure your browser is configured to handle multimedia.

   a. Navigate the Web until you locate the multimedia clip.

   b. Click the multimedia link to start the clip.

INDEPENDENT
CHALLENGE 1

One of the useful features of the Mosaic Web browser is its ability to annotate the contents of Web pages. These annotations do not affect the Web page itself, of course. Rather, the annotations are stored locally so that when Mosaic tries to access the page, it checks to see whether any annotations have been entered for it. If so, it places a hypertext jump on the page linking the page to the annotated text. If you are using a program other than Mosaic, your instructor can help you find the appropriate annotation commands.

To complete this independent challenge:

1 Start Mosaic and access the Web page you're interested in.

2 From the Mosaic menu, choose Annotate. The Annotate dialog box appears. Your browser's command might be different.

3 Type the text you want to add to the page in the box labeled "Enter the Annotation Text."

4 Type your name in the Author box and a title for the annotation in the Title box. These two strings identify the author of the annotation and describe the contents.

5 Click Commit to add the annotation to the Web page.

When you scroll to the bottom of the page, you should see a new hypertext link appended to the document. The link is connected to your annotation. Clicking the link opens a new page displaying your annotated text.

As you become more experienced with hypertext, you can use the the hypertext programming language, HTML (which stands for Hypertext Markup Language), to enhance your annotations. With HTML you can create annotated texts that include their own hypertext links or inline images. In the second independent challenge, you'll get a chance to write your own HTML code.

INDEPENDENT
CHALLENGE 2

Not all Web pages are found on remote servers. You can create your own Web pages and store them on your computer. Doing so requires that you enter a few HTML commands. HTML is a relatively simple programming language that is still very powerful. Teaching HTML is beyond the scope of this book, but it is well

worth the effort to learn it. You can view an introduction to HTML at the URL http://www.ncsa.uiuc.edu/General/Internet/WWW/HTMLQuickRef.html. Another way of learning HTML is to view the source code for the different Web documents you encounter. To view the source code select the command Document Source from the Mosaic File menu. If you are using a program other than Mosaic, the command might be different; see your instructor. Try creating a page of your own that accesses some of the Federal government home pages. To do this you need a text editor such as the Windows Notepad program.

To complete this independent challenge:

1 Using a text editor, enter the following text into a text file:
```
<html>
<head> <title>Federal Government Info Page</title>
</head>
<h1>Federal Home Pages </h1>
<a href="http://www.whitehouse.gov/"> The White House
</a>
<br>
<a href="http://thomas.loc.gov"> Legislative Information
</a>
<br>
<a href="gopher://ftp.senate.gov:70/"> The Senate Gopher
</a>
<br>
<a href="http://lcweb.loc.gov/homepage/lchp.html"> The
Library of Congress </a>
</html>
```

2 Save the text file with the name gov.htm.

3 Start your browser.

4 From the File menu choose Open Local File and open the gov.htm file you've just created. Your browser's commands might be different.

5 Mosaic loads the local file and displays links to four government pages: the White House, the Legislative Server, the Senate Gopher, and the Library of Congress home page. Test each of the links to verify that you've entered them correctly.

Congratulations! You've created your first Web page. Is this page available to the rest of the Internet? You'll have to talk to your instructor to find out whether your computer can act as a Web server and make this page accessible to other users. For now, it is certainly available to you if no one else.

Bibliography

Branwyn, G., Carton, S. (1995). *Mosaic Quick Tour for Mac.* North Carolina: Ventana Press

Branwyn, G., Carton, S. (1995). *Mosaic Quick Tour for Windows.* North Carolina: Ventana Press

Braun, E. (1994). *The Internet Directory.* New York: Fawcett Columbine.

Dougherty, D., Koman, R. (1994) *The Mosaic Handbook.* California: O'Reilly & Associates

Fraase, M. (1995). *The Mac Internet Tour Guide.* North Carolina: Ventana Press

Fraase, M. (1995). *The PC Internet Tour Guide.* North Carolina: Ventana Press

Fraase, M. (1995). *The Windows Internet Tour Guide.* North Carolina: Ventana Press

Gilster, P. (1994). *The Internet Navigator.* New York: John Wiley & Sons Inc.

Harley, H., Stout, R. (1994). *The Internet Complete Reference.* New York: Osborne McGraw-Hill

Krol, E. (1994). *The Whole Internet Catalog.* California. O'Reilly & Associates.

Solomon, D. W. (1990). *Using UNIX.* Indiana: QUE Corporation.

Turlington, S. (1995). *Walking the World Wide Web.* North Carolina: Ventana Press

Popular Web Sites

Government	URL	DESCRIPTION
CIA Home Page	http://www.ic.gov/	Observe what the Central Intelligence Agency is up to
FBI Home Page	http://naic.nasa.gov/fbi/	Information from the offices of the Federal Bureau of Investigation
Library of Congress	http://www.loc.gov/	Tour the Library of Congress Home Page
Senate Gopher	gopher://gopher.senate.gov/	Information on the activities of the United States Senate
Smithsonian Institution	http://www.si.edu/	Drop by the Smithsonian Institution's Home Page
Thomas	http://thomas.loc.gov/	Information on the activities of the House of Representatives
U.S. Bureau of the Census	http://www.census.gov/	United States Census Bureau Information
White House Home Page	http://www.whitehouse.gov/	The White House home page with information on the Clinton Administration

Business		
AT&T 800 Directory	http://att.net/dir800	Browse AT&T's directory of 800 numbers
CareerMosaic	http://www.careermosaic.com/cm/	Career and employment information
Commerce Net	http://www.commerce.net	Information on doing business on the Internet
Entrepreneurs	http://sashimi.wwa.com/~notime/eotw/EOTW.html	Information for the entrepreneur
Internal Revenue Service	http://www.ustreas.gov/treasury/bureaus/irs/irs.html	The Home Page for the Internal Revenue Service (IRS)
Internet Business Center	http://www.tig.com/IBC/	Another great source of information for those wishing to do business on the Internet
Internet Shopping Network	https://www.internet.net/	Do your shopping on the Internet. Not free.
QuoteCom Home Page	http://www.quote.com/	Download the latest Stock Market quotes

Science

Biosciences	http://golgi.harvard.edu/biopages.html	Information on the bioscience resources available on the Internet
Dinosaur Hall	http://ucmp1.berkeley.edu/exhibittext/dinosaur.html	The Dinosaurs make their return on the WWW
EnviroWeb	http://envirolink.org/	Information of environmental studies on the Internet
Meterology	http://www.met.fu-berlin.de/DataSources/MetIndex.html	Find out what the weather is like outside the Internet
Nine Planets	http://seds.lpl.arizona.edu/nineplanets/nineplanets/nineplanets.html	A multimedia tour of the Solar System
The Fractal Microscope	http://www.ncsa.uiuc.edu/Edu/Fractal/Fractal_Home.html	Explore the beautiful world of Fractal Mathematics
Xerox PARC Map Viewer	http://pubweb.parc.xerox.com/map	View a map of any location in the world

Entertainment

Games Domain	http://wcl-rs.bham.ac.uk/GamesDomain	Role playing games available on the WWW
Interesting Places for Kids	http://www.crc.ricoh.com/people/steve/kids.html	Web pages designed for and by kids
Letterman's Top Ten List	http://www.cbs.com/lateshow/ttlist.html	View Dave Letterman's popular Top Ten lists
Movie Browser	http://www.msstate.edu/Movies/moviequery.html	Information about films, actors and directors
Time Magazine	http://www.timeinc.com/time/universe.html	Web pages dedicated to the publication of Time Inc.
Warner Bros. Records	http://www.iuma.com/Warner/	Download music clips from your favorite artists
WebMuseum	http://mistral.enst.fr/	Tour the Louvre and Paris on the WWW
World Wide Web of Sports	http://www.tns.lcs.mit.edu/cgi-bin/sports	Get the latest sport information

Subject Catalogs

CERN Subject Catalog	http://info.cern.ch/hypertext/DataSources/bySubject/Overview.html	One of the standard Web subject catalogs from CERN.
EINet Galaxy	http://galaxy.einet.net/	Contains a wealth of interesting Web pages
The Whole Internet Catalog	http://www.digital.com/gnn/wic/index.html	Based on the popular Internet guide
Yahoo	http://akebono.stanford.edu/yahoo/	Over 32,000 popular Web pages listed

Search Tools

CUI Catalog	http://info.cern.ch/hypertext/DataSources/bySubject/Overview.html	The CUI WWW search tool
The Lycos Home Page	http://lycos.cs.cmu.edu/	A popular Internet search tool located at Carnegie-Mellon
WebCrawler	http://webcrawler.cs.washington.edu/WebCrawler/WebQuery.html	Contains a searchable database of over 350,000 Web documents
World Wide Yellow Pages	http://www.yellow.com	A list of all the businesses on the WWW
World Wide Web Worm	http://www.cs.colorado.edu/home/mcbryan/WWWW.html	A powerful search tool that scans Web pages for certain keywords

Index

Special Characters

&, 32-33
*, 99
^, 52-53, 90
>, 32-33, 80-81
?, 99

A

accounts, guest, 88-89
Address Book, 64-67
    creating aliases with, 64-65
    creating distribution lists with, 66-67
aliases. *See also* mailing lists
    and Address Book, 64-67
    creating, 35, 64
    domain name, 20-21
    and e-mail, 35
anonymous FTP servers, 92-93. *See also*
    Archie; FTP
argument, 13. *See also* commands
Archie, 127-135
    cancelling searches in, 129
    clients, 128-129, 134-135
    mailing results of searches in, 130-131
    output, controlling, 130-131
    search criteria, establishing, 132-133
        sending through e-mail, 148
    searching in, 128-129
    search parameters in, 130-131
    search types in, 131
    servers, 128-129
        commands, 133
    set command, 130-131
Arpanet, 5
articles, 72-73. *See also* Usenet
    moving through, 80-81
    posting, 82-83
    quoted lines in, 80-81
    reading, 80-81
    removing unwanted, 83
    saving, 80
    searching for text strings in, 86
    sorting, 78-79
    viewing list of, 78-79
article selection level, 76-77
    commands, 79
ascii files, 93. *See also* files, text
attachment numbers, 60-61

B

binary files, 93
    and Gopher, 118-119
    transferring, 100-101
Bitnet, 37
bookmarks, 122-123, 152
browsers, 152-153. *See also* Mosaic

C

Cc field, 29
clients
    Archie, 128-129, 134-135
    definition of, 6-7
    Gopher, 108-109
    WAIS, 140
command-driven interface, 12-13
commands, 12-13
    case-sensitive, 15, 32, 77, 94, 143
    cd, 16-17
    context-sensitive, 53
    help for, 17, 33
    INFO DATABASE, 45, 48
    ls, 14-15
    mail, 30-31
    mget, 96, 98-99
    mkdir, 16-17
    more, 80-81
    nslookup, 18-19
    in Pine, 52-53
    SUBSCRIBE, 42-43
    UNIX, 17
        parts of, 13
    UNSUBSCRIBE, 43
command switches, 16-17. *See also*
    parameters
    e-mail, 31
compressed files, 100-101
    formats, 101
cross-posting, 82-83
CUI World Web Catalog, 160-161

D

Date field, 29
directories
    browsing through contents of, 59
    changing, 16-17, 97
    creating, 16-17
    listing contents of, 14-15
    local, 96-97
    remote, 96-97
    returning to home, 101
    showing current, in FTP, 95
    viewing, 14-15
directory tree, 14-15
    FTP, 94-95
    moving through, 16
distribution lists, 35. *See also* aliases
    creating, with Address Book, 66-67
    modifying, 67
domain names, 18-19
    aliases, 20-21
    of Gopher servers, 115
    looking up, 18-19
    top-level, 20-21
downloading, 96
    binary files, 100-101, 118-119
    multiple files, 98-99
    text files, 96-97
Duke University, 73

E

e-mail, 27-70. *See also* distribution lists
  addresses, 29-31
    finding, 126
    grouping, 35
  and Archie searches, 148
  cancelling, 31
  commands, 32
  command switches, 31
  deleting messages, 35
  exporting messages, 60-61
  fields, 28-29
  headers, 28-29
  mailboxes, 32-33
  message parts, 28-29
  new messages in, 32-33
  and non-text files
    attaching, 58-59
    saving, 60-61
  Pine program, 49-70
  printing, 56-57
  quitting, 32-33
  replying to, 34-35
    including previous message in, 56-57
  saving messages as files, 60-61
  sending, 30-31
    to multiple users, 66-67
  signatures, 28-29, 40-41, 48
  unread messages in, 32-33
  viewing messages, 32-33
emoticons, 38-39
engines, 160-161. *See also* World Wide Web, searching
Eudora, 51
exporting, 61
expunge, 55

F

Fast Player, 162
fields, 28-29
file server, 6
files
  archives, 45
  binary, 93, 100-101, 118-119

  compressed, 100-101
  keyword descriptions of, 132-133
  non-text
    attaching to e-mail, 58-59
    saving attached, 60-61
    viewing, 60
  obtaining, with FTP, 92-93
  overwriting, 97
  searching contents of, 140-145
  size of, information on, 100
  text, 93
    downloading, 96-99
    viewing contents of, 97
  types of, 93
  uploading, with FTP, 103
  viewers, 152
flames, 38
folders, 33. *See also* e-mail; mailboxes
  creating, 62-63
  in Pine, 54-55, 62-63
From field, 29
FTP (file transfer protocol), 21, 87, 92-103
  commands, 94, 96
  directory trees, moving through, 94-95
  downloading with
    binary files, 100-101
    text files, 96-99
  etiquette, 117
  file size information in, 100
  ftpmail, 106
  via Gopher, 116-119
  obtaining files with, 92-93, 96-101
  quitting, 98-99
  and README files, 94-95
  servers, anonymous, 92-93
  suspending/returning to, 102-103
  transfer modes, 100-101
  uploading with, 103

G

Gopher, 107-126
  accessing, 108-109
  advantages of, 107-108
  and Archie, 127-135

  bookmarks, 122-123
  cancelling operations in, 111
  client software, 109
  clients, using, 108-109
  commands, 110, 112, 123
  FTP with, 116-119
  history of, 113
  labels in, 118
  for Macintosh computers, 118-119
  menus in, 107-109
    customizing, 122-123
    icons, 158
    item types in, 118-119
    moving through, 112-113
    searching contents of, 127, 136-139
  newsgroups, 121
  quitting, 122
  servers, 108-109
    connecting to remote, 114-115
  suspending/returning to, 123
  Telnet access to, 109-110
  text files in, 110-111
    commands for, 110
  and Veronica, 136-139
  and WAIS, 140-145
  Web connections to, 158-159
gopherspace, 114
  searching, 136-139
graphical user interface (GUI), 12-13. *See also* Mosaic
graphics
  attaching files to e-mail, 58-61
  obtaining with FTP, 100-101
  in the Web, 152-153
guest accounts, 88-89

H

headers, 28-29
  newsgroup article, 80-81
  searching in, 63

host
    address, 18-21
    definition of, 6-7
    names, 18-19
HTML (Hypertext Markup Language),
    157, 168
HTTP (Hypertext Transfer Protocol), 157
hypermedia, 151
hypertext documents, 150-151. *See also*
    World Wide Web
    addresses of, 156-157
    transfer protocol, 157

I

icons, 150-151
Inbox folder, 54
inline images, 152-153. *See also* graphics
interest groups. *See* mailing lists; Usenet
interface, 12-13
    command-driven, 12-13
    graphical user, 12-13
    menu-driven, 12-13
Internet. *See also* FTP; Gopher; Telnet;
    World Wide Web
    acronyms, 39
    access to, 8-9
    advantages of, 4-5
    basic tools, 4-5
    Business Directory, 164
    etiquette, 38-39
    history of, 5
    Hunt, 126, 148
    logging on to, 10-11
        remote hosts, 88-89
    logging out of, 22
    Phone Book, 126
    searching on, 127-148
    service providers, 9
    structure of, 4-7
IP (Internet Protocol) address, 18-19
    looking up, 18-19, 91

J

jumping, 150-151. *See also* World
    Wide Web

K

keywords, 45
    in Archie, 128-129
    identifying files by, 132-133

L

libraries
    and Internet access, 8
    and Telnet, 88-89, 120-121
Library of Congress, 89
links, 150-151, 155
Listserv, 36-37. *See also* mailing lists
    commands, 42, 44, 45
    file archives, 45
    finding mailing list topics with, 40-41
list server, 36-37, 40-45
    address, 44-45
logging on, 10-11
    to commercial services, 11
    to Telnet, 88-89
logging off, 22
    automatic, 22
Lynx, 152-153, 154

M

Macgopher, 109
Macintosh computers
    and Gopher, 109, 118-119
    off-line mail readers for, 51
    and WAIS, 141
MacWais, 141
mailboxes, 32-33
    multiple, 33
mailers, 27. *See also* Pine mail program
    and off-line mail readers, 51

mailing lists, 27, 36-45
    addresses, 44-45
    and Bitnet, 37
    examples of, 36
    etiquette of, 38-39
    and file archives, 45
    finding, 40-41
    listing, 41
    and Listserv, 36-37, 40-45
    and list servers, 36-37
    subscribing to, 42-43
    suspending receipt of, 43
    unsubscribing to, 43
    using, 44-45
.mailrc file, 35
menu-driven interface, 12-13
menus
    choosing items in, 50
    in Gopher, 108-109
        moving through, 112-113
    searching, with Veronica, 136-139
    submenus in, 108-109
    tree, 112
Message-Id field, 29
MIME (Multipurpose Internet Mail
    Extensions), 58-59
modems, 7, 8
moderators, 36-37. *See also* mailing lists
Mosaic, 152-157
    features of, 152
    and Gopher, accessing, 158-159
    moving through the Web with,
        156-157
    multimedia files in, 162-163
    page elements in, 155
    printing pages in, 156-157
    starting, 154-155
MpegPlay, 162
multimedia, 151, 162-163
    saving files to disk, 163

N

NASA Space Link, 89
National Science Foundation, 5
netiquette, 38-39
    FTP, 117
networks
    connecting to, 7
    etiquette of, 38-39
    history of, 5
    protocols, 19
    terminology, 6-7
newbies, 38
newsgroups, 72-73
    article selection list, 78-79
    articles, reading, 80-81
    categories of, 74-75
    commands for, 77
    distributions, selecting, 82-83
    finding, 74-75
    Gopher, about, 121
    listing available, 74-75
    quitting, 82-83
    subscribing to, 76-77
        automatically, 74-75
    unsubscribing to, 75
    the Web, about, 151
newsgroup selection level commands,
    76-77
.newsrc file, 75
newsreaders, 72-73
    browsers as, 158
    command levels, 76-77
    and threading, 78-79
news servers, 72-73
NSFnet, 5

O

on-line services, 8-9
operating systems, 12-13

P

page(s)
    article list, 78-79
    elements of, in Mosaic, 155
    in Gopher, 108-109
    home, 154
    title, 108-109
    in the Web, 150-151
        annotating, 168
        creating, 168
paging level, 76-77
    commands, 80-81
    posting articles with, 82-83
    reading articles with, 80-81
parameters, 130-131. *See also* switches
    and Archie clients, 134-135
    and Veronica, 138-139
passwords, 10-11
    choosing, 11
PCGopher, 109
Pegasus Mail, 51
Pine mail program, 49-70
    Address Book, 64-67
    ^ symbol in, 52-53
    command list, 50-53
    Compose Message commands, 53
    Current Message commands, 57
    deleting messages, 55
    Folder Index screen commands, 54
    Folder List screen commands, 62-63
    folders in, 54-55
        creating/using, 62-63
    key combinations in, 52-53
    Main Menu, 50-51
    moving through messages in, 57
    non-text files
        attaching to messages, 58-59
        saving, 60-61
    quitting, 52-53
    printing messages with, 56-57

    replying to messages with, 56-57
    saving messages as files, 60-61
    sending messages with, 52-53
        to multiple users, 53
    sorting messages, 55
    starting, 50-51
    status bar, 50-51
    text files, inserting, 59
    upgrades, acquiring, 70
    versions of, 58
    viewing messages with, 54-55
pkzip program, 101
pointers, 108-109
port numbers, 88-89
posting, 72-73, 76
    to multiple newsgroups, 82-83
prompts
    command, 13
    definition of, 10
    UNIX mail (&), 32-33
protocols, 19. *See also* FTP; HTTP; TCP/IP

Q

Quick Time, 162

R

README files, 94-95
Received field, 29
Return-Path field, 29
rn program, 72
robots, 160
rtin program, 72

S

saved-mail folder, 54
search criteria, 128-129

search(es)
    in Archie, 128-135
        criteria, 128-129, 132-133
        parameters, 130-131
    for article subjects, 86
    boolean operators in, 138-139
    commands for, 45
    engines, 160-161
    exact, 131
    in file archives, 45, 48
    for message headers, 63
    for mailing list topics, 40-41
    sub, 131
    subcase, 131
    in Veronica, 136-139
    in WAIS, 140-145
    in the Web, 160-161
    whatis, 132-133
sent-mail folder, 54
servers, 6-7
    anonymous FTP, 92-93
    Archie, 128-129
    directory of, 142
    file, 6
    Gopher, 114-115
    list, 36-37
    news, 72-73
signatures, 28-29
    creating, 48
    deleting, 40-41
smileys, 38-39
Software Description Database, 132-133
software progams, downloading with FTP,
    100-101
sound files, 100-101
Sound Machine, 162
sources, 140-141. *See also* WAIS
    listing available, 142-143
Sparkle, 162
spiders, 160
Stuffit-Lite program, 101
subdirectories, 14-15
Subject field, 29
subscribers, 36-37. *See also* mailing lists

SWAIS, 141, 143
    commands, 144
switches, command, 16-17. *See also*
  parameters

T

TCP/IP (Transmission Control
  Protocol/Internet Protocol), 19
Telnet, 87-91
    to Archie servers, 128-129
    accessing with Gopher, 120-121
    commands, 91
    disconnecting from, 121
    Gopher servers via, 108
    logging on to, 88-89
    sites, popular, 89
    suspending/returning to, 90-91
terminal, 6-7
    types, 91
text editors, 75, 82-83
text files, 93, 96-99
    in Gopher, 108-111
threads, 78-79. *See also* newsgroups
    cancelling, 86
tin program, 72
To field, 29
toolbars, 152
trn program, 72
    article selection level commands, 79
    case-sensitivity of, 77
    commands, to send articles, 83
    finding newsgroups with, 74-75
    searching with, 86
TurboGopher, 109

U

United States
    Department of Defense, 5
    House of Representatives, 115
    Senate, 115
University of Minnesota, 113, 115
University of North Carolina, 73

UNIX, 12-17
    commands, 16-17
        parts of, 13
    compression formats, 101
    Mail, 27-48. *See also* e-mail
    mh (mail handler), 51
    newsreaders, 72-73
    text editors, 75
uploading, 96-97, 103
URL (Uniform Resource Locator), 156-157
Usenet, 71-86
    history of, 73
user names, 10-11
"user unknown" message, 11

V

Veronica, 127, 136-139
    advanced searching with, 138-139
    advantages of, 136
    starting, 136-137
video clips, obtaining, 100-101
    viewing, 162-163
viewers, 162-163
vi program, 75
virus-checking software, 103
VT100 terminals, 91

W

WAIS (Wide Area Information Service), 127,
  140-145
    client software, 141
    connecting to, 140-141
    listing sources in, 144
    public-access clients, 140
    searching in, 144-145
    selecting sources in, 142-143
    SWAIS commands, 144
WAISSearch, 141
Washington University Services, 89
Weather Reports, 89
Web. *See* World Wide Web

WELL, The (The Whole Earth 'Lectronic Links), 115

Whole Internet Catalog, 164

wildcards, 99

Wingopher, 109

WinWais, 141

World, 115

World Wide Web, 149-168

   annotating pages in, 168

   Best of the, 164

   browsers, 152-153

      starting, 154-155

   communication methods, 158-159

creating pages in, 168

document locations, 156-157

and Gopher, accessing, 158-159

home page, 154-155

and HTTP, 157

and Mosaic, 152-155

moving through, 156-157

multimedia in, 162-163

printing pages in, 156-157

searching, 160-161

search pages, 161

Servers, 164

source code, viewing, 168

structure of, 150-151

   URLs, 156-159, 164

Wplany, 162

X

Xgopher, 109

XWAIS, 141

X-Windows, 13